4

PROGRAMMER'S GUIDE: SYSTEM SERVICES AND APPLICATION PACKAGING TOOLS

UNIX
SYSTEM LABORATORIES

Published by Prentice Hall, Inc.
A Simon & Schuster Company
Englewood Cliffs, NJ 07632

P R E N T I C E   H A L L

ORDERING INFORMATION

UNIX® SYSTEM V RELEASE 4.2 DOCUMENTATION

To order single copies of UNIX® SYSTEM V Release 4.2 documentation, please call (515) 284-6761.

ATTENTION DOCUMENTATION MANAGERS AND TRAINING DIRECTORS:
For bulk purchases in excess of 30 copies, please write to:

Corporate Sales Department
PTR Prentice Hall
113 Sylvan Avenue
Englewood Cliffs, N.J. 07632

or

Phone: (201) 592-2863
FAX: (201) 592-2249

ATTENTION GOVERNMENT CUSTOMERS:

For GSA and other pricing information, please call (201) 461-7107.

Prentice-Hall International (UK) Limited, *London*
Prentice-Hall of Australia Pty. Limited, *Sydney*
Prentice-Hall Canada Inc., *Toronto*
Prentice-Hall Hispanoamericana, S.A., *Mexico*
Prentice-Hall of India Private Limited, *New Delhi*
Prentice-Hall of Japan, Inc., *Tokyo*
Simon & Schuster Asia Pte. Ltd., *Singapore*
Editora Prentice-Hall do Brasil, Ltda., *Rio de Janeiro*

AT&T UNIX® System V Release 4

General Use and System Administration

UNIX® System V Release 4 Network User's and Administrator's Guide
UNIX® System V Release 4 Product Overview and Master Index
UNIX® System V Release 4 System Administrator's Guide
UNIX® System V Release 4 System Administrator's Reference Manual
UNIX® System V Release 4 User's Guide
UNIX® System V Release 4 User's Reference Manual

General Programmer's Series

UNIX® System V Release 4 Programmer's Guide: ANSI C
  and Programming Support Tools
UNIX® System V Release 4 Programmer's Guide: Character User Interface
  (FMLI and ETI)
UNIX® System V Release 4 Programmer's Guide: Networking Interfaces
UNIX® System V Release 4 Programmer's Guide: POSIX Conformance
UNIX® System V Release 4 Programmer's Guide: System Services
  and Application Packaging Tools
UNIX® System V Release 4 Programmer's Reference Manual

System Programmer's Series

UNIX® System V Release 4 ANSI C Transition Guide
UNIX® System V Release 4 BSD / XENIX® Compatibility Guide
UNIX® System V Release 4 Device Driver Interface / Driver−Kernel
  Interface (DDI / DKI) Reference Manual
UNIX® System V Release 4 Migration Guide
UNIX® System V Release 4 Programmer's Guide: STREAMS

 Available from Prentice Hall

Contents

9   Modifying the sysadm Interface

10   Data Validation Tools

System Services and Application Packaging Tools

Figures and Tables

Preface

Purpose

This guide is designed to give you information about application programming in a UNIX system environment. It does not attempt to teach you how to write programs. Rather, it is intended to supplement texts on programming by concentrating on the other elements that are part of getting application programs into operation.

Audience and Prerequisite Knowledge

As the title suggests, we are addressing application programmers. No special level of programming involvement is assumed. We hope the book will be useful to people who work on or manage large application development projects.

Programmers in the expert class, or those engaged in developing system software, may find this guide lacks the depth of information they need. For them we recommend the *Programmer's Reference Manual*.

Knowledge of terminal use, of a UNIX system editor, and of the UNIX system directory/file structure is assumed. If you feel shaky about your mastery of these basic tools, you might want to look over the *User's Guide* before tackling this one.

Organization

This material is organized into ten chapters as follows:

- Chapter 1 — Introduction to Application Programming

  Briefly describes what application programming is, UNIX system tools and where to read about them, and languages supported in the UNIX system environment and where to read about them.

- Chapter 2 — Application Programming in the UNIX System Environment

  This chapter introduces the system calls and other system services you can use to develop and package application programs.

- Chapters 3 through 10 — Support Tools and Descriptions

  Includes detailed information about the use of many of the UNIX system tools and system services.

At the end of the text is an appendix showing a sample application that pulls together a lot of the tools described in the Guide; an appendix of manual pages unique to *System Services and Application Packaging Tools*; an appendix of case studies; and an index.

The C Connection

The UNIX system supports many programming languages, and C compilers are available on many different operating systems. Nevertheless, the relationship between the UNIX operating system and C has always been and remains very close. Most of the code in the UNIX operating system is written in the C language, and over the years many organizations using the UNIX system have come to use C for an increasing portion of their application code. Thus, while this guide is intended to be useful to you no matter what language(s) you are using, you will find that, unless there is a specific language-dependent point to be made, the examples assume you are programming in C. The *Programmer's Guide: ANSI C and Programming Support Tools* gives you detailed information on C language programming in the UNIX environment.

Hardware/Software Dependencies

Nearly all the text in this book is accurate for any computer running UNIX System V Release 4.0, with the exception of hardware-specific information such as addresses.

If you find commands that work a little differently in your UNIX system environment, it may be because you are running under a different release of the software. If some commands just don't seem to exist at all, they may be members of packages not installed on your system. If you do find yourself trying to execute a non-existent command, talk to the administrators of your system to find out what you have available.

Notation Conventions

Whenever the text includes examples of output from the computer and/or commands entered by you, we follow the standard notation scheme that is common throughout UNIX system documentation:

- All computer input and output is shown in a constant-width font. Commands that you type in from your terminal are shown in constant-width type. Text that is printed on your terminal by the computer is shown in constant-width type.

- Comments added to a display to show that part of the display has been omitted are shown in *italic* type and are indented to separate them from the text that represents computer output or input. Comments that explain the input or output are shown in the same type font as the rest of the display.

  An italic font is used to show substitutable text elements, such as the word "*filename.*"

- Because you are expected to press the RETURN key after entering a command or menu choice, the RETURN key is not explicitly shown in these cases. If, however, during an interactive session, you are expected to press RETURN without having typed any text, the notation is shown.

- Control characters are shown by the string "CTRL-" followed by the appropriate character, such as D (this is known as CTRL-D). To enter a control character, hold down the key marked "CTRL" (or "CONTROL") and press the "D" key.

- The standard default prompt signs for an ordinary user and root are the dollar sign ($) and the pound sign (#).

- When the # prompt is used in an example, the command illustrated may be executed only by root.

Command References

When commands are mentioned in a section of the text for the first time, a reference to the manual section where the command is formally described is included in parentheses: command(section). The numbered sections are located in the following manuals:

Sections (1, 1C, 1G)	*User's Reference Manual*
Sections (1, 1M), (4), (5), (7), (8)	*System Administrator's Reference Manual*
Sections (1), (2), (3), (4), (5)	*Programmer's Reference Manual*

Note that Section 1 is listed for all the manuals. Section 1 of the *User's Reference Manual* describes commands appropriate for general users. Section 1 of the *Programmer's Reference Manual* describes commands appropriate for programmers. Section 1 of the *System Administrator's Reference Manual* describes commands appropriate for system administrators.

Information in the Examples

While every effort has been made to present displays of information just as they appear on your terminal, it is possible that your system may produce slightly different output. Some displays depend on a particular machine configuration that may differ from yours. Changes between releases of the UNIX system software may cause small differences in what appears on your terminal.

Where complete code samples are shown, we have tried to make sure they compile and work as represented. Where code fragments are shown, while we can't say that they have been compiled, we have attempted to maintain the same standards of coding accuracy for them.

1 Introduction to Application Programming

Introduction

This chapter introduces application programming in a UNIX system environment.

It briefly describes what application programming is and then moves on to a discussion on UNIX system tools and where you can read about them, and to languages supported in the UNIX system environment and where you can read about them.

Throughout this chapter and the rest of the Guide, you will find pointers and references to other guides and manuals where information is described in detail. In particular, you will find numerous references to the *Programmer's Guide: ANSI C and Programming Support Tools*. The *Programmer's Guide: ANSI C and Programming Support Tools* and the *Programmer's Guide: System Services and Application Packaging Tools* are closely connected. Much of the information from both used to be in the Release 3.2 version of the *Programmer's Guide*. For Release 4.0 of UNIX, the information has been divided into two guides.

This guide concentrates on an application programmer's view of how to develop and package application software under UNIX System V, using the system services provided by the kernel.

The *Programmer's Guide: ANSI C and Programming Support Tools* describes the C programming environment, libraries, compiler, link editor, and file formats. It also describes the tools provided in the UNIX System/C environment for building, analyzing, debugging, and maintaining programs.

If you are unsure of which book to reference, check the *Product Overview and Master Index*. It explains how the document set is organized and where to find specific information.

Application Programming

This Guide discusses programming where the objective is to produce programs (applications) that will run on a UNIX system computer.

Programmers working in this environment are developing applications for the benefit of other, nonprogramming users. Most large commercial computer applications involve a team of applications development programmers. They may be employees of the end-user organization or they may work for a software development firm. Some of the people working in this environment may be more in the project management area than working programmers.

Application programming has some of the following characteristics:

- Applications are often large and are developed by a team of people who write requirements, designs, tests, and end-user documents. This implies use of a project management methodology, including version control (described in the *Programmer's Guide: ANSI C and Programming Support Tools*), change requests, tracking, and so on.

- Applications must be developed more robustly.

  - They must be easy to use, implying character or graphical user interfaces.

  - They must check all incoming data for validity (for example, using the data validation tools described in Chapter 10).

  - They should be able to handle large amounts of data.

- Applications must be easy to install and administer (see Chapter 8, "Packaging Application Software" and Chapter 9, "Modifying the sysadm Interface").

UNIX System Tools and Where You Can Read About Them

Let's clarify the term "UNIX system tools." In the narrowest sense, it means an existing piece of software used as a component in a new task. In a broader context, the term is often used to refer to elements of the UNIX system that might also be called features, utilities, programs, filters, commands, languages, functions, and so on. It gets confusing because any of the things that might be called by one or more of these names can be, and often are, used in the narrow way as part of the solution to a programming problem.

Tools Covered and Not Covered in This Guide

The *Programmer's Guide: System Services and Application Packaging Tools* is about tools used in the process of creating programs in a UNIX system environment, so let's take a minute to talk about which tools we mean, which ones are not going to be covered in this book, and where you might find information about those not covered here. Actually, the subject of things not covered in this guide might be even more important to you than the things that are. We couldn't possibly cover everything you ever need to know about UNIX system tools in this one volume.

Tools not covered in this text:

- the login procedure

- UNIX system editors and how to use them

- how the file system is organized and how you move around in it

- shell programming

Information about these subjects can be found in the *User's Guide* and a number of commercially available texts.

Tools that are covered in this text apply to applications. Each application performs a different function, but goes through the same basic steps: input, processing, and output. These tools help you accomplish these steps.

Tools for packaging applications software and customizing the user interface are also covered in this text.

Languages Supported in a UNIX System Environment and Where You Can Read About Them

In this section we describe a variety of languages supported in the UNIX system environment.

By "languages" we mean those offered by AT&T for use on a computer running a current release of UNIX System V. Since these are separately purchasable items, not all of them will necessarily be installed on your machine. On the other hand, you may have languages available on your machine that came from another source and are not mentioned in this discussion.

The C Language

C is intimately associated with the UNIX system since it was originally developed for use in recoding the UNIX system kernel. If you need to use a lot of UNIX system function calls for low-level I/O, memory or device management, or interprocess communication, C is a logical first choice. Most programs, however, don't require such direct interfaces with the operating system, so the decision to choose C might better be based on one or more of the following characteristics:

- a variety of data types: characters, integers of various sizes, and floating point numbers
- low-level constructs (most of the UNIX system kernel is written in C)
- derived data types such as arrays, functions, pointers, structures, and unions
- multidimensional arrays
- scaled pointers and the ability to do pointer arithmetic
- bitwise operators
- a variety of flow-of-control statements: if, if-else, switch, while, do-while, and for
- a high degree of portability

A difficulty with C is that it takes a fairly concentrated use of the language over a period of several months to reach your full potential as a C programmer. If you are a casual programmer, you might make life easier for yourself if you choose a less demanding language.

Refer to the *Programmer's Guide: ANSI C and Programming Support Tools* for complete details on C.

Shell

You can use the shell to create programs (new commands). Such programs are also called shell procedures. Refer to the *User's Guide* for information on how to create and execute shell programs using commands, variables, positional parameters, return codes, and basic programming control structures.

awk

awk (its name is an acronym constructed from the initials of its developers) scans an input file for lines that match pattern(s) described in a specification file. On finding a line that matches a pattern, awk performs actions also described in the specification. It is not uncommon that an awk program can be written in a couple of lines to do functions that would take a couple of pages to describe in a programming language like FORTRAN or C. For example, consider a case where you have a set of records that consist of a key field and a second field that represents a quantity, and the task is to output the sum of the quantities for each key. The pseudocode for such a program might look like this:

```
SORT RECORDS
Read the first record into a hold area;
Read additional records until EOF;
{
If the key matches the key of the record in the hold area,
    add the quantity to the quantity field of the held record;
If the key does not match the key of the held record,
    write the held record,
    move the new record to the hold area;
}
At EOF, write out the last record from the hold area.
```

An awk program to accomplish this task would look like this:

```
        { qty[$1] += $2 }
END     { for (key in qty) print key, qty[key] }
```

This illustrates only one characteristic of awk; its ability to work with associative arrays. With awk, the input file does not have to be sorted, which is a requirement of the pseudoprogram.

For detailed information on awk, see the "awk" chapter in the *User's Guide* and awk(1) in the *User's Reference Manual*.

lex

lex is a lexical analyzer that can be added to C or FORTRAN programs. A lexical analyzer is interested in the vocabulary of a language rather than its grammar, which is a system of rules defining the structure of a language. lex can produce C language subroutines that recognize regular expressions specified by the user, take some action when a regular expression is recognized, and pass the output stream on to the next program.

For detailed information on lex, see the "lex" chapter in the *Programmer's Guide: ANSI C and Programming Support Tools* and lex(1) in the *Programmer's Reference Manual*.

yacc

yacc (Yet Another Compiler Compiler) is a tool for describing an input language to a computer program. yacc produces a C language subroutine that parses an input stream according to rules laid down in a specification file. The yacc specification file establishes a set of grammatical rules together with actions to be taken when tokens in the input match the rules. lex may be used with yacc to control the input process and pass tokens to the parser that applies the grammatical rules.

For detailed information on yacc, see the yacc chapter in the *Programmer's Guide: ANSI C and Programming Support Tools* and yacc(1) in the *Programmer's Reference Manual*.

m4

m4 is a macro processor that can be used as a preprocessor for assembly language and C programs. For details, see the m4 chapter of the *Programmer's Guide: ANSI C and Programming Support Tools* and m4(1) in the *Programmer's Reference Manual*.

bc and dc

bc enables you to use a computer terminal as you would a programmable calculator. You can edit a file of mathematical computations and call bc to execute them. The bc program uses dc. You can use dc directly, if you want, but it takes a little getting used to since it works with reverse Polish notation. That means you enter numbers into a stack followed by the operator. bc and dc are described in Section 1 of the *User's Reference Manual*.

curses

Actually a library of C functions, curses is included in this list because the set of functions just about amounts to a sublanguage for dealing with terminal screens. If you are writing programs that include interactive user screens, you will want to become familiar with this group of functions.

For detailed information on curses, see the *Programmer's Guide: Character User Interfce (FMLI and ETI)*

FMLI

The Form and Menu Language Interpreter (FMLI) is a high-level programming tool having two main parts:

- The Form and Menu Language, a programming language for writing scripts that define how an application will be presented to users. The syntax of the Form and Menu Language is very similar to that of the UNIX system shell programming language, including variable setting and evaluation, built-in commands and functions, use of and escape from special characters, redirection of input and output, conditional statements, interrupt signal handling, and the ability to set various terminal attributes. The Form and Menu Language also includes sets of "descriptors," which are used to define or customize attributes of frames and other objects in your application.

- The Form and Menu Language Interpreter, fmli, which is a command interpreter that sets up and controls the video display screen on a terminal, using instructions from your scripts to supplement FMLI's predefined screen control mechanisms. FMLI scripts can also invoke UNIX system commands and C executables, either in the background or in full screen mode. The Form and Menu Language Interpreter operates similarly to the UNIX command interpreter sh. At run time it parses the scripts you have written, thus giving you the advantages of quick prototyping and easy maintenance.

FMLI provides a framework for developers to write applications and application interfaces that use menus and forms. It controls many aspects of screen management for you. That means that you do not have to be concerned with the low-level details of creating or placing frames, providing users with a means of navigating between or within frames, or processing the use of forms and menus. Nor do you need to worry about on which kind of terminal your application will be run. FMLI takes care of all that for you.

For details see the FMLI chapter in the *Programmer's Guide: Character User Interface (FMLI and ETI)*

ETI

The Extended Terminal Interface (ETI) is a set of C library routines that promote the development of application programs displaying and manipulating windows, panels, menus, and forms and that run under the UNIX system.

ETI consists of

- the low-level (curses) library
- the panel library
- the menu library
- the form library
- the TAM Transition library

The routines are C functions and macros; many of them resemble routines in the standard C library. For example, there's a routine printw that behaves much like printf and another routine getch that behaves like getc. The automatic teller program at your bank might use printw to print its menus and getch to accept your requests for withdrawals (or, better yet, deposits). A visual screen editor like the UNIX system screen editor vi might also use these and other ETI routines.

A major feature of ETI is cursor optimization. Cursor optimization minimizes the amount a cursor has to move around a screen to update it. For example, if you designed a screen editor program with ETI routines and edited the sentence

        ETI is a great package for creating forms and menus.

to read

        ETI is the best package for creating forms and menus.

the program would change only "the best" in place of "a great." The other characters would be preserved. Because the amount of data transmitted—the output—is minimized, cursor optimization is also referred to as output optimization.

Cursor optimization takes care of updating the screen in a manner appropriate for the terminal on which an ETI program is run. This means that ETI can do whatever is required to update many different terminal types. It searches the terminfo database to find the correct description for a terminal.

How does cursor optimization help you and those who use your programs? First, it saves you time in describing in a program how you want to update screens. Second, it saves a user's time when the screen is updated. Third, it reduces the load on your UNIX system's communication lines when the updating takes place. Fourth, you don't have to worry about the myriad of terminals on which your program might be run.

Here's a simple ETI program. It uses some of the basic ETI routines to move a cursor to the middle of a terminal screen and print the character string BullsEye. For now, just look at their names and you will get an idea of what each of them does:

Figure 1-1: A Simple ETI Program

```
#include <curses.h>

main()
{
    initscr();

    move( LINES/2 - 1, COLS/2 - 4 );
    addstr("Bulls");
    refresh();
    addstr("Eye");
    refresh();
    endwin();
}
```

For complete information on ETI, refer to the ETI chapter in the *Programmer's Guide: Character User Interface (FMLI and ETI)*.

XWIN Graphical Windowing System

The XWIN Graphical Windowing System is a network-transparent window system. X display servers run on computers with either monochrome or color bit-map display hardware. The server distributes user input to and accepts output requests from various application programs (referred to as "clients"). Each client is located on either the same machine or on another machine in the network.

The clients use Xlib, a C library routine, to interface with the window system by means of a stream connection.

"Widgets" are a set of code and data that provide the look and feel of a user interface. The C library routines used for creating and managing widgets are called the X Intrinsics. They are built on top of the X Window System, monitor events related to user interactions, and dispatch the correct widget code to handle the display. Widgets can then call application-registered routines (called callbacks) to handle the specific application semantics of an interaction. The X Intrinsics also monitor application-registered, nongraphical events and dispatch application routines to handle them. These features allow programmers to use this implementation of an OPEN LOOK toolkit in data base management, network management, process control, and other applications requiring response to external events.

Clients sometimes use a higher level library of the X Intrinsics and a set of widgets in addition to xlib. Refer to the *XWIN Graphical Windowing System* for general information about the design of X. The *Xlib–C Language Interface* is a reference guide to the low-level C language interface to the XWIN System protocol.

OPEN LOOK Graphical User Interface

The OPEN LOOK Graphical User Interface is a software application that creates a user-friendly graphical environment for the UNIX system. It replaces the traditional UNIX system commands with with graphics that include windows, menus, icons, and other symbols. Using a hand-held pointing device (a "mouse"), you manipulate windows by moving them, changing their size and running them in the background. You can have multiple applications running at the same time by creating more than one window on your screen.

For more information, refer to the *OPEN LOOK Graphical User Interface User's Guide* and the *OPEN LOOK Graphical User Interface Programmer's Guide/Reference Manual*.

2 Application Programming in the UNIX System Environment

Package Development and Installation   2-27

Introduction

This chapter discusses programming where the objective is to produce programs (applications) that will run on a UNIX system computer.

The chapter introduces the system calls and other system services you can use to develop and package application programs.

The first section lists the system calls in functional groups, and includes brief discussions of error handling, processes, and signals. For details, see Section 2 of the *Programmer's Reference Manual*.

The "Developing Application Software" section introduces such topics as file and record locking, interprocess communication, symbolic links, virtual memory, the process scheduler, and data validation.

The "Package Development and Installation" section introduces how to package applications software and customize the user interface.

The chapter's aim is to give you some sense of the situations in which you use these tools, and how the tools fit together.

System Calls

UNIX system calls are the interface between the kernel and the user programs that run on top of it. read, write, and the other system calls in Section 2 of the *Programmer's Reference Manual* define what the UNIX system is. Everything else is built on their foundation. Strictly speaking, they are the only way to access such facilities as the file system, interprocess communication primitives, and multitasking mechanisms.

Of course, most programs do not need to invoke system calls directly to gain access to these facilities. If you are writing a C program, for example, you can use the library functions described in Section 3 of the *Programmer's Reference Manual*. When you use these functions, the details of their implementation on the UNIX system are transparent to the program, for example, that the system call read underlies the fread implementation in the standard C library. In other words, the program will generally be portable to any system, UNIX or not, with a conforming C implementation. (See Chapter 2 of the *Programmer's Guide: ANSI C and Programming Support Tools* for a discussion of the standard C library.)

In contrast, programs that invoke system calls directly are portable only to other UNIX or UNIX-like systems; for that reason, you would not use read in a program that performed a simple input/output operation. Other operations, however, including most multitasking mechanisms, do require direct interaction with the UNIX system kernel. These operations are the subject of the first part of this book.

A C program is automatically linked with the system calls you have invoked when you compile the program. The procedure may be different for programs written in other languages. Check the *Programmer's Guide: ANSI C and Programming Support Tools* for details on the language you are using.

Error Handling

UNIX system calls that are not able to complete successfully almost always return a value of −1 to your program. (If you look through the system calls in Section 2, you will see that there are a few calls for which no return value is defined, but they are the exceptions.) In addition to the −1 that is returned to the program, the unsuccessful system call places an integer in an externally declared variable, errno. In a C program, you can determine the value in errno if your program contains the statement

```
#include <errno.h>
```

The value in errno is not cleared on successful calls, so your program should check it only if the system call returned a −1. The errors are described in intro(2) of the *Programmer's Reference Manual*.

The C language function perror(3C) can be used to print an error message (on stderr) based on the value of errno.

Basic File I/O

These system calls perform basic operations on UNIX system files.

Figure 2-1: Basic File I/O System Calls

Function Name(s)	Purpose
open	open a file for reading or writing
close	close a file descriptor
read	read from a file
write	write to a file
creat	create a new file or rewrite an existing one
unlink	remove directory entry
lseek	move read/write file pointer

Advanced File I/O

These system calls allow creation of new directories (and other things), linking to existing files, and obtaining or modifying file status information.

Figure 2-2: Advanced File I/O System Calls

Function Name(s)	Purpose
link	link to a file
access	determine accessibility of a file
mknod	make a directory, a special, or ordinary file
chmod, fchmod	change mode of file
chown, lchown, fchown	change owner and group of a file
utime	set file access and modification times
stat, lstat, fstat	get file status
fcntl	file control
ioctl	device control
fpathconf, pathconf	get configurable path name variables
getdents	read directory entries and put in file system-independent format
mkdir	make a directory
readlink	read the value of a symbolic link
rename	change the name of a file
rmdir	remove a directory
symlink	make a symbolic link to a file

Terminal I/O

These system calls deal with a general terminal interface that is provided to control asynchronous communications ports.

Figure 2-3: Terminal I/O System Calls

Function Name(s)	Purpose
tcgetattr, tcsetattr	get and set terminal attributes
tcsendbreak, tcdrain, tcflush, tcflow	line control functions
cfgetospeed, cfgetispeed, cfsetispeed, cfsetospeed	get and set baud rate functions
tcgetpgrp, tcsetpgrp	get and set terminal foreground process group ID
tcgetsid	get terminal session ID

Processes

These system calls control user processes.

Figure 2-4: Process System Calls

Function Name(s)	Purpose
fork	create a new process
exec, execl, execv, execle, execve, execlp, execvp	execute a file
exit, _exit	terminate process
wait	wait for child process to stop or terminate
setuid, setgid	set user and group IDs
setpgrp	set process group ID

Figure 2-4: Process System Calls (continued)

chdir, fchdir	change working directory
chroot	change root directory
nice	change priority of a process
getcontext, setcontext	get and set current user context
getgroups, setgroups	get or set supplementary group access list IDs
getpid, getpgrp, getppid, getpgid	get process, process group, and parent process IDs
getuid, geteuid, getgid, getegid	get real user, effective user, real group, and effect
pause	suspend process until signal
priocntl	process scheduler control
setpgid	set process group ID
setsid	set session ID
waitid	wait for a child process to change state
kill	send a signal to a process or group of processes

Overview of Processes

Whenever you execute a command in the UNIX system you are initiating a process that is numbered and tracked by the operating system. A flexible feature of the UNIX system is that processes can be generated by other processes. This happens more than you might ever be aware of. For example, when you log in to your system you are running a process, very probably the shell. If you then use an editor such as vi, take the option of invoking the shell from vi, and execute the ps command, you will see a display something like that in Figure 2-5 (which shows the results of a ps −f command):

Figure 2-5: Process Status

UID	PID	PPID	C	STIME	TTY	TIME	COMD
abc	24210	1	0	06:13:14	tty29	0:05	-sh
abc	24631	24210	0	06:59:07	tty29	0:13	vi c2.uli
abc	28441	28358	80	09:17:22	tty29	0:01	ps -f
abc	28358	24631	2	09:15:14	tty29	0:01	sh -i

As you can see, user abc (who went through the steps described above) now has four processes active. It is an interesting exercise to trace the chain that is shown in the Process ID (PID) and Parent Process ID (PPID) columns. The shell that was started when user abc logged on is process 24210; its parent is the initialization process (process ID 1). Process 24210 is the parent of process 24631, and so on.

The four processes in the example above are all UNIX system shell-level commands, but you can spawn new processes from your own program. You might think, "Well, it's one thing to switch from one program to another when I'm at my terminal working interactively with the computer; but why would a program want to run other programs, and if one does, why wouldn't I just put everything together into one big executable module?"

Overlooking the case where your program is itself an interactive application with diverse choices for the user, your program may need to run one or more other programs based on conditions it encounters in its own processing. (If it's the end of the month, go do a trial balance, for example.) The usual reasons why it might not be practical to create one large executable are:

- The load module may get too big to fit in the maximum process size for your system.

- You may not have control over the object code of all the other modules you want to include.

Suffice it to say, there are legitimate reasons why this creation of new processes might need to be done. There are two ways to do it:

- exec(2)—stop this process and start another
- fork(2)—start an additional copy of this process

exec(2)

exec is the name of a family of functions that includes execl, execv, execle, execve, execlp, and execvp. They all have the function of transforming the calling process into a new process. The reason for the variety is to provide different ways of pulling together and presenting the arguments of the function. An example of one version (execl) might be:

```
execl("/usr/bin/prog2", "prog", progarg1, progarg2, (char *)0);
```

For execl the argument list is

/usr/bin/prog2	path name of the new process file
prog	the name the new process gets in its argv[0]
progarg1, progarg2	arguments to prog2 as char *'s
(char *)0	a null char pointer to mark the end of the arguments

Check the exec(2) manual page in the *Programmer's Reference Manual* for the rest of the details. The key point of the exec family is that there is no return from a successful execution: the new process overlays the process that makes the exec system call. The new process also takes over the Process ID and other attributes of the old process. If the call to exec is unsuccessful, control is returned to your program with a return value of −1. You can check errno to learn why it failed.

fork(2)

The fork system call creates a new process that is an exact copy of the calling process. The new process is known as the child process; the caller is known as the parent process. The one major difference between the two processes is that the child gets its own unique process ID. When the fork process has completed successfully, it returns a 0 to the child process and the child's process ID to the parent. If the idea of having two identical processes seems a little funny, consider this:

- Because the return value is different between the child process and the parent, the program can contain the logic to determine different paths.

- The child process could say, "Okay, I'm the child. I'm supposed to issue an exec for an entirely different program."

- The parent process could say, "My child is going to be execing a new process. I'll issue a wait until I get word that that process is finished."

Your code might include statements like this:

Figure 2-6: Example of fork

```
#include <errno.h>

int ch_stat, ch_pid, status;
char *progarg1;
char *progarg2;
void exit();
extern int errno;

    if ((ch_pid = fork()) < 0)
    {
        /* Could not fork...
           check errno
        */
    }
    else if (ch_pid == 0)                        /* child */
    {
        (void)execl("/usr/bin/prog2","prog",progarg1,progarg2,(char *)0);
        exit(2);    /* execl() failed */
    }
    else                /* parent */
    {
        while ((status = wait(&ch_stat)) != ch_pid)
        {
            if (status < 0 && errno == ECHILD)
                break;
            errno = 0;
        }
    }
```

Because the child process ID is taken over by the new exec'd process, the parent knows the ID. What this boils down to is a way of leaving one program to run another, returning to the point in the first program where processing left off. By the way, this is exactly what the function system in the standard C library does.

Keep in mind that the fragment of code above includes a minimum amount of checking for error conditions. There is also potential confusion about open files and which program is writing to a file. Leaving out the possibility of named files, the new process created by the fork or exec has the three standard files that are automatically opened: stdin, stdout, and stderr. If the parent has buffered output that should appear before output from the child, the buffers must be flushed before the fork. Also, if the parent and the child process both read input from a stream, whatever is read by one process will be lost to the other. That is, once something has been delivered from the input buffer to a process the pointer has moved on.

Basic Interprocess Communication

These system calls connect processes so they can communicate. pipe is the system call for creating an interprocess channel. dup is the call for duplicating an open file descriptor. (These IPC mechanisms are not applicable for processes on separate hosts.)

Advanced Interprocess Communication

These system calls support interprocess messages, semaphores, and shared memory and are effective in data base management. (These IPC mechanisms are also not applicable for processes on separate hosts.)

Figure 2-7: Advanced Interprocess Communication System Calls

Function Name(s)	Purpose
msgget	get message queue
msgctl	message control operations
msgop	message operations
semget	get set of semaphores
semctl	semaphore control operations
semop	semaphore operations
shmget	get shared memory segment identifier
shmctl	shared memory control operations
shmop	shared memory operations

Memory Management

These system calls give you access to virtual memory facilities.

Figure 2-8: Memory Management System Calls

Function Name(s)	Purpose
getpagesize	get system page size
memcntl	memory management control
mmap	map pages of memory
mprotect	set protection of memory mapping
munmap	unmap pages of memory
plock	lock process, text, or data in memory
brk, sbrk	change data segment space allocation

File System Control

These system calls allow you to control various aspects of the file system.

Figure 2-9: File System Control System Calls

Function Name(s)	Purpose
ustat	get file system statistics
sync	update super block
mount, unmount	mount/unmount a file system
statfs, fstatfs	get file system information
sysfs	get file system type information

Signals

Signals are messages passed by the UNIX system to running processes.

Figure 2-10: Signal System Calls

Function Name(s)	Purpose
sigaction	detailed signal management
sigaltstack	set and/or get signal alternate stack context
signal, sigset, sighold, sigrelse, sigignore, sigpause	simplified signal management
sigpending	examine signals that are blocked and pending
sigprocmask	change or examine signal mask
sigsend, sigsendset	send a signal to a process or group of processes
sigsuspend	install a signal mask and suspend process until signal

Signals Overview

The system defines a set of signals that may be delivered to a process. Signal delivery resembles the occurrence of a hardware interrupt: the signal is normally blocked from further occurrence, the current process context is saved, and a new one is built. A process may specify the handler to which a signal is delivered, or specify that the signal is to be blocked or ignored. A process may also specify that a default action is to be taken when signals occur.

Some signals will cause a process to exit when they are not caught. This may be accompanied by creation of a core image file, containing the current memory image of the process for use in post-mortem debugging. A process may choose to have signals delivered on a special stack, so that sophisticated software stack manipulations are possible.

All signals have the same priority. If multiple signals are pending simultaneously, the order in which they are delivered to a process is implementation specific. Signal routines normally execute with the signal that caused their invocation to be blocked, but other signals may yet occur. Mechanisms are provided whereby critical sections of code may protect themselves against the occurrence of specified signals.

Signal Types

The signals defined by the system fall into one of five classes: hardware conditions, software conditions, input/output notification, process control, or resource control. The set of signals is defined in the file <signal.h>.

Hardware signals are derived from exceptional conditions which may occur during execution. Such signals include SIGFPE representing floating point and other arithmetic exceptions, SIGILL for illegal instruction execution, SIGSEGV for addresses outside the currently assigned area of memory or for accesses that violate memory protection constraints and SIGBUS for accesses that result in hardware related errors. Other, more CPU-specific hardware signals exist, such as SIGABRT, SIGEMT, and SIGTRAP.

Software signals reflect interrupts generated by user request: SIGINT for the normal interrupt signal; SIGQUIT for the more powerful quit signal, that normally causes a core image to be generated; SIGHUP and SIGTERM that cause graceful process termination, either because a user has hung up, or by user or program request; and SIGKILL, a more powerful termination signal which a process cannot catch or ignore. Programs may define their own asynchronous events using SIGUSR1 and SIGUSR2. Other software signals (SIGALRM, SIGVTALRM, SIGPROF) indicate the expiration of interval timers.

A process can request notification via a SIGPOLL signal when input or output is possible on a descriptor, or when a non-blocking operation completes. A process may request to receive a SIGURG signal when an urgent condition arises.

A process may be stopped by a signal sent to it or the members of its process group. The SIGSTOP signal is a powerful stop signal, because it cannot be caught. Other stop signals SIGTSTP, SIGTTIN, and SIGTTOU are used when a user request, input request, or output request respectively is the reason for stopping the process. A SIGCONT signal is sent to a process when it is continued from a stopped state. Processes may receive notification with a SIGCHLD signal when a child process changes state, either by stopping or by terminating.

Exceeding resource limits may cause signals to be generated. SIGXCPU occurs when a process nears its CPU time limit and SIGXFSZ warns that the limit on file size creation has been reached.

Signal Handlers

A process has a handler associated with each signal. The handler controls the way the signal is delivered. The call

```
#include <signal.h>

struct sigaction {
        void        (*sa_handler)();
        sigset_t    sa_mask;
        int         sa_flags;
};

sigaction(signo, sa, osa)
        int signo;
        struct sigaction *sa;
        struct sigaction *osa;
```

assigns interrupt handler address `sa_handler` to signal *signo*. Each handler address specifies either an interrupt routine for the signal, that the signal is to be ignored, or that a default action (usually process termination) is to occur if the signal occurs. The constants `SIG_IGN` and `SIG_DFL` used as values for `sa_handler` cause ignoring or defaulting of a condition.

> **NOTE** There are two things that must be done to reset a signal handler from within a signal handler. Resetting the routine that catches the signal [`signal(n, SIG_DFL);`] is only the first. It's also necessary to unblock the blocked signal, which is done with `sigprocmask`.

`sa_mask` specifies the set of signals to be masked when the handler is invoked; it implicitly includes the signal which invoked the handler. Five operations are permitted on signal sets. The set will be emptied by a call to `sigemptyset`. It will be filled with every signal currently supported by a call to `sigfillset`. Specific signals may be added or deleted with calls to `sigaddset` and `sigdelset` respectively. Set membership can be tested with `sigismember`. Signals sets should always be initialized with a call to `sigemptyset` or `sigfillset`.

`sa_flags` specifies special properties of the signal, such as whether system calls should be restarted if the signal handler returns, if the signal action should be reset to `SIG_DFL` when it is caught, and whether the handler should operate on the normal run-time stack or a special signal stack (see below).

If *osa* is nonzero, the previous signal action is returned.

When a signal condition arises for a process, the signal is added to a set of signals pending for the process. If the signal is not currently blocked by the process then it will be delivered. The process of signal delivery adds the signal to be delivered and those signals specified in the associated signal handler's `sa_mask` to a set of those masked for the process, saves the current process context, and places the process in the context of the signal handling routine. The call is arranged so that if the signal handling routine exits normally the signal mask will be restored and the process will resume execution in the original context. If the process wishes to resume in a different context, then it must arrange to restore the signal mask itself.

The mask of blocked signals is independent of handlers for delays. It delays the delivery of signals much as a raised hardware interrupt priority level delays hardware interrupts. Preventing an interrupt from occurring by changing the handler is analogous to disabling a device from further interrupts.

The signal handling routine `sa_handler` is called by a C call of the form

```
(*sa_handler)(signo, infop, ucp);
        int signo;
        siginfo_t *infop;
        ucontext_t *ucp;
```

signo gives the number of the signal that occurred. *infop* is either equal to 0, or points to a structure that contains information detailing the reason why the signal was generated. This information must be explicitly asked for when the signal's action is specified. The *ucp* parameter is a pointer to a structure containing the process's context prior to the delivery of the signal, and will be used to restore the process's context upon return from the signal handler.

Sending Signals

A process can send a signal to another process or group of processes with the calls:

```
kill(pid, signo);
        int pid, signo;

sigsend(idtype, id, signo);
        idtype_t idtype;
        id_t id;
```

Unless the process sending the signal is privileged, its real or effective user ID must be equal to the receiving process's real or saved user ID.

Signals can also be sent from from a terminal device to the process group or session leader associated with the terminal. See `termio(7)`.

Protecting Critical Sections

To block a section of code against one or more signals, a `sigprocmask` call may be used to add a set of signals to the existing mask, and return the old mask:

```
sigprocmask(SIG_BLOCK, mask, omask);
        sigset_t *mask;
        sigset_t *omask;
```

The old mask can then be restored later with `sigprocmask`,

```
sigprocmask(SIG_UNBLOCK, mask, omask);
        sigset_t *mask;
        sigset_t *omask;
```

The `sigprocmask` call can be used to read the current mask without changing it by specifying null pointer as its second argument.

It is possible to check conditions with some signals blocked, and then to pause waiting for a signal and restoring the mask, by using:

```
sigsuspend(mask);
        sigset_t *mask;
```

Signal Stacks

Applications that maintain complex or fixed size stacks can use the call

```
struct sigaltstack {
        caddr_t      ss_sp;
        int     ss_size;
        int     ss_flags;
};
sigaltstack(ss, oss)
        struct sigaltstack *ss;
        struct sigaltstack *oss;
```

to provide the system with a stack based at `ss_sp` of size `ss_size` for delivery of signals. The system automatically adjusts for direction of stack growth. `ss_flags` indicates whether the process is currently on the signal stack, and whether the signal stack is disabled.

When a signal is to be delivered and the process has requested that it be delivered on the alternate stack (see `sigaction` above), the system checks whether the process is on a signal stack. If it is not, then the process is switched to the signal stack for delivery, with the return from the signal arranged to restore the previous stack.

If the process wishes to take a nonlocal exit from the signal routine, or run code from the signal stack that uses a different stack, a `sigaltstack` call should be used to reset the signal stack.

Miscellaneous System Calls

These are system calls for such things as administration, timing, and other miscellaneous purposes.

Figure 2-11: Miscellaneous System Calls

Function Names(s)	Purpose
ulimit	get and set user limits
alarm	set a process alarm clock
getmsg	get next message off a stream
getrlimit, setrlimit	control maximum system resource consumption
uname	get/set name of current UNIX system
putmsg	send a message on a stream
profil	execution time profile
sysconf	method for application's determination of value for system configuration
uadmin	administrative control
time	get time
stime	set time
acct	enable or disable process accounting
sys3b	machine-specific functions

Developing Application Software

Each application performs a different function, but goes through the same basic steps: input, processing, and output. This section briefly describes tools you can use to accomplish these steps. Then it refers you to other chapters in this book or to other documents for more details.

For the input and output steps, most applications interact with an end user at a terminal.

During the processing step, sometimes an application needs access to special services provided by the operating system (for example, to interact with the file system, control processes, manage memory, and more). Some of these services are provided through system calls and some through libraries of functions. (System calls are grouped by function in the previous section of this book.) Some system call services and libraries for validating data are described in detail later in this book.

File and Record Locking

The provision for locking files, or portions of files, is primarily used to prevent the sort of error that can occur when two or more users of a file try to update information at the same time. The classic example is the airlines reservation system where two ticket agents each assign a passenger to Seat A, Row 5 on the 5 o'clock flight to Detroit. A locking mechanism is designed to prevent such mishaps by blocking Agent B from even seeing the seat assignment file until Agent A's transaction is complete.

File locking and record locking are really the same thing, except that file locking implies the whole file is affected; record locking means that only a specified portion of the file is locked. (Remember, in the UNIX system, file structure is undefined; a record is a concept of the programs that use the file.)

Two types of locks are available: read locks and write locks. If a process places a read lock on a file, other processes can also read the file but all are prevented from writing to it, that is, changing any of the data. If a process places a write lock on a file, no other processes can read or write in the file until the lock is removed. Write locks are also known as exclusive locks. The term shared lock is sometimes applied to read locks.

Another distinction needs to be made between mandatory and advisory locking. Mandatory locking means that the discipline is enforced automatically for the system calls that read, write, or create files. This is done through a permission flag established by the file's owner (or the superuser). Advisory locking means that the processes that use the file take the responsibility for setting and removing locks as needed. Thus, mandatory may sound like a simpler and better deal, but it isn't so. The mandatory locking capability is included in the system to comply with an agreement with /usr/group, an organization that represents the interests of UNIX system users. The principal weakness in the mandatory method is that the lock is in place only while the single system call is being made. It is extremely common for a single transaction to require a series of reads and writes before it can be considered complete. In cases like this, the term atomic is used to describe a transaction that must be viewed as an indivisible unit. The preferred way to manage locking in such a circumstance is to make certain the lock is in place before any I/O starts, and that it is not removed until the transaction is done. That calls for locking of the advisory variety.

Where to Find More Information

There is an example of file and record locking in the sample application in Appendix A. Chapter 3 in this book is a detailed discussion of the subject with a number of examples. The manual pages that apply to this facility are fcntl(2), fcntl(5), lockf(3), and chmod(2) in the *Programmer's Reference Manual*. fcntl(2) is the system call for file and record locking (although it isn't limited to that only) fcntl(5) tells you the file control options. The subroutine lockf(3) can also be used to lock sections of a file or an entire file. Setting chmod so that all portions of a file are locked will ensure that parts of files are not corrupted.

Interprocess Communications

Pipes, named pipes, and signals are all forms of interprocess communication. Business applications running on a UNIX system computer, however, often need more sophisticated methods of communication. In applications, for example, where fast response is critical, a number of processes may be brought up at the start of a business day to be constantly available to handle transactions on demand. This cuts out initialization time that can add seconds to the time required to deal with the transaction. To go back to the ticket reservation example again for a moment, if a customer calls to reserve a seat on the 5 o'clock flight to Detroit, you don't want to have to say, "Yes, sir. Just hang on a minute while I start up the reservations program." In transaction-driven systems, the normal mode of processing is to have all the components of the application standing by waiting for some sort of an indication that there is work to do.

To meet requirements of this type, the UNIX system offers a set of nine system calls and their accompanying header files, all under the umbrella name of interprocess communications (IPC).

The IPC system calls come in sets of three; one set each for messages, semaphores, and shared memory. These three terms define three different styles of communication between processes:

messages   Communication is in the form of data stored in a buffer. The buffer can be either sent or received.

semaphores   Communication is in the form of positive integers with a value between 0 and 32,767. Semaphores may be contained in an array the size of which is determined by the system administrator. The default maximum size for the array is 25.

shared memory   Communication takes place through a common area of main memory. One or more processes can attach a segment of memory and as a consequence can share whatever data is placed there.

The sets of IPC system calls are:

```
msgget    semget    shmget
msgctl    semctl    shmctl
msgop     semop     shmop
```

The get calls each return to the calling program an identifier for the type of IPC facility that is being requested.

The ctl calls provide a variety of control operations that include obtaining (IPC_STAT), setting (IPC_SET) and removing (IPC_RMID), the values in data structures associated with the identifiers picked up by the get calls.

The op manual pages describe calls that are used to perform the particular operations characteristic of the type of IPC facility being used. msgop has calls that send or receive messages. semop (the only one of the three that is actually the name of a system call) is used to increment or decrement the value of a semaphore, among other functions. shmop has calls that attach or detach shared memory segments.

Where to Find More Information

Chapter 4 in this book gives a detailed description of IPC, with many code examples that use the IPC system calls. An example of the use of some IPC features is included in the liber application in Appendix A. The system calls are described in Section 2 of the *Programmer's Reference Manual*.

Process Scheduler

The UNIX system scheduler determines when processes run. It maintains process priorities based on configuration parameters, process behavior, and user requests; it uses these priorities to assign processes to the CPU.

Scheduler functions give users absolute control over the order in which certain processes run and the amount of time each process may use the CPU before another process gets a chance.

By default, the scheduler uses a time-sharing policy. A time-sharing policy adjusts process priorities dynamically in an attempt to give good response time to interactive processes and good throughput to CPU-intensive processes.

The scheduler offers a real-time scheduling policy as well as a time-sharing policy. Real-time scheduling allows users to set fixed priorities— priorities that the system does not change. The highest priority real-time user process always gets the CPU as soon as it is runnable, even if system processes are runnable. An application can therefore specify the exact order in which processes run. An application may also be written so that its real-time processes have a guaranteed response time from the system.

For most UNIX system environments, the default scheduler configuration works well and no real-time processes are needed: administrators need not change configuration parameters and users need not change scheduler properties of their processes. However, for some applications with strict timing constraints, real-time processes are the only way to guarantee that the application's requirements are met.

Where to Find More Information

Chapter 5 in this book gives detailed information on the process scheduler, along with relevant code examples. See also priocntl(1) in the *User's Reference Manual*, priocntl(2) in the *Programmer's Reference Manual*, and dispadmin(1M) in the *System Administrator's Reference Manual*.

Symbolic Links

A symbolic link is a special type of file that represents another file. The data in a symbolic link consists of the path name of a file or directory to which the symbolic link file refers. The link that is formed is called symbolic to distinguish it from a regular (also called a hard) link. A symbolic link differs functionally from a regular link in three major ways.

- Files from different file systems may be linked.

- Directories, as well as regular files, may be symbolically linked by any user.

- A symbolic link can be created even if the file it represents does not exist.

When a user creates a regular link to a file, a new directory entry is created containing a new file name and the inode number of an existing file. The link count of the file is incremented.

In contrast, when a user creates a symbolic link, (using the ln(1) command with the −s option) both a new directory entry and a new inode are created. A data block is allocated to contain the path name of the file to which the symbolic link refers. The link count of the referenced file is not incremented.

Symbolic links can be used to solve a variety of common problems. For example, it frequently happens that a disk partition (such as root) runs out of disk space. With symbolic links, an administrator can create a link from a directory on that file system to a directory on another file system. Such a link provides extra disk space and is, in most cases, transparent to both users and programs.

Symbolic links can also help deal with the built-in path names that appear in the code of many commands. Changing the path names would require changing the programs and recompiling them. With symbolic links, the path names can effectively be changed by making the original files symbolic links that point to new files.

In a shared resource environment like RFS, symbolic links can be very useful. For example, if it is important to have a single copy of certain administrative files, symbolic links can be used to help share them. Symbolic links can also be used to share resources selectively. Suppose a system administrator wants to do a remote mount of a directory that contains sharable devices. These devices must be in /dev on the client system, but this system has devices of its own so the administrator does not want to mount the directory onto /dev. Rather than do this, the administrator can mount the directory at a location other than /dev and then use symbolic links in the /dev directory to refer to these remote devices. (This is similar to the problem of built-in path names since it is normally assumed that devices reside in the /dev directory.)

Finally, symbolic links can be valuable within the context of the virtual file system (VFS) architecture. With VFS new services, such as higher performance files, network IPC, and FACE servers, may be provided on a file system basis. Symbolic links can be used to link these services to home directories or to places that make more sense to the application or user. Thus, you might create a data base index file in a RAM-based file system type and symbolically link it to the place where the data base server expects it and manages it.

Where to Find More Information

Chapter 6 in this book discusses symbolic links in detail. Refer to symlink(2) in the *Programmer's Reference Manual* for information on creating symbolic links. See also stat(2), rename(2), link(2), readlink(2), and unlink(2) in the same manual.

Memory Management

The UNIX system includes a complete set of memory-mapping mechanisms. Process address spaces are composed of a vector of memory pages, each of which can be independently mapped and manipulated. The memory-management facilities

- unify the system's operations on memory

- provide a set of kernel mechanisms powerful and general enough to support the implementation of fundamental system services without special-purpose kernel support

- maintain consistency with the existing environment, in particular using the UNIX file system as the name space for named virtual-memory objects

The system's virtual memory consists of all available physical memory resources including local and remote file systems, processor primary memory, swap space, and other random-access devices. Named objects in the virtual memory are referenced though the UNIX file system. However, not all file system objects are in the virtual memory; devices that UNIX cannot treat as storage, such as terminal and network device files, are not in the virtual memory. Some virtual memory objects, such as private process memory and shared memory segments, do not have names.

The Memory Mapping Interface

The applications programmer gains access to the facilities of the virtual memory system through several sets of system calls.

- mmap establishes a mapping between a process's address space and a virtual memory object.

- mprotect assigns access protection to a block of virtual memory

- munmap removes a memory mapping

- getpagesize returns the system-dependent size of a memory page.

- mincore tells whether mapped memory pages are in primary memory

Where to Find More Information

Chapter 7 in this book gives a detailed description of the virtual memory system. Refer to mmap(2), mprotect(2), munmap(2), getpagesize(2), and mincore(2) in the *Programmer's Reference Manual* for these manual pages.

Data Validation Tools

Data validation tools are written to help you write any administrative programs and routines that are part of your software package (this is known as package administration). They help standardize the appearance of administration interaction in the UNIX system environment and also simplify development of scripts and programs requiring administrator input.

There are two types of data validation tools:

- shell commands (to be used in shell scripts)
- visual tools (to be used in FMLI form definitions)

The shell commands perform a series of tasks; the visual tools perform a subsection of the full series. These tasks are:

- prompting a user for input
- validating the answer
- formatting and printing a help message when requested
- formatting and presenting an error message when validation fails
- returning the input if it passes validation
- allowing a user to quit the process

Where to Find More Information

Chapter 10 in this book describes the characteristics of these tools and introduces you to the available tools for all two types. For details on a specific tool, refer to Appendix B. It contains the manual pages for ckdate(1), ckgid(1), ckint(1), ckkeywd(1), ckpath(1), ckrange(1), ckstr(1), cktime(1), ckuid(1), ckyorn(1), dispgid(1), and dispuid(1). The visual tools are also documented in the Section 1 manual pages.

Package Development and Installation

This section gives the software package developer information on the interfaces provided by SVR4, specifically package software for SVR4 and how to modify the administrator's interface.

The interface modification tools allow you to generate files to deliver as part of your package. When these files are installed, your package administration tasks are added to the interface.

Packaging Application Software

Packaging software that will be installed on a computer running UNIX SVR4 differs from packaging in a pre-SVR4 environment. Pre-SVR4 packages deliver information to the system through script actions, but an SVR4 package does this through package information files.

A software package is made up of a group of components that together create the software. These components naturally include the executables that comprise the software, but they also include at least two information files and can optionally include other information files and scripts.

The contents of a package fall into three categories:

- required components
- optional package information files
- optional package scripts

A packaging tool, the pkgmk command, is provided to help automate package creation. It gathers the components of a package on the development machine and copies and formats them onto the installation medium.

The installation tool, the pkgadd command, copies the package from the installation medium onto a system and performs system housekeeping routines that concern the package.

Where to Find More Information

Chapter 8 in this book gives complete details on packaging application software. Appendix C contains package installation case studies. For details on a specific tool, refer to Appendix B. It contains the manual pages for admin(4), compver(4), copyright(4), depend(4), installf(1M), pkgadd(1M), pkgask(1M), pkgchk(1M), pkginfo(1), pkginfo(4), pkgmap(4), pkgmk(1), pkgparam(1), pkgproto(1), pkgrm(1M), pkgtrans(1), prototype(4), removef(1M), and space(4).

Modifying the sysadm Interface

The UNIX system provides a menu interface to the most common administrative procedures. It is invoked by executing sysadm and is referred to as the sysadm interface.

You can deliver additions or changes to this interface as part of your application software package. Creating the necessary information for an interface modification can be done using the tools UNIX provides.

Two commands can be used to modify the interface. edsysadm allows you to make changes or additions to the interface. It is interactive (much like the sysadm command itself) and presents a series of prompts for information. Which prompts appear depend on your response to them. The delsysadm command deletes menus or tasks from the interface. In addition to these commands, a group of data validation tools are provided to simplify and standardize the programming of administrative interaction.

When you execute edsysadm to define menus and tasks and save those definitions to be included in your application software package, it creates the package description file, the menu information file, and a prototype file.

- The package description file contains information used by edsysadm to change interface modifications already saved for packaging.

- The menu information file contains the menu or task name, where it is located in the interface structure and, for tasks, what executable to use when the task is invoked.

■ The prototype file created by edsysadm contains entries for all of the interface modification components that must be packaged with your software (for example, the menu information file and, for tasks, the executables).

You must take a number of steps if you intend to modify the sysadm interface by adding the administration to your package. You have to

■ plan your package administration

■ write your administration actions

■ write your help messages

■ package your interface modifications

Where to Find More Information

Chapter 9 in this book gives complete details on modifying the sysadm interface. For details on a specific tool, refer to Appendix B. It contains the manual pages for delsysadm(1M) and edsysadm(1M). The *System Administrator's Guide* gives a complete description of the interface and how to use it. See also the *Programmer's Guide: Character User Interface (FMLI and ETI)* for complete information on FMLI.

3 File and Record Locking

Introduction

Mandatory and advisory file and record locking both are available on current releases of the UNIX system. The intent of this capability to is provide a synchronization mechanism for programs accessing the same stores of data simultaneously. Such processing is characteristic of many multiuser applications, and the need for a standard method of dealing with the problem has been recognized by standards advocates like /usr/group, an organization of UNIX system users from businesses and campuses across the country.

Advisory file and record locking can be used to coordinate self-synchronizing processes. In mandatory locking, the standard I/O subroutines and I/O system calls enforce the locking protocol. In this way, at the cost of a little efficiency, mandatory locking double checks the programs against accessing the data out of sequence.

The remainder of this chapter describes how file and record locking capabilities can be used. Examples are given for the correct use of record locking. Misconceptions about the amount of protection that record locking affords are dispelled. Record locking should be viewed as a synchronization mechanism, not a security mechanism.

The manual pages for the fcntl(2) system call, the lockf(3) library function, and fcntl(5) data structures and commands are referred to throughout this section. You should read them before continuing.

Terminology

Before discussing how record locking should be used, let us first define a few terms.

Record

A contiguous set of bytes in a file. The UNIX operating system does not impose any record structure on files. This may be done by the programs that use the files.

Cooperating Processes

Processes that work together in some well-defined fashion to accomplish the tasks at hand. Processes that share files must request permission to access the files before using them. File access permissions must be carefully set to restrict noncooperating processes from accessing those files. The term process will be used interchangeably with cooperating process to refer to a task obeying such protocols.

Read (Share) Locks

These are used to gain limited access to sections of files. When a read lock is in place on a record, other processes may also read lock that record, in whole or in part. No other process, however, may have or obtain a write lock on an overlapping section of the file. If a process holds a read lock it may assume that no other process will be writing or updating that record at the same time. This access method also permits many processes to read the given record. This might be necessary when searching a file, without the contention involved if a write or exclusive lock were to be used.

Write (Exclusive) Locks

These are used to gain complete control over sections of files. When a write lock is in place on a record, no other process may read or write lock that record, in whole or in part. If a process holds a write lock it may assume that no other process will be reading or writing that record at the same time.

Advisory Locking

A form of record locking that does not interact with the I/O subsystem. Advisory locking is not enforced, for example, by creat(2), open(2), read(2), or write(2). The control over records is accomplished by requiring an appropriate record lock request before I/O operations. If appropriate requests are always made by all processes accessing the file, then the accessibility of the file will be controlled by the interaction of these requests. Advisory locking depends on the individual processes to enforce the record locking protocol; it does not require an accessibility check at the time of each I/O request.

Mandatory Locking

A form of record locking that does interact with the I/O subsystem. Access to locked records is enforced by the creat, open, read, and write(2) system calls. If a record is locked, then access of that record by any other process is restricted according to the type of lock on the record. The control over records should still be performed explicitly by requesting an appropriate record lock before I/O operations, but an additional check is made by the system before each I/O operation to ensure the record locking protocol is being honored. Mandatory locking offers an extra synchronization check, but at the cost of some additional system overhead.

File Protection

There are access permissions for UNIX system files to control who may read, write, or execute such a file. These access permissions may only be set by the owner of the file or by the superuser. The permissions of the directory in which the file resides can also affect the ultimate disposition of a file. Note that if the directory permissions allow anyone to write in it, then files within the directory may be removed, even if those files do not have read, write or execute permission for that user. Any information that is worth protecting, is worth protecting properly. If your application warrants the use of record locking, make sure that the permissions on your files and directories are set properly. A record lock, even a mandatory record lock, will only protect the portions of the files that are locked. Other parts of these files might be corrupted if proper precautions are not taken.

Only a known set of programs and/or administrators should be able to read or write a data base. This can be done easily by setting the set-group-ID bit of the data base accessing programs; see chmod(1). The files can then be accessed by a known set of programs that obey the record locking protocol. An example of such file protection, although record locking is not used, is the mail(1) command. In that command only the particular user and the mail command can read and write in the unread mail files.

Opening a File for Record Locking

The first requirement for locking a file or segment of a file is having a valid open file descriptor. If read locks are to be done, then the file must be opened with at least read accessibility and likewise for write locks and write accessibility. For our example we will open our file for both read and write access:

```
#include <stdio.h>
#include <errno.h>
#include <fcntl.h>

int fd;              /* file descriptor */
char *filename;

main(argc, argv)
int argc;
char *argv[];
{
        extern void exit(), perror();

        /* get data base file name from command line and open the
         * file for read and write access.
         */
        if (argc < 2) {
            (void) fprintf(stderr, "usage: %s filename\n", argv[0]);
            exit(2);
            }
        filename = argv[1];
        fd = open(filename, O_RDWR);
        if (fd < 0) {
            perror(filename);
            exit(2);
            }
        .
        .
        .
```

The file is now open for us to perform both locking and I/O functions. We then proceed with the task of setting a lock.

 NOTE Mapped files cannot be locked: if a file has been mapped, any attempt to use file or record locking on the file fails. See mmap(2).

Setting a File Lock

There are several ways for us to set a lock on a file. In part, these methods depend on how the lock interacts with the rest of the program. There are also questions of performance as well as portability. Two methods will be given here, one using the fcntl(2) system call, the other using the /usr/group standards compatible lockf library function call.

Locking an entire file is just a special case of record locking. For both these methods the concept and the effect of the lock are the same. The file is locked starting at a byte offset of zero (0) until the end of the maximum file size. This point extends beyond any real end of the file so that no lock can be placed on this file beyond this point. To do this the value of the size of the lock is set to zero. The code using the fcntl system call is as follows:

```
#include <fcntl.h>
#define MAX_TRY    10
int try;
struct flock lck;

try = 0;

/* set up the record locking structure, the address of which
 * is passed to the fcntl system call.
 */
lck.l_type = F_WRLCK;    /* setting a write lock */
lck.l_whence = 0;        /* offset l_start from beginning of file */
lck.l_start = 0L;
lck.l_len = 0L;          /* until the end of the file address space */

/* Attempt locking MAX_TRY times before giving up.
 */
while (fcntl(fd, F_SETLK, &lck) < 0) {
        if (errno == EAGAIN || errno == EACCES) {
                /* there might be other errors cases in which
                 * you might try again.
                 */
                if (++try < MAX_TRY) {
                        (void) sleep(2);
                        continue;
                }
                (void) fprintf(stderr,"File busy try again later!\n");
                return;
        }
        perror("fcntl");
        exit(2);
}
        .
        .
        .
```

This portion of code tries to lock a file. This is attempted several times until one of the following things happens:

- the file is locked

- an error occurs

- it gives up trying because MAX_TRY has been exceeded

To perform the same task using the `lockf` function, the code is as follows:

```
#include <unistd.h>
#define MAX_TRY      10
int try;
try = 0;

/* make sure the file pointer
 * is at the beginning of the file.
 */
lseek(fd, 0L, 0);

/* Attempt locking MAX_TRY times before giving up.
 */
while (lockf(fd, F_TLOCK, 0L) < 0) {
        if (errno == EAGAIN || errno == EACCES) {
                /* there might be other errors cases in which
                 * you might try again.
                 */
                if (++try < MAX_TRY) {
                        sleep(2);
                        continue;
                }
                (void) fprintf(stderr,"File busy try again later!\n");
                return;
        }
        perror("lockf");
        exit(2);
}
        .
        .
        .
```

It should be noted that the `lockf` example appears to be simpler, but the `fcntl(2)` example exhibits additional flexibility. Using the `fcntl(2)` method, it is possible to set the type and start of the lock request simply by setting a few structure variables. `lockf` merely sets write (exclusive) locks; an additional system call, `lseek`, is required to specify the start of the lock.

Setting and Removing Record Locks

Locking a record is done the same way as locking a file except for the differing starting point and length of the lock. We will now try to solve an interesting and real problem. There are two records (these records may be in the same or different file) that must be updated simultaneously so that other processes get a consistent view of this information. (This type of problem comes up, for example, when updating the interrecord pointers in a doubly linked list.) To do this you must decide the following questions:

- What do you want to lock?
- For multiple locks, in what order do you want to lock and unlock the records?
- What do you do if you succeed in getting all the required locks?
- What do you do if you fail to get all the locks?

In managing record locks, you must plan a failure strategy if you cannot obtain all the required locks. It is because of contention for these records that we have decided to use record locking in the first place. Different programs might:

- wait a certain amount of time, and try again
- abort the procedure and warn the user
- let the process sleep until signaled that the lock has been freed
- some combination of the above

Let us now look at our example of inserting an entry into a doubly linked list. For the example, we will assume that the record after which the new record is to be inserted has a read lock on it already. The lock on this record must be changed or promoted to a write lock so that the record may be edited.

Promoting a lock (generally from read lock to write lock) is permitted if no other process is holding a read lock in the same section of the file. If there are processes with pending write locks that are sleeping on the same section of the file, the lock promotion succeeds and the other (sleeping) locks wait. Promoting (or demoting) a write lock to a read lock carries no restrictions. In either case, the lock is merely reset with the new lock type. Because the /usr/group lockf function does not have read locks, lock promotion is not applicable to that call. An example of record locking with lock promotion follows:

```
struct record {
        .
        .                    /* data portion of record */
        .
        long prev;    /* index to previous record in the list */
        long next;    /* index to next record in the list */
};

/* Lock promotion using fcntl(2)
 * When this routine is entered it is assumed that there are read
 * locks on "here" and "next".
 * If write locks on "here" and "next" are obtained:
 *     Set a write lock on "this".
 *     Return index to "this" record.
 * If any write lock is not obtained:
 *     Restore read locks on "here" and "next".
 *     Remove all other locks.
 *     Return a -1.
 */
long
set3lock (this, here, next)
long this, here, next;
{
        struct flock lck;

        lck.l_type = F_WRLCK;    /* setting a write lock */
        lck.l_whence = 0;        /* offset l_start from beginning of file */
        lck.l_start = here;
        lck.l_len = sizeof(struct record);

        /* promote lock on "here" to write lock */
        if (fcntl(fd, F_SETLKW, &lck) < 0) {
                return (-1);
        }
        /* lock "this" with write lock */
        lck.l_start = this;
        if (fcntl(fd, F_SETLKW, &lck) < 0) {
                /* Lock on "this" failed;
                 * demote lock on "here" to read lock.
                 */
                lck.l_type = F_RDLCK;
                lck.l_start = here;
                (void) fcntl(fd, F_SETLKW, &lck);
                return (-1);
        }
        /* promote lock on "next" to write lock */
```

(continued on next page)

System Services and Application Packaging Tools

```
        lck.l_start = next;
        if (fcntl(fd, F_SETLKW, &lck) < 0) {
                /* Lock on "next" failed;
                 * demote lock on "here" to read lock,
                 */
                lck.l_type = F_RDLCK;
                 lck.l_start = here;
                (void) fcntl(fd, F_SETLK, &lck);
                /* and remove lock on "this".
                 */
                lck.l_type = F_UNLCK;
                lck.l_start = this;
                (void) fcntl(fd, F_SETLK, &lck);
                return (-1);/* cannot set lock, try again or quit */
        }

        return (this);
}
```

The locks on these three records were all set to wait (sleep) if another process was blocking them from being set. This was done with the F_SETLKW command. If the F_SETLK command was used instead, the fcntl system calls would fail if blocked. The program would then have to be changed to handle the blocked condition in each of the error return sections.

Let us now look at a similar example using the lockf function. Since there are no read locks, all (write) locks will be referenced generically as locks.

```
/* Lock promotion using lockf(3)
 * When this routine is entered it is assumed that there are
 * no locks on "here" and "next".
 * If locks are obtained:
 *     Set a lock on "this".
 *     Return index to "this" record.
 * If any lock is not obtained:
 *     Remove all other locks.
 *     Return a -1.
 */

#include <unistd.h>

long
set3lock (this, here, next)
long this, here, next;

{

        /* lock "here" */
        (void) lseek(fd, here, 0);
        if (lockf(fd, F_LOCK, sizeof(struct record)) < 0) {
                return (-1);
        }
        /* lock "this" */
        (void) lseek(fd, this, 0);
        if (lockf(fd, F_LOCK, sizeof(struct record)) < 0) {
                /* Lock on "this" failed.
                 * Clear lock on "here".
                 */
                (void) lseek(fd, here, 0);
                (void) lockf(fd, F_ULOCK, sizeof(struct record));
                return (-1);

        }

        /* lock "next" */
        (void) lseek(fd, next, 0);
        if (lockf(fd, F_LOCK, sizeof(struct record)) < 0) {

                /* Lock on "next" failed.
                 * Clear lock on "here",
                 */
                (void) lseek(fd, here, 0);
                (void) lockf(fd, F_ULOCK, sizeof(struct record));
```

(continued on next page)

System Services and Application Packaging Tools

```
                 /* and remove lock on "this".
                  */
                 (void) lseek(fd, this, 0);
                 (void) lockf(fd, F_ULOCK, sizeof(struct record));
                 return (-1);/* cannot set lock, try again or quit */

          }

       return (this);

  }
```

Locks are removed in the same manner as they are set, only the lock type is different (F_UNLCK or F_ULOCK). An unlock cannot be blocked by another process and will only affect locks that were placed by this process. The unlock only affects the section of the file defined in the previous example by lck. It is possible to unlock or change the type of lock on a subsection of a previously set lock. This may cause an additional lock (two locks for one system call) to be used by the operating system. This occurs if the subsection is from the middle of the previously set lock.

Getting Lock Information

You can determine which processes, if any, are blocking a lock from being set. This can be used as a simple test or as a means to find locks on a file. A lock is set up as in the previous examples and the F_GETLK command is used in the fcntl call. If the lock passed to fcntl would be blocked, the first blocking lock is returned to the process through the structure passed to fcntl. That is, the lock data passed to fcntl is overwritten by blocking lock information. This information includes two pieces of data that have not been discussed yet, l_pid and l_sysid, that are only used by F_GETLK. (For systems that do not support a distributed architecture the value in l_sysid should be ignored.) These fields uniquely identify the process holding the lock.

If a lock passed to fcntl using the F_GETLK command would not be blocked by another process's lock, then the l_type field is changed to F_UNLCK and the remaining fields in the structure are unaffected. Let us use this capability to print all the segments locked by other processes. Note that if there are several read locks over the same segment only one of these will be found.

```
struct flock lck;

/* Find and print "write lock" blocked segments of this file. */
        (void) printf("sysid   pid type    start   length\n");
        lck.l_whence = 0;
        lck.l_start = 0L;
        lck.l_len = 0L;
        do {
                lck.l_type = F_WRLCK;
                (void) fcntl(fd, F_GETLK, &lck);
                if (lck.l_type != F_UNLCK) {
                        (void) printf("%5d %5d   %c  %8d %8d\n",
                                lck.l_sysid,
                                lck.l_pid,
                                (lck.l_type == F_WRLCK) ? 'W' : 'R',
                                lck.l_start,
                                lck.l_len);
                        /* if this lock goes to the end of the address
                         * space, no need to look further, so break out.
                         */
                        if (lck.l_len == 0)
                                break;
                        /* otherwise, look for new lock after the one
                         * just found.
                         */
                        lck.l_start += lck.l_len;
                }
        } while (lck.l_type != F_UNLCK);
```

fcntl with the F_GETLK command will always return correctly (that is, it will
not sleep or fail) if the values passed to it as arguments are valid.

The lockf function with the F_TEST command can also be used to test if there
is a process blocking a lock. This function does not, however, return the information about where the lock actually is and which process owns the lock. A
routine using lockf to test for a lock on a file follows:

```
/* find a blocked record. */
/* seek to beginning of file */
(void) lseek(fd, 0, 0L);
/* set the size of the test region to zero (0)
 * to test until the end of the file address space.
 */
if (lockf(fd, F_TEST, 0L) < 0) {
        switch (errno) {
                case EACCES:
                case EAGAIN:
                (void) printf("file is locked by another process\n");
                break;
                case EBADF:
                /* bad argument passed to lockf */
                perror("lockf");
                break;
                default:
                (void) printf("lockf: unknown error <%d>\n", errno);
                break;
                }

        }
```

When a process forks, the child receives a copy of the file descriptors that the parent has opened. The parent and child also share a common file pointer for each file. If the parent were to seek to a point in the file, the child's file pointer would also be at that location. This feature has important implications when using record locking. The current value of the file pointer is used as the reference for the offset of the beginning of the lock, as described by l_start, when using a l_whence value of 1. If both the parent and child process set locks on the same file, there is a possibility that a lock will be set using a file pointer that was reset by the other process. This problem appears in the lockf(3) function call as well and is a result of the /usr/group requirements for record locking. If forking is used in a record locking program, the child process should close and reopen the file if either locking method is used. This will result in the creation of a new and separate file pointer that can be manipulated without this problem occurring. Another solution is to use the fcntl system call with a l_whence value of 0 or 2. This makes the locking function atomic, so that even processes sharing file pointers can be locked without difficulty.

Deadlock Handling

There is a certain level of deadlock detection/avoidance built into the record locking facility. This deadlock handling provides the same level of protection granted by the /usr/group standard lockf call. This deadlock detection is only valid for processes that are locking files or records on a single system. Deadlocks can only potentially occur when the system is about to put a record locking system call to sleep. A search is made for constraint loops of processes that would cause the system call to sleep indefinitely. If such a situation is found, the locking system call will fail and set errno to the deadlock error number. If a process wishes to avoid the use of the systems deadlock detection it should set its locks using F_GETLK instead of F_GETLKW.

Selecting Advisory or Mandatory Locking

The use of mandatory locking is not recommended for reasons that will be made clear in a subsequent section. Whether or not locks are enforced by the I/O system calls is determined at the time the calls are made by the permissions on the file; see chmod(2). For locks to be under mandatory enforcement, the file must be a regular file with the set-group-ID bit on and the group execute permission off. If either condition fails, all record locks are advisory. Mandatory enforcement can be assured by the following code:

```
#include <sys/types.h>
#include <sys/stat.h>

int mode;
struct stat buf;
            .
            .
            .
        if (stat(filename, &buf) < 0) {
                perror("program");
                exit (2);
        }
        /* get currently set mode */
        mode = buf.st_mode;
        /* remove group execute permission from mode */
        mode &= ~(S_IEXEC>>3);
        /* set 'set group id bit' in mode */
        mode |= S_ISGID;
        if (chmod(filename, mode) < 0) {
                perror("program");
                exit(2);
        }
            .
            .
            .
```

Files that are to be record locked should never have any type of execute permission set on them. This is because the operating system does not obey the record locking protocol when executing a file.

The chmod(1) command can also be easily used to set a file to have mandatory locking. This can be done with the command:

    chmod +l *file*

The ls(1) command shows this setting when you ask for the long listing format:

    ls −l *file*

causes the following to be printed:

    −rw−−−l−−−   1   *user*   *group*   *size*   *mod_time*   *file*

Caveat Emptor—Mandatory Locking

- Mandatory locking only protects those portions of a file that are locked. Other portions of the file that are not locked may be accessed according to normal UNIX system file permissions.

- If multiple reads or writes are necessary for an atomic transaction, the process should explicitly lock all such pieces before any I/O begins. Thus advisory enforcement is sufficient for all programs that perform in this way.

- As stated earlier, arbitrary programs should not have unrestricted access permission to files that are important enough to record lock.

- Advisory locking is more efficient because a record lock check does not have to be performed for every I/O request.

Record Locking and Future Releases of the UNIX System

Provisions have been made for file and record locking in a UNIX system environment. In such an environment the system on which the locking process resides may be remote from the system on which the file and record locks reside. In this way multiple processes on different systems may put locks upon a single file that resides on one of these or yet another system. The record locks for a file reside on the system that maintains the file. It is also important to note that deadlock detection/avoidance is only determined by the record locks being held by and for a single system. Therefore, it is necessary that a process only hold record locks on a single system at any given time for the deadlock mechanism to be effective. If a process needs to maintain locks over several systems, it is suggested that the process avoid the sleep-when-blocked features of `fcntl` or `lockf` and that the process maintain its own deadlock detection. If the process uses the sleep-when-blocked feature, then a timeout mechanism should be provided by the process so that it does not hang waiting for a lock to be cleared.

4 Interprocess Communication

Introduction

UNIX System V Release 4.0 provides several mechanisms that allow processes to exchange data and synchronize execution. The simpler of these mechanisms are pipes, named pipes, and signals. These are limited, however, in what they can do. For instance,

- Pipes do not allow unrelated processes to communicate.

- Named pipes allow unrelated processes to communicate, but they cannot provide private channels for pairs of communicating processes; that is, any process with appropriate permission may read from or write to a named pipe.

- Sending signals, via the `kill` system call, allows arbitrary processes to communicate, but the message consists only of the signal number.

Release 4.0 also provides an InterProcess Communication (IPC) package that supports three, more versatile types of interprocess communication. For example,

- Messages allow processes to send formatted data streams to arbitrary processes.

- Semaphores allow processes to synchronize execution.

- Shared memory allows processes to share parts of their virtual address space.

When implemented as a unit, these three mechanisms share common properties such as

- each mechanism contains a "get" system call to create a new entry or retrieve an existing one

- each mechanism contains a "control" system call to query the status of an entry, to set status information, or to remove the entry from the system

- each mechanism contains an "operations" system call to perform various operations on an entry

This chapter describes the system calls for each of these three forms of IPC.

This information is for programmers who write multiprocess applications. These programmers should have a general understanding of what semaphores are and how they are used.

Information from other sources would also be helpful. See the ipcs(1) and ipcrm(1) manual pages in the *User's Reference Manual* and the following manual pages in the *Programmer's Reference Manual*:

```
intro(2)
msgget(2)        msgctl(2)        msgop(2)
semget(2)        semctl(2)        semop(2)
shmget(2)        shmctl(2)        shmop(2)
```

Included in this chapter are several example programs that show the use of these IPC system calls. Since there are many ways to accomplish the same task or requirement, keep in mind that the example programs were written for clarity and not for program efficiency. Usually, system calls are embedded within a larger user-written program that makes use of a particular function provided by the calls.

Messages

The message type of IPC allows processes (executing programs) to communicate through the exchange of data stored in buffers. This data is transmitted between processes in discrete portions called messages. Processes using this type of IPC can send and receive messages.

Before a process can send or receive a message, it must have the UNIX operating system generate the necessary software mechanisms to handle these operations. A process does this using the msgget system call. In doing this, the process becomes the owner/creator of a message queue and specifies the initial operation permissions for all processes, including itself. Subsequently, the owner/creator can relinquish ownership or change the operation permissions using the msgctl system call. However, the creator remains the creator as long as the facility exists. Other processes with permission can use msgctl to perform various other control functions.

Processes which have permission and are attempting to send or receive a message can suspend execution if they are unsuccessful at performing their operation. That is, a process which is attempting to send a message can wait until it becomes possible to post the message to the specified message queue; the receiving process isn't involved (except indirectly, e.g., if the consumer isn't consuming, the queue space will eventually be exhausted) and vice versa. A process which specifies that execution is to be suspended is performing a "blocking message operation." A process which does not allow its execution to be suspended is performing a "nonblocking message operation."

A process performing a blocking message operation can be suspended until one of three conditions occurs:

- It is successful.
- It receives a signal.
- The message queue is removed from the system.

System calls make these message capabilities available to processes. The calling process passes arguments to a system call, and the system call either successfully or unsuccessfully performs its function. If the system call is successful, it performs its function and returns applicable information. Otherwise, a known error code (−1) is returned to the process, and an external error number variable, errno, is set accordingly.

Using Messages

Before a message can be sent or received, a uniquely identified message queue and data structure must be created. The unique identifier is called the message queue identifier (msqid); it is used to identify or refer to the associated message queue and data structure.

The message queue is used to store (header) information about each message being sent or received. This information, which is for internal use by the system, includes the following for each message:

- pointer to the next message on queue

- message type

- message text size

- message text address

There is one associated data structure for the uniquely identified message queue. This data structure contains the following information related to the message queue:

- operation permissions data (operation permission structure)

- pointer to first message on the queue

- pointer to last message on the queue

- current number of bytes on the queue

- number of messages on the queue

- maximum number of bytes on the queue

- process identification (PID) of last message sender

- PID of last message receiver

- last message send time

- last message receive time

- last change time

NOTE All include files discussed in this chapter are located in the /usr/include or /usr/include/sys directories.

The structure definition for the associated data structure is as follows:

```
struct msqid_ds
{
        struct ipc_perm  msg_perm;    /* operation permission struct */
        struct msg       *msg_first;  /* ptr to first message on q */
        struct msg       *msg_last;   /* ptr to last message on q */
        ulong            msg_cbytes;  /* current # bytes on q */
        ulong            msg_qnum;    /* # of messages on q */
        ulong            msg_qbytes;  /* max # of bytes on q */
        pid_t            msg_lspid;   /* pid of last msgsnd */
        pid_t            msg_lrpid;   /* pid of last msgrcv */
        time_t           msg_stime;   /* last msgsnd time */
        long             msg_pad1;    /* reserved for time_t expansion */
        time_t           msg_rtime;   /* last msgrcv time */
        long             msg_pad2;    /* time_t expansion */
        time_t           msg_ctime;   /* last change time */
        long             msg_pad3;    /* time expansion */
        long             msg_pad4[4]; /* reserve area*/
};
```

It is located in the <sys/msg.h> header file. Note that the msg_perm member of this structure uses ipc_perm as a template. Figure 4-1 shows the breakout for the operation permissions data structure.

The definition of the ipc_perm data structure is as follows:

Figure 4-1: `ipc_perm` **Data Structure**

```
struct ipc_perm
{
        uid_t     uid;      /* owner's user id */
        gid_t     gid;      /* owner's group id */
        uid_t     cuid;     /* creator's user id */
        gid_t     cgid;     /* creator's group id */
        mode_t    mode;     /* access modes */
        ulong     seq;      /* slot usage sequence number */
        key_t     key;      /* key */
        long      pad[4];   /*reserve area */
};
```

It is located in the `<sys/ipc.h>` header file and is common to all IPC facilities.

The `msgget` system call is used to perform one of two tasks:

- to get a new message queue identifier and create an associated message queue and data structure for it

- to return an existing message queue identifier that already has an associated message queue and data structure

Both tasks require a `key` argument passed to the `msgget` system call. For the first task, if the `key` is not already in use for an existing message queue identifier , a new identifier is returned with an associated message queue and data structure created for the `key`. This occurs as long as no system-tunable parameters would be exceeded and a control command `IPC_CREAT` is specified in the `msgflg` argument passed in the system call.

There is also a provision for specifying a `key` of value zero, known as the private `key` (`IPC_PRIVATE`). When specified, a new identifier is always returned with an associated message queue and data structure created for it unless a system-tunable parameter would be exceeded. The `ipcs` command will show the `KEY` field for the `msqid` as all zeros.

For the second task, if a message queue identifier exists for the `key` specified, the value of the existing identifier is returned. If you do not want to have an existing message queue identifier returned, a control command (`IPC_EXCL`) can be specified (set) in the msgflg argument passed to the system call. ("Using msgget" describes how to use this system call.)

When performing the first task, the process that calls msgget becomes the owner/creator, and the associated data structure is initialized accordingly. Remember, ownership can be changed but the creating process always remains the creator. The message queue creator also determines the initial operation permissions for it.

Once a uniquely identified message queue and data structure are created, msgop (message operations) and msgctl (message control) can be used.

Message operations, as mentioned before, consist of sending and receiving messages. The msgsnd and msgrcv system calls are provided for each of these operations (see "Operations for Messages" for details of these system calls).

The msgctl system call permits you to control the message facility in the following ways:

- by retrieving the data structure associated with a message queue identifier (IPC_STAT)

- by changing operation permissions for a message queue (IPC_SET)

- by changing the size (msg_qbytes) of the message queue for a particular message queue identifier (IPC_SET)

- by removing a particular message queue identifier from the UNIX operating system along with its associated message queue and data structure (IPC_RMID)

See "Controlling Message Queues" for msgctl system call details.

Getting Message Queues

This section describes how to use the msgget system call. The accompanying program illustrates its use.

Using msgget

The synopsis found in the msgget(2) entry in the *Programmer's Reference Manual* is as follows:

```
#include  <sys/types.h>
#include  <sys/ipc.h>
#include  <sys/msg.h>

int  msgget  (key, msgflg)
key_t  key;
int msgflg;
```

All of these include files are located in the /usr/include/sys directory of the UNIX operating system.

The following line in the synopsis:

```
int msgget (key, msgflg)
```

informs you that msgget is a function with two formal arguments that returns an integer-type value. The next two lines:

```
key_t   key;
int msgflg;
```

declare the types of the formal arguments. key_t is defined by a typedef in the <sys/types.h> header file to be an integral type.

The integer returned from this function upon successful completion is the message queue identifier that was discussed earlier. Upon failure, the external variable errno is set to indicate the reason for failure, and the value -1 (which is not a valid msqid) is returned.

As declared, the process calling the msgget system call must supply two arguments to be passed to the formal key and msgflg arguments.

A new msqid with an associated message queue and data structure is provided if either

- **key** is equal to IPC_PRIVATE,

or

- **key** is a unique integer and the control command IPC_CREAT is specified in the **msgflg** argument.

The value passed to the **msgflg** argument must be an integer-type value that will specify the following:

- operations permissions

- control fields (commands)

Operation permissions determine the operations that processes are permitted to perform on the associated message queue. "Read" permission is necessary for receiving messages or for determining queue status by means of a **msgctl** IPC_STAT operation. "Write" permission is necessary for sending messages. Figure 4-2 reflects the numeric values (expressed in octal notation) for the valid operation permissions codes.

Figure 4-2: Operation Permissions Codes

Operation Permissions	Octal Value
Read by User	00400
Write by User	00200
Read by Group	00040
Write by Group	00020
Read by Others	00004
Write by Others	00002

A specific value is derived by adding or bitwise ORing the octal values for the operation permissions wanted. That is, if read by user and read/write by others is desired, the code value would be 00406 (00400 plus 00006). There are constants located in the <sys/msg.h> header file which can be used for the user operations permissions. They are as follows:

```
MSG_W  0200  /* write permissions by owner */

MSG_R  0400  /* read permissions by owner */
```

Control flags are predefined constants (represented by all uppercase letters). The flags which apply to the `msgget` system call are `IPC_CREAT` and `IPC_EXCL` and are defined in the `<sys/ipc.h>` header file.

The value for `msgflg` is therefore a combination of operation permissions and control commands. After determining the value for the operation permissions as previously described, the desired flag(s) can be specified. This is accomplished by adding or bitwise ORing (|) them with the operation permissions; the bit positions and values for the control commands in relation to those of the operation permissions make this possible.

The `msgflg` value can easily be set by using the flag names in conjunction with the octal operation permissions value:

```
msqid = msgget (key, (IPC_CREAT | 0400));

msqid = msgget (key, (IPC_CREAT | IPC_EXCL | 0400));
```

As specified by the `msgget`(2) page in the *Programmer's Reference Manual*, success or failure of this system call depends upon the argument values for `key` and `msgflg` or system-tunable parameters. The system call will attempt to return a new message queue identifier if one of the following conditions is true:

■ `key` is equal to `IPC_PRIVATE`

■ `key` does not already have a message queue identifier associated with it and (`msgflg` and `IPC_CREAT`) is "true" (not zero).

The `key` argument can be set to `IPC_PRIVATE` like this:

```
msqid = msgget (IPC_PRIVATE, msgflg);
```

The system call will always be attempted. Exceeding the `MSGMNI` system-tunable parameter always causes a failure. The `MSGMNI` system-tunable parameter determines the systemwide number of unique message queues that may be in use at any given time.

`IPC_EXCL` is another control command used in conjunction with `IPC_CREAT`. It will cause the system call to return an error if a message queue identifier already exists for the specified `key`. This is necessary to prevent the process from thinking that it has received a new identifier when it has not. In other words, when both `IPC_CREAT` and `IPC_EXCL` are specified, a new message queue identifier is returned if the system call is successful.

Refer to the msgget(2) page in the *Programmer's Reference Manual* for specific, associated data structure initialization for successful completion. The specific failure conditions and their error names are contained there also.

Example Program

Figure 4-3 is a menu-driven program. It allows all possible combinations of using the msgget system call to be exercised.

From studying this program, you can observe the method of passing arguments and receiving return values. The user-written program requirements are pointed out.

This program begins (lines 4-8) by including the required header files as specified by the msgget(2) entry in the *Programmer's Reference Manual*. Note that the <sys/errno.h> header file is included as opposed to declaring errno as an external variable; either method will work.

Variable names have been chosen to be as close as possible to those in the synopsis for the system call. Their declarations are self explanatory. These names make the programs more readable are perfectly legal since they are local to the program. The variables declared for this program and what they are used for are as follows:

key used to pass the value for the desired key

opperm used to store the desired operation permissions

flags used to store the desired control commands (flags)

opperm_flags
used to store the combination from the logical ORing of the opperm and flags variables; it is then used in the system call to pass the msgflg argument

msqid used for returning the message queue identification number for a successful system call or the error code (−1) for an unsuccessful one.

The program begins by prompting for a hexadecimal key, an octal operation permissions code, and finally for the control command combinations (flags) which are selected from a menu (lines 15-32). All possible combinations are allowed even though they might not be viable. This allows errors to be observed for illegal combinations.

Next, the menu selection for the flags is combined with the operation permissions, and the result is stored in the `opperm_flags` variable (lines 36-51).

The system call is made next, and the result is stored in the `msqid` variable (line 53).

Since the `msqid` variable now contains a valid message queue identifier or the error code (−1), it is tested to see if an error occurred (line 55). If `msqid` equals −1, a message indicates that an error resulted, and the external `errno` variable is displayed (line 57).

If no error occurred, the returned message queue identifier is displayed (line 61).

The example program for the `msgget` system call follows. We suggest you name the program file `msgget.c` and the executable file `msgget`.

Figure 4-3: `msgget` **System Call Example**

```
1      /*This is a program to illustrate
2      **the message get, msgget(),
3      **system call capabilities.*/

4      #include    <stdio.h>
5      #include    <sys/types.h>
6      #include    <sys/ipc.h>
7      #include    <sys/msg.h>
8      #include    <errno.h>

9      /*Start of main C language program*/
10     main()
11     {
12         key_t key;
13         int opperm, flags;
14         int msqid, opperm_flags;
15         /*Enter the desired key*/
16         printf("Enter the desired key in hex = ");
17         scanf("%x", &key);


18         /*Enter the desired octal operation
19          permissions.*/
20         printf("\nEnter the operation\n");
```

(continued on next page)

Figure 4-3: msgget **System Call Example** (continued)

```
21      printf("permissions in octal = ");
22      scanf("%o", &opperm);

23      /*Set the desired flags.*/
24      printf("\nEnter corresponding number to\n");
25      printf("set the desired flags:\n");
26      printf("No flags              = 0\n");
27      printf("IPC_CREAT             = 1\n");
28      printf("IPC_EXCL              = 2\n");
29      printf("IPC_CREAT and IPC_EXCL = 3\n");
30      printf("          Flags       = ");

31      /*Get the flag(s) to be set.*/
32      scanf("%d", &flags);

33      /*Check the values.*/
34      printf ("\nkey =0x%x, opperm = 0%o, flags = 0%o\n",
35          key, opperm, flags);

36      /*Incorporate the control fields (flags) with
37        the operation permissions*/
38      switch (flags)
39      {
40      case 0:    /*No flags are to be set.*/
41          opperm_flags = (opperm | 0);
42          break;
43      case 1:    /*Set the IPC_CREAT flag.*/
44          opperm_flags = (opperm | IPC_CREAT);
45          break;
46      case 2:    /*Set the IPC_EXCL flag.*/
47          opperm_flags = (opperm | IPC_EXCL);
48          break;
49      case 3:    /*Set the IPC_CREAT and IPC_EXCL flags.*/
50          opperm_flags = (opperm | IPC_CREAT | IPC_EXCL);
51      }

52      /*Call the msgget system call.*/
53      msqid = msgget (key, opperm_flags);

54      /*Perform the following if the call is unsuccessful.*/
55      if(msqid == -1)
56      {
57          printf ("\nThe msgget call failed, error number = %d\n", errno);
58      }
59      /*Return the msqid upon successful completion.*/
60      else
```

(continued on next page)

Figure 4-3: msgget **System Call Example** (continued)

```
61              printf ("\nThe msqid - %d\n", msqid);
62          exit(0);
63      )
```

Controlling Message Queues

This section describes how to use the msgctl system call. The accompanying program illustrates its use.

Using msgctl

The synopsis found in the msgctl(2) entry in the *Programmer's Reference Manual* is as follows:

```
#include <sys/types.h>
#include <sys/ipc.h>
#include <sys/msg.h>

int msgctl (msqid, cmd, buf)
int msqid, cmd;
struct msqid_ds *buf;
```

The msgctl system call requires three arguments to be passed to it; it returns an integer-type value.

When successful, it returns a zero value; when unsuccessful, it returns a −1.

The msqid variable must be a valid, non-negative, integer value. In other words, it must have already been created by using the msgget system call.

The cmd argument can be any one of the following values:

IPC_STAT   return the status information contained in the associated data structure for the specified message queue identifier, and place it in the data structure pointed to by the buf pointer in the user memory area.

IPC_SET   for the specified message queue identifier, set the effective user and group identification, operation permissions, and the number of bytes for the message queue to the values contained in the data structure pointed to by the buf pointer in the user memory area.

IPC_RMID   remove the specified message queue identifier along with its associated message queue and data structure.

A process must have an effective user identification of OWNER/CREATOR or superuser to perform an IPC_SET or IPC_RMID control command. Read permission is required to perform the IPC_STAT control command.

The details of this system call are discussed in the following example program. If you need more information on the logic manipulations in this program, read the msgget(2) section of the *Programmer's Reference Manual*; it goes into more detail than would be practical for this document.

Example Program

Figure 4-4 is a menu-driven program. It allows all possible combinations of using the msgctl system call to be exercised.

From studying this program, you can observe the method of passing arguments and receiving return values. The user-written program requirements are pointed out.

This program begins (lines 5-9) by including the required header files as specified by the msgctl(2) entry in the *Programmer's Reference Manual*. Note in this program that errno is declared as an external variable, and therefore, the <sys/errno.h> header file does not have to be included.

Variable and structure names have been chosen to be as close as possible to those in the synopsis for the system call. Their declarations are self explanatory. These names make the program more readable and are perfectly legal since they are local to the program. The variables declared for this program and what they are used for are as follows:

uid	used to store the IPC_SET value for the effective user identification
gid	used to store the IPC_SET value for the effective group identification
mode	used to store the IPC_SET value for the operation permissions
bytes	used to store the IPC_SET value for the number of bytes in the message queue (msg_qbytes)
rtrn	used to store the return integer value from the system call
msqid	used to store and pass the message queue identifier to the system call
command	used to store the code for the desired control command so that subsequent processing can be performed on it
choice	used to determine which member is to be changed for the IPC_SET control command
msqid_ds	used to receive the specified message queue identifier's data structure when an IPC_STAT control command is performed
buf	a pointer passed to the system call which locates the data structure in the user memory area where the IPC_STAT control command is to place its return values or where the IPC_SET command gets the values to set

Note that the msqid_ds data structure in this program (line 16) uses the data structure, located in the <sys/msg.h> header file of the same name, as a template for its declaration.

The next important thing to observe is that although the buf pointer is declared to be a pointer to a data structure of the msqid_ds type, it must also be initialized to contain the address of the user memory area data structure (line 17). Now that all of the required declarations have been explained for this program, this is how it works.

First, the program prompts for a valid message queue identifier which is stored in the msqid variable (lines 19, 20). This is required for every msgctl system call.

Then the code for the desired control command must be entered (lines 21-27) and stored in the command variable. The code is tested to determine the control command for subsequent processing.

If the IPC_STAT control command is selected (code 1), the system call is performed (lines 37, 38) and the status information returned is printed out (lines 39-46); only the members that can be set are printed out in this program. Note that if the system call is unsuccessful (line 106), the status information of the last successful call is printed out. In addition, an error message is displayed and the errno variable is printed out (line 108). If the system call is successful, a message indicates this along with the message queue identifier used (lines 110-113).

If the IPC_SET control command is selected (code 2), the first thing is to get the current status information for the message queue identifier specified (lines 50-52). This is necessary because this example program provides for changing only one member at a time, and the system call changes all of them. Also, if an invalid value happened to be stored in the user memory area for one of these members, it would cause repetitive failures for this control command until corrected. The next thing the program does is to prompt for a code corresponding to the member to be changed (lines 53-59). This code is stored in the choice variable (line 60). Now, depending upon the member picked, the program prompts for the new value (lines 66-95). The value is placed into the appropriate member in the user memory area data structure, and the system call is made (lines 96-98). Depending upon success or failure, the program returns the same messages as for IPC_STAT above.

If the IPC_RMID control command (code 3) is selected, the system call is performed (lines 100-103), and the msqid along with its associated message queue and data structure are removed from the UNIX operating system. Note that the buf pointer is ignored in performing this control command, and its value can be zero or NULL. Depending upon the success or failure, the program returns the same messages as for the other control commands.

The example program for the msgctl system call follows. We suggest that you name the source program file msgctl.c and the executable file msgctl.

Figure 4-4: `msgctl` **System Call Example**

```
1      /*This is a program to illustrate
2      **the message control, msgctl(),
3      **system call capabilities.
4      */

5      /*Include necessary header files.*/
6      #include    <stdio.h>
7      #include    <sys/types.h>
8      #include    <sys/ipc.h>
9      #include    <sys/msg.h>

10     /*Start of main C language program*/
11     main()
12     {
13         extern int errno;
14         int uid, gid, mode, bytes;
15         int rtrn, msqid, command, choice;
16         struct msqid_ds msqid_ds, *buf;
17         buf = &msqid_ds;

18         /*Get the msqid, and command.*/
19         printf("Enter the msqid = ");
20         scanf("%d", &msqid);
21         printf("\nEnter the number for\n");
22         printf("the desired command:\n");
23         printf("IPC_STAT    = 1\n");
24         printf("IPC_SET     = 2\n");
25         printf("IPC_RMID    = 3\n");
26         printf("Entry       = ");
27         scanf("%d", &command);

28         /*Check the values.*/
29         printf ("\nmsqid =%d, command = %d\n",
30             msqid, command);

31         switch (command)
32         {
33         case 1:    /*Use msgctl() to duplicate
34             the data structure for
35                 msqid in the msqid_ds area pointed
36                 to by buf and then print it out.*/
37             rtrn = msgctl(msqid, IPC_STAT,
38                 buf);
39             printf ("\nThe USER ID = %d\n",
```

(continued on next page)

Figure 4-4: msgctl **System Call Example** (continued)

```
40              buf->msg_perm.uid);
41          printf ("The GROUP ID = %d\n",
42              buf->msg_perm.gid);
43          printf ("The operation permissions = 0%o\n",
44              buf->msg_perm.mode);
45          printf ("The msg_qbytes = %d\n",
46              buf->msg_qbytes);
47          break;
48      case 2:     /*Select and change the desired
49                      member(s) of the data structure.*/
50          /*Get the original data for this msqid
51              data structure first.*/
52          rtrn = msgctl(msqid, IPC_STAT, buf);
53          printf("\nEnter the number for the\n");
54          printf("member to be changed:\n");
55          printf("msg_perm.uid    = 1\n");
56          printf("msg_perm.gid    = 2\n");
57          printf("msg_perm.mode   = 3\n");
58          printf("msg_qbytes      = 4\n");
59          printf("Entry           = ");

60          scanf("%d", &choice);
61          /*Only one choice is allowed per
62            pass as an illegal entry will
63                cause repetitive failures until
64            msqid_ds is updated with
65                IPC_STAT.*/

66          switch(choice){
67          case 1:
68              printf("\nEnter USER ID = ");
69              scanf ("%ld", &uid);
70              buf->msg_perm.uid =(uid_t)uid;
71              printf("\nUSER ID = %d\n",
72                  buf->msg_perm.uid);
73              break;
74          case 2:
75              printf("\nEnter GROUP ID = ");
76              scanf("%d", &gid);
77              buf->msg_perm.gid = gid;
78              printf("\nGROUP ID = %d\n",
79                  buf->msg_perm.gid);
80              break;
81          case 3:
```

(continued on next page)

Figure 4-4: msgctl **System Call Example** (continued)

```
82                  printf("\nEnter MODE - ");
83                  scanf("%o", &mode);
84                  buf->msg_perm.mode = mode;
85                  printf("\nMODE - 0%o\n",
86                      buf->msg_perm.mode);
87                  break;
88              case 4:
89                  printf("\nEnter msq_bytes - ");
90                  scanf("%d", &bytes);
91                  buf->msg_qbytes = bytes;
92                  printf("\nmsg_qbytes - %d\n",
93                      buf->msg_qbytes);
94                  break;
95              }

96              /*Do the change.*/
97              rtrn = msgctl(msqid, IPC_SET,
98                  buf);
99              break;

100         case 3:    /*Remove the msqid along with its
101                       associated message queue
102                       and data structure.*/
103             rtrn = msgctl(msqid, IPC_RMID, (struct msqid_ds *) NULL);
104         }
105         /*Perform the following if the call is unsuccessful.*/
106         if(rtrn == -1)
107         {
108             printf ("\nThe msgctl call failed, error number - %d\n", errno);
109         }
110         /*Return the msqid upon successful completion.*/
111         else
112             printf ("\nMsgctl was successful for msqid - %d\n",
113                 msqid);
114         exit (0);
115     }
```

Operations for Messages

This section describes how to use the msgsnd and msgrcv system calls. The accompanying program illustrates their use.

Using msgop

The synopsis found in the msgop(2) entry in the *Programmer's Reference Manual* is as follows:

```
#include <sys/types.h>
#include <sys/ipc.h>
#include <sys/msg.h>

int msgsnd (msqid, msgp, msgsz, msgflg)
int msqid;
struct msgbuf *msgp;
int msgsz, msgflg;

int msgrcv (msqid, msgp, msgsz, msgtyp, msgflg)
int msqid;
struct msgbuf *msgp;
int msgsz;
long msgtyp;
int msgflg;
```

Sending a Message

The msgsnd system call requires four arguments to be passed to it. It returns an integer value.

When successful, it returns a zero value; when unsuccessful, msgsnd returns a −1.

The msqid argument must be a valid, non-negative, integer value. In other words, it must have already been created by using the msgget system call.

The msgp argument is a pointer to a structure in the user memory area that contains the type of the message and the message to be sent.

The `msgsz` argument specifies the length of the character array in the data structure pointed to by the `msgp` argument. This is the length of the message. The maximum `size` of this array is determined by the `MSGMAX` system-tunable parameter.

The `msgflg` argument allows the "blocking message operation" to be performed if the `IPC_NOWAIT` flag is not set ((`msgflg` and `IPC_NOWAIT`)= = 0); the operation would block if the total number of bytes allowed on the specified message queue are in use (`msg_qbytes` or `MSGMNB`), or the total system-wide number of messages on all queues is equal to the system- imposed limit (`MSGTQL`). If the `IPC_NOWAIT` flag is set, the system call will fail and return a −1.

The `msg_qbytes` data structure member can be lowered from `MSGMNB` by using the `msgctl` `IPC_SET` control command, but only the superuser can raise it afterwards.

Further details of this system call are discussed in the following program. If you need more information on the logic manipulations in this program, read "Using `msgget`". It goes into more detail than would be practical for every system call.

Receiving Messages

The `msgrcv` system call requires five arguments to be passed to it; it returns an integer value.

When successful, it returns a value equal to the number of bytes received; when unsuccessful it returns a −1.

The `msqid` argument must be a valid, non-negative, integer value. In other words, it must have already been created by using the `msgget` system call.

The `msgp` argument is a pointer to a structure in the user memory area that will receive the message type and the message text.

The `msgsz` argument specifies the length of the message to be received. If its value is less than the message in the array, an error can be returned if desired (see the `msgflg` argument below).

The `msgtyp` argument is used to pick the first message on the message queue of the particular type specified. If it is equal to zero, the first message on the queue is received; if it is greater than zero, the first message of the same type is received; if it is less than zero, the lowest type that is less than or equal to its absolute value is received.

The msgflg argument allows the "blocking message operation" to be performed if the IPC_NOWAIT flag is not set ((msgflg and IPC_NOWAIT) == 0); the operation would block if there is not a message on the message queue of the desired type (msgtyp) to be received. If the IPC_NOWAIT flag is set, the system call will fail immediately when there is not a message of the desired type on the queue. msgflg can also specify that the system call fail if the message is longer than the size to be received; this is done by not setting the MSG_NOERROR flag in the msgflg argument ((msgflg and MSG_NOERROR)) == 0). If the MSG_NOERROR flag is set, the message is truncated to the length specified by the msgsz argument of msgrcv.

Further details of this system call are discussed in the following program. If you need more information on the logic manipulations in this program read "Using msgget". It goes into more detail than would be practical for every system call.

Example Program

Figure 4-5 is a menu-driven program. It allows all possible combinations of using the msgsnd and msgrcv system calls to be exercised.

From studying this program, you can observe the method of passing arguments and receiving return values. The user-written program requirements are pointed out.

This program begins (lines 5-9) by including the required header files as specified by the msgop(2) entry in the *Programmer's Reference Manual*. Note that in this program errno is declared as an external variable; therefore, the <sys/errno.h> header file does not have to be included.

Variable and structure names have been chosen to be as close as possible to those in the synopsis. Their declarations are self explanatory. These names make the program more readable and are perfectly legal since they are local to the program. The variables declared for this program and what they are used for are as follows:

sndbuf   used as a buffer to contain a message to be sent (line 13); it uses the msgbuf1 data structure as a template (lines 10-13). The msgbuf1 structure (lines 10-13) is a duplicate of the msgbuf structure contained in the <sys/msg.h> header file, except that the size of the character array for mtext is tailored to fit this application. The msgbuf structure should

<table>
<tr><td></td><td>not be used directly because <code>mtext</code> has only one element that would limit the size of each message to one character. Instead, declare your own structure. It should be identical to <code>msgbuf</code> except that the size of the <code>mtext</code> array should fit your application.</td></tr>
<tr><td><code>rcvbuf</code></td><td>used as a buffer to receive a message (line 13); it uses the <code>msgbuf1</code> data structure as a template (lines 10-13)</td></tr>
<tr><td><code>msgp</code></td><td>used as a pointer (line 13) to both the <code>sndbuf</code> and <code>rcvbuf</code> buffers</td></tr>
<tr><td><code>i</code></td><td>used as a counter for inputting characters from the keyboard, storing them in the array, and keeping track of the message length for the <code>msgsnd</code> system call; it is also used as a counter to output the received message for the <code>msgrcv</code> system call</td></tr>
<tr><td><code>c</code></td><td>used to receive the input character from the <code>getchar</code> function (line 50)</td></tr>
<tr><td><code>flag</code></td><td>used to store the code of <code>IPC_NOWAIT</code> for the <code>msgsnd</code> system call (line 61)</td></tr>
<tr><td><code>flags</code></td><td>used to store the code of the <code>IPC_NOWAIT</code> or <code>MSG_NOERROR</code> flags for the <code>msgrcv</code> system call (line 117)</td></tr>
<tr><td><code>choice</code></td><td>used to store the code for sending or receiving (line 30)</td></tr>
<tr><td><code>rtrn</code></td><td>used to store the return values from all system calls</td></tr>
<tr><td><code>msqid</code></td><td>used to store and pass the desired message queue identifier for both system calls</td></tr>
<tr><td><code>msgsz</code></td><td>used to store and pass the <code>size</code> of the message to be sent or received</td></tr>
<tr><td><code>msgflg</code></td><td>used to pass the value of flag for sending or the value of flags for receiving</td></tr>
<tr><td><code>msgtyp</code></td><td>used for specifying the message type for sending or for picking a message type for receiving.</td></tr>
</table>

Note that a `msqid_ds` data structure is set up in the program (line 21) with a pointer initialized to point to it (line 22); this will allow the data structure members affected by message operations to be observed. They are observed by using the `msgctl (IPC_STAT)` system call to get them for the program to print them out (lines 80-92 and lines 160-167).

The first thing the program prompts for is whether to send or receive a message. A corresponding code must be entered for the desired operation; it is stored in the choice variable (lines 23-30). Depending upon the code, the program proceeds as in the following `msgsnd` or `msgrcv` sections.

`msgsnd`

When the code is to send a message, the `msgp` pointer is initialized (line 33) to the address of the send data structure, `sndbuf`. Next, a message type must be entered for the message; it is stored in the variable `msgtyp` (line 42), and then (line 43) it is put into the `mtype` member of the data structure pointed to by `msgp`.

The program now prompts for a message to be entered from the keyboard and enters a loop of getting and storing into the `mtext` array of the data structure (lines 48-51). This will continue until an end-of-file is recognized which, for the `getchar` function, is a control-D (CTRL-D) immediately following a carriage return (<CR>).

The message is immediately echoed from the `mtext` array of the `sndbuf` data structure to provide feedback (lines 54-56).

The next and final thing that must be decided is whether to set the `IPC_NOWAIT` flag. The program does this by requesting that a code of a 1 be entered for yes or anything else for no (lines 57-65). It is stored in the flag variable. If a 1 is entered, `IPC_NOWAIT` is logically ORed with `msgflg`; otherwise, `msgflg` is set to zero.

The `msgsnd` system call is performed (line 69). If it is unsuccessful, a failure message is displayed along with the error number (lines 70-72). If it is successful, the returned value is printed and should be zero (lines 73-76).

Every time a message is successfully sent, three members of the associated data structure are updated. They are:

`msg_qnum`	represents the total number of messages on the message queue; it is incremented by one.
`msg_lspid`	contains the process identification (PID) number of the last process sending a message; it is set accordingly.
`msg_stime`	contains the time in seconds since January 1, 1970, Greenwich Mean Time (GMT) of the last message sent; it is set accordingly.

These members are displayed after every successful message send operation (lines 79-92).

`msgrcv`

When the code is to receive a message, the program continues execution as in the following paragraphs.

The `msgp` pointer is initialized to the `rcvbuf` data structure (line 99).

Next, the message queue identifier of the message queue from which to receive the message is requested; it is stored in `msqid` (lines 100-103).

The message type is requested; it is stored in `msgtyp` (lines 104-107).

The code for the desired combination of control flags is requested next; it is stored in flags (lines 108-117). Depending upon the selected combination, `msgflg` is set accordingly (lines 118-131).

Finally, the number of bytes to be received is requested; it is stored in `msgsz` (lines 132-135).

The `msgrcv` system call is performed (line 142). If it is unsuccessful, a message and error number is displayed (lines 143-145). If successful, a message indicates so, and the number of bytes returned and the `msg` type returned (because the value returned may be different from the value requested) is displayed followed by the received message (lines 150-156).

When a message is successfully received, three members of the associated data structure are updated. They are:

`msg_qnum`	contains the number of messages on the message queue; it is decremented by one.

msg_lrpid   contains the PID of the last process receiving a message; it is set accordingly.

msg_rtime   contains the time in seconds since January 1, 1970, Greenwich Mean Time (GMT) that the last process received a message; it is set accordingly.

Figure 4-5 shows the msgop system calls. We suggest that you put the program into a source file called msgop.c and then compile it into an executable file called msgop.

Figure 4-5: msgop **System Call Example**

```
1     /*This is a program to illustrate
2     **the message operations, msgop(),
3     **system call capabilities.
4     */

5     /*Include necessary header files.*/
6     #include    <stdio.h>
7     #include    <sys/types.h>
8     #include    <sys/ipc.h>
9     #include    <sys/msg.h>

10    struct msgbuf1 {
11         long    mtype;
12         char    mtext[8192];
13    } sndbuf, rcvbuf, *msgp;

14    /*Start of main C language program*/
15    main()
16    {
17         extern int errno;
18         int i, c, flag, flags, choice;
19         int rtrn, msqid, msgsz, msgflg;
20         long mtype, msgtyp;
21         struct msqid_ds msqid_ds, *buf;
22         buf = &msqid_ds;

23         /*Select the desired operation.*/
24         printf("Enter the corresponding\n");
25         printf("code to send or\n");
26         printf("receive a message:\n");
```

(continued on next page)

Figure 4-5: msgop **System Call Example** (continued)

```
27        printf("Send          = 1\n");
28        printf("Receive       = 2\n");
29        printf("Entry         = ");
30        scanf("%d", &choice);

31        if(choice == 1) /*Send a message.*/
32        {
33            msgp = &sndbuf; /*Point to user send structure.*/

34            printf("\nEnter the msqid of\n");
35            printf("the message queue to\n");
36            printf("handle the message = ");
37            scanf("%d", &msqid);

38            /*Set the message type.*/
39            printf("\nEnter a positive integer\n");
40            printf("message type (long) for the\n");
41            printf("message = ");
42            scanf("%ld", &msgtyp);
43            msgp->mtype = msgtyp;

44            /*Enter the message to send.*/
45            printf("\nEnter a message: \n");

46            /*A control-d (^d) terminates as
47              EOF.*/

48            /*Get each character of the message
49              and put it in the mtext array.*/
50            for(i = 0; ((c = getchar()) != EOF); i++)
51                sndbuf.mtext[i] = c;

52            /*Determine the message size.*/
53            msgsz = i;

54            /*Echo the message to send.*/
55            for(i = 0; i < msgsz; i++)
56                putchar(sndbuf.mtext[i]);

57            /*Set the IPC_NOWAIT flag if
58              desired.*/
59            printf("\nEnter a 1 if you want \n");
60            printf("the IPC_NOWAIT flag set:  ");
61            scanf("%d", &flag);
```

(continued on next page)

Figure 4-5: msgop **System Call Example** (continued)

```
62              if(flag == 1)
63                  msgflg = IPC_NOWAIT;
64              else
65                  msgflg = 0;

66              /*Check the msgflg.*/
67              printf("\nmsgflg = 0%o\n", msgflg);

68              /*Send the message.*/
69              rtrn = msgsnd(msqid, msgp, msgsz, msgflg);
70              if(rtrn == -1)
71              printf("\nMsgsnd failed.  Error = %d\n",
72                  errno);
73              else {
74                  /*Print the value of test which
75                      should be zero for successful.*/
76                  printf("\nValue returned = %d\n", rtrn);

77                  /*Print the size of the message
78                   sent.*/
79                  printf("\nMsgsz = %d\n", msgsz);

80                  /*Check the data structure update.*/
81                  msgctl(msqid, IPC_STAT, buf);

82                  /*Print out the affected members.*/

83                  /*Print the incremented number of
84                   messages on the queue.*/
85                  printf("\nThe msg_qnum = %d\n",
86                      buf->msg_qnum);
87                  /*Print the process id of the last sender.*/
88                  printf("The msg_lspid = %d\n",
89                      buf->msg_lspid);
90                  /*Print the last send time.*/
91                  printf("The msg_stime = %d\n",
92                      buf->msg_stime);
93              }
94          }

95          if(choice == 2)  /*Receive a message.*/
96          {
97              /*Initialize the message pointer
98               to the receive buffer.*/
```

(continued on next page)

Figure 4-5: msgop **System Call Example** (continued)

```
 99          msgp = &rcvbuf;

100          /*Specify the message queue which contains
101                the desired message.*/
102          printf("\nEnter the msqid = ");
103          scanf("%d", &msqid);

104          /*Specify the specific message on the queue
105                by using its type.*/
106          printf("\nEnter the msgtyp = ");
107          scanf("%ld", &msgtyp);

108          /*Configure the control flags for the
109                desired actions.*/
110          printf("\nEnter the corresponding code\n");
111          printf("to select the desired flags: \n");
112          printf("No flags                    = 0\n");
113          printf("MSG_NOERROR                 = 1\n");
114          printf("IPC_NOWAIT                  = 2\n");
115          printf("MSG_NOERROR and IPC_NOWAIT  = 3\n");
116          printf("              Flags         = ");
117          scanf("%d", &flags);

118          switch(flags) {
119          case 0:
120              msgflg = 0;
121              break;
122          case 1:
123              msgflg = MSG_NOERROR;
124              break;
125          case 2:
126              msgflg = IPC_NOWAIT;
127              break;
128          case 3:
129              msgflg = MSG_NOERROR | IPC_NOWAIT;
130              break;
131          }

132          /*Specify the number of bytes to receive.*/
133          printf("\nEnter the number of bytes\n");
134          printf("to receive (msgsz) = ");
135          scanf("%d", &msgsz);

136          /*Check the values for the arguments.*/
```

(continued on next page)

System Services and Application Packaging Tools

Figure 4-5: msgop **System Call Example** (continued)

```
137          printf("\nmsqid =%d\n", msqid);
138          printf("\nmsgtyp = %ld\n", msgtyp);
139          printf("\nmsgsz = %d\n", msgsz);
140          printf("\nmsgflg = 0%o\n", msgflg);

141          /*Call msgrcv to receive the message.*/
142          rtrn = msgrcv(msqid, msgp, msgsz, msgtyp, msgflg);

143          if(rtrn == -1)  {
144              printf("\nMsgrcv failed., Error = %d\n", errno);
145          }
146          else {
147              printf ("\nMsgctl was successful\n");
148              printf("for msqid = %d\n",
149                  msqid);

150              /*Print the number of bytes received,
151                 it is equal to the return
152                 value.*/
153              printf("Bytes received = %d\n", rtrn);

154              /*Print the received message.*/
155              for(i = 0; i<rtrn; i++)
156                  putchar(rcvbuf.mtext[i]);
157          }
158          /*Check the associated data structure.*/
159          msgctl(msqid, IPC_STAT, buf);
160          /*Print the decremented number of messages.*/
161          printf("\nThe msg_qnum = %d\n", buf->msg_qnum);
162          /*Print the process id of the last receiver.*/
163          printf("The msg_lrpid = %d\n", buf->msg_lrpid);
164          /*Print the last message receive time*/
165          printf("The msg_rtime = %d\n", buf->msg_rtime);
166      }
167  }
```

Semaphores

The semaphore type of IPC allows processes (executing programs) to communicate through the exchange of semaphore values. Since many applications require the use of more than one semaphore, the UNIX operating system has the ability to create sets or arrays of semaphores. A semaphore set can contain one or more semaphores up to a limit set by the system administrator. The tunable parameter, SEMMSL, has a default value of 25. Semaphore sets are created by using the semget (semaphore get) system call.

The process performing the semget system call becomes the owner/creator, determines how many semaphores are in the set, and sets the initial operation permissions for all processes, including itself. This process can subsequently relinquish ownership of the set or change the operation permissions using the semctl(semaphore control) system call. The creating process always remains the creator as long as the facility exists. Other processes with permission can use semctl to perform other control functions.

Any process can manipulate the semaphore(s) if the owner of the semaphore grants permission. Each semaphore within a set can be incremented and decremented with the semop(2) system call (documented in the *Programmer's Reference Manual*).

To increment a semaphore, an integer value of the desired magnitude is passed to the semop system call. To decrement a semaphore, a minus (−) value of the desired magnitude is passed.

The UNIX operating system ensures that only one process can manipulate a semaphore set at any given time. Simultaneous requests are performed sequentially in an arbitrary manner.

A process can test for a semaphore value to be greater than a certain value by attempting to decrement the semaphore by one more than that value. If the process is successful, then the semaphore value is greater than that certain value. Otherwise, the semaphore value is not. While doing this, the process can have its execution suspended (IPC_NOWAIT flag not set) until the semaphore value would permit the operation (other processes increment the semaphore), or the semaphore facility is removed.

The ability to suspend execution is called a "blocking semaphore operation." This ability is also available for a process which is testing for a semaphore equal to zero; only read permission is required for this test; it is accomplished by passing a value of zero to the semop (semaphore operation) system call.

On the other hand, if the process is not successful and did not request to have its execution suspended, it is called a "nonblocking semaphore operation." In this case, the process is returned a known error code (−1), and the external `errno` variable is set accordingly.

The blocking semaphore operation allows processes to communicate based on the values of semaphores at different points in time. Remember also that IPC facilities remain in the UNIX operating system until removed by a permitted process or until the system is reinitialized.

Operating on a semaphore set is done by using the `semop` system call.

When a set of semaphores is created, the first semaphore in the set is semaphore number zero. The last semaphore number in the set is numbered one less than the total in the set.

A single system call can be used to perform a sequence of these "blocking/nonblocking operations" on a set of semaphores. When performing a sequence of operations, the blocking/nonblocking operations can be applied to any or all of the semaphores in the set. Also, the operations can be applied in any order of semaphore number. However, no operations are done until they can all be done successfully. For example, if the first three of six operations on a set of ten semaphores could be completed successfully, but the fourth operation would be blocked, no changes are made to the set until all six operations can be performed without blocking. Either the operations are successful and the semaphores are changed, or one ("nonblocking") operation is unsuccessful and none are changed. In short, the operations are "atomically performed."

Remember, any unsuccessful nonblocking operation for a single semaphore or a set of semaphores causes immediate return with no operations performed at all. When this occurs, an error code (−1) is returned to the process, and the external variable `errno` is set accordingly.

System calls (documented in the *Programmer's Reference Manual*) make these semaphore capabilities available to processes. The calling process passes arguments to a system call, and the system call either successfully or unsuccessfully performs its function. If the system call is successful, it performs its function and returns the appropriate information. Otherwise, a known error code (-1) is returned to the process, and the external variable `errno` is set accordingly.

Using Semaphores

Before semaphores can be used (operated on or controlled) a uniquely identified data structure and semaphore set (array) must be created. The unique identifier is called the semaphore set identifier (semid); it is used to identify or refer to a particular data structure and semaphore set.

The semaphore set contains a predefined number of structures in an array, one structure for each semaphore in the set. The number of semaphores (nsems) in a semaphore set is user selectable. The following members are in each structure within a semaphore set:

- semaphore value

- PID performing last operation

- number of processes waiting for the semaphore value to become greater than its current value

- number of processes waiting for the semaphore value to equal zero

There is one associated data structure for the uniquely identified semaphore set. This data structure contains the following information related to the semaphore set:

- operation permissions data (operation permissions structure)

- pointer to first semaphore in the set (array)

- number of semaphores in the set

- last semaphore operation time

- last semaphore change time

The C programming language data structure definition for the semaphore set (array member) is as follows:

```
struct sem
{
        ushort   semval;          /* semaphore value */
        pid_t    sempid;          /* pid of last operation */
        ushort   semncnt;         /* # awaiting semval > cval */
        ushort   semzcnt;         /* # awaiting semval - 0 */
};
```

It is located in the <sys/sem.h> header file.

Likewise, the structure definition for the associated semaphore data structure is as follows:

```
struct semid_ds
{
        struct ipc_perm sem_perm;    /* operation permission struct */
        struct sem      *sem_base;   /* ptr to first semaphore in set */
        ushort          sem_nsems;   /* # of semaphores in set */
        time_t          sem_otime;   /* last semop time */
        long            sem_pad1;    /* reserved for time_t expansion */
        time_t          sem_ctime;   /* last change time */
        long            sem_pad2;    /*time_t expansion */
        long            sem_pad3[4]; /* reserve area */
};
```

It is also located in the <sys/sem.h> header file. Note that the sem_perm member of this structure uses ipc_perm as a template. Figure 4-1 shows the breakout for the operation permissions data structure.

The ipc_perm data structure is the same for all IPC facilities; it is located in the <sys/ipc.h> header file and is shown in the "Messages" section.

The semget system call is used to perform two tasks:

■ to get a new semaphore set identifier and create an associated data structure and semaphore set for it

■ to return an existing semaphore set identifier that already has an associated data structure and semaphore set

The task performed is determined by the value of the key argument passed to the semget system call. For the first task, if the key is not already in use for an existing semid and the IPC_CREAT flag is set, a new semid is returned with an associated data structure and semaphore set created for it provided no system tunable parameter would be exceeded.

There is also a provision for specifying a key of value zero (0), which is known as the private key (IPC_PRIVATE). When specified, a new identifier is always returned with an associated data structure and semaphore set created for it, unless a system-tunable parameter would be exceeded. The ipcs command will show the key field for the semid as all zeros.

When performing the first task, the process which calls semget becomes the owner/creator, and the associated data structure is initialized accordingly. Remember, ownership can be changed, but the creating process always remains the creator (see "Controlling Semaphores"). The creator of the semaphore set also determines the initial operation permissions for the facility.

For the second task, if a semaphore set identifier exists for the key specified, the value of the existing identifier is returned. If you do not want to have an existing semaphore set identifier returned, a control command (IPC_EXCL) can be specified (set) in the semflg argument passed to the system call. The system call will fail if it is passed a value for the number of semaphores (nsems) that is greater than the number actually in the set; if you do not know how many semaphores are in the set, use 0 for nsems. ("Using semget" describes how to use this system call.)

Once a uniquely identified semaphore set and data structure are created, semop (semaphore operations) and semctl (semaphore control) can be used.

Semaphore operations consist of incrementing, decrementing, and testing for zero. The semop system call is used to perform these operations (see "Operations on Semaphores" for details of this system call).

The semctl system call permits you to control the semaphore facility in the following ways:

- by returning the value of a semaphore (GETVAL)

- by setting the value of a semaphore (SETVAL)

- by returning the PID of the last process performing an operation on a semaphore set (GETPID)

- by returning the number of processes waiting for a semaphore value to become greater than its current value (GETNCNT)

- by returning the number of processes waiting for a semaphore value to equal zero (GETZCNT)

- by getting all semaphore values in a set and placing them in an array in user memory (GETALL)

- by setting all semaphore values in a semaphore set from an array of values in user memory (SETALL)

- by retrieving the data structure associated with a semaphore set (IPC_STAT)

- by changing operation permissions for a semaphore set (IPC_SET)

- by removing a particular semaphore set identifier from the UNIX operating system along with its associated data structure and semaphore set (IPC_RMID)

See "Controlling Semaphores" for details of the semctl system call.

Getting Semaphores

This section describes how to use the semget system call. The accompanying program illustrates its use.

Using semget

The synopsis found in the semget(2) entry in the *Programmer's Reference Manual* is as follows:

```
#include  <sys/types.h>
#include  <sys/ipc.h>
#include  <sys/sem.h>

int  semget (key, nsems, semflag)
key_t  key;
int nsems, semflag;
```

The following line in the synopsis:

```
int semget (key, nsems, semflg)
```

informs you that semget is a function with three formal arguments that returns an integer-type value. The next two lines:

```
key_t  key;
int nsems, semflg;
```

declare the types of the formal arguments. key_t is defined by a typedef in the <sys/types.h> header file to be an integer.

The integer returned from this system call upon successful completion is the semaphore set identifier that was discussed above.

The process calling the semget system call must supply three actual arguments to be passed to the formal key, nsems, and semflg arguments.

A new semid with an associated semaphore set and data structure is created if either

- key is equal to IPC_PRIVATE,

or

- key is a unique integer and semflg ANDed with IPC_CREAT is "true."

The value passed to the semflg argument must be an integer that will specify the following:

- operation permissions

■ control fields (commands)

Figure 4-6 reflects the numeric values (expressed in octal notation) for the valid operation permissions codes.

Figure 4-6: Operation Permissions Codes

Operation Permissions	Octal Value
Read by User	00400
Alter by User	00200
Read by Group	00040
Alter by Group	00020
Read by Others	00004
Alter by Others	00002

A specific value is derived by adding or bitwise ORing the values for the operation permissions wanted. That is, if read by user and read/alter by others is desired, the code value would be 00406 (00400 plus 00006). There are constants #define'd in the <sys/sem.h> header file which can be used for the user (OWNER). They are as follows:

```
SEM_A    0200    /* alter permission by owner */
SEM_R    0400    /* read permission by owner */
```

Control flags are predefined constants (represented by all uppercase letters). The flags that apply to the semget system call are IPC_CREAT and IPC_EXCL and are defined in the <sys/ipc.h> header file.

The value for semflg is, therefore, a combination of operation permissions and control commands. After determining the value for the operation permissions as previously described, the desired flag(s) can be specified. This specification is accomplished by adding or bitwise ORing (|) them with the operation permissions; the bit positions and values for the control commands in relation to those of the operation permissions make this possible.

The semflg value can easily be set by using the flag names in conjunction with the octal operation permissions value:

```
semid = semget (key, nsems, (IPC_CREAT | 0400));
semid = semget (key, nsems, (IPC_CREAT | IPC_EXCL | 0400));
```

As specified by the semget(2) entry in the *Programmer's Reference Manual*, success or failure of this system call depends upon the actual argument values for key, nsems, and semflg, and system-tunable parameters. The system call will attempt to return a new semaphore set identifier if one of the following conditions is true:

- key is equal to IPC_PRIVATE

- key does not already have a semaphore set identifier associated with it and (semflg & IPC_CREAT) is "true" (not zero).

The key argument can be set to IPC_PRIVATE like this:

```
semid = semget(IPC_PRIVATE, nsems, semflg);
```

Exceeding the SEMMNI, SEMMNS, or SEMMSL system-tunable parameters will always cause a failure. The SEMMNI system-tunable parameter determines the maximum number of unique semaphore sets (semid's) that may be in use at any given time. The SEMMNS system-tunable parameter determines the maximum number of semaphores in all semaphore sets system wide. The SEMMSL system-tunable parameter determines the maximum number of semaphores in each semaphore set.

IPC_EXCL is another control command used in conjunction with IPC_CREAT. It will cause the system call to return an error if a semaphore set identifier already exists for the specified key provided. This is necessary to prevent the process from thinking that it has received a new (unique) identifier when it has not. In other words, when both IPC_CREAT and IPC_EXCL are specified, a new semaphore set identifier is returned if the system call is successful. Any value for semflg returns a new identifier if the key equals zero (IPC_PRIVATE) and no system- tunable parameters are exceeded.

Refer to the semget(2) manual page in the *Programmer's Reference Manual* for specific associated data structure initialization for successful completion. The specific failure conditions and their error names are contained there also.

Example Program

Figure 4-7 is a menu-driven program. It allows all possible combinations of using the `semget` system call to be exercised.

From studying this program, you can observe the method of passing arguments and receiving return values. The user-written program requirements are pointed out.

This program begins (lines 4-8) by including the required header files as specified by the `semget`(2) entry in the *Programmer's Reference Manual*. Note that the `<sys/errno.h>` header file is included as opposed to declaring `errno` as an external variable; either method will work.

Variable names have been chosen to be as close as possible to those in the synopsis. Their declarations are self explanatory. These names make the program more readable and are perfectly legal since they are local to the program. The variables declared for this program and what they are used for are as follows:

`key`	used to pass the value for the desired key
`opperm`	used to store the desired operation permissions
`flags`	used to store the desired control commands (flags)
`opperm_flags`	
	used to store the combination from the logical ORing of the `opperm` and `flags` variables; it is then used in the system call to pass the `semflg` argument
`semid`	used for returning the semaphore set identification number for a successful system call or the error code (−1) for an unsuccessful one.

The program begins by prompting for a hexadecimal `key`, an octal operation permissions code, and the control command combinations (flags) which are selected from a menu (lines 15-32). All possible combinations are allowed even though they might not be viable. This allows observing the errors for illegal combinations.

Next, the menu selection for the flags is combined with the operation permissions; the result is stored in `opperm_flags` (lines 36-52).

Then, the number of semaphores for the set is requested (lines 53-57); its value is stored in nsems.

The system call is made next; the result is stored in the semid (lines 60, 61).

Since the semid variable now contains a valid semaphore set identifier or the error code (−1), it is tested to see if an error occurred (line 63). If semid equals −1, a message indicates that an error resulted and the external errno variable is displayed (line 65). Remember that the external errno variable is only set when a system call fails; it should only be examined immediately following system calls.

If no error occurred, the returned semaphore set identifier is displayed (line 69).

The example program for the semget system call follows. We suggest that you name the source program file semget.c and the executable file semget.

Figure 4-7: semget **System Call Example**

```
1     /*This is a program to illustrate
2     **the semaphore get, semget(),
3     **system call capabilities.*/

4     #include    <stdio.h>
5     #include    <sys/types.h>
6     #include    <sys/ipc.h>
7     #include    <sys/sem.h>
8     #include    <errno.h>

9     /*Start of main C language program*/
10    main()
11    {
12        key_t key;      /*declare as long integer*/
13        int opperm, flags, nsems;
14        int semid, opperm_flags;

15        /*Enter the desired key*/
16        printf("\nEnter the desired key in hex = ");
17        scanf("%x", &key);

18        /*Enter the desired octal operation
19            permissions.*/
20        printf("\nEnter the operation\n");
```

(continued on next page)

Figure 4-7: semget **System Call Example** (continued)

```
21        printf("permissions in octal - ");
22        scanf("%o", &opperm);

23        /*Set the desired flags.*/
24        printf("\nEnter corresponding number to\n");
25        printf("set the desired flags:\n");
26        printf("No flags              = 0\n");
27        printf("IPC_CREAT             = 1\n");
28        printf("IPC_EXCL              = 2\n");
29        printf("IPC_CREAT and IPC_EXCL  = 3\n");
30        printf("           Flags      = ");
31        /*Get the flags to be set.*/
32        scanf("%d", &flags);

33        /*Error checking (debugging)*/
34        printf ("\nkey =0x%x, opperm = 0%o, flags = %d\n",
35             key, opperm, flags);
36        /*Incorporate the control fields (flags) with
37             the operation permissions.*/
38        switch (flags)
39        {
40        case 0:    /*No flags are to be set.*/
41            opperm_flags = (opperm | 0);
42            break;
43        case 1:    /*Set the IPC_CREAT flag.*/
44            opperm_flags = (opperm | IPC_CREAT);
45            break;
46        case 2:    /*Set the IPC_EXCL flag.*/
47            opperm_flags = (opperm | IPC_EXCL);
48            break;
49        case 3: /*Set the IPC_CREAT and IPC_EXCL
50                  flags.*/
51            opperm_flags = (opperm | IPC_CREAT | IPC_EXCL);
52        }

53        /*Get the number of semaphores for this set.*/
54        printf("\nEnter the number of\n");
55        printf("desired semaphores for\n");
56        printf("this set (25 max) = ");
57        scanf("%d", &nsems);

58        /*Check the entry.*/
59        printf("\nNsems = %d\n", nsems);
```

(continued on next page)

Figure 4-7: semget **System Call Example** (continued)

```
60      /*Call the semget system call.*/
61      semid = semget(key, nsems, opperm_flags);

62      /*Perform the following if the call is unsuccessful.*/
63      if(semid == -1)
64      {
65          printf("The semget call failed, error number = %d\n", errno);
66      }
67      /*Return the semid upon successful completion.*/
68      else
69          printf("\nThe semid = %d\n", semid);
70      exit(0);
71      }
```

Controlling Semaphores

This section describes how to use the semctl system call. The accompanying
program illustrates its use.

Using semctl

The synopsis found in the semctl(2) entry in the *Programmer's Reference Manual*
is as follows:

```
#include <sys/types.h>
#include <sys/ipc.h>
#include <sys/sem.h>

int semctl (semid, semnum, cmd, arg)
int semid, cmd;
int semnum;
union semun
{
        int val;
        struct semid_ds *buf;
        ushort *array;
} arg;
```

The semctl system call requires four arguments to be passed to it, and it returns an integer value.

The semid argument must be a valid, non-negative, integer value that has already been created by using the semget system call.

The semnum argument is used to select a semaphore by its number. This relates to sequences of operations (atomically performed) on the set. When a set of semaphores is created, the first semaphore is number 0, and the last semaphore is numbered one less than the total in the set.

The cmd argument can be replaced by one of the following values:

GETVAL	return the value of a single semaphore within a semaphore set
SETVAL	set the value of a single semaphore within a semaphore set
GETPID	return the PID of the process that performed the last operation on the semaphore within a semaphore set
GETNCNT	return the number of processes waiting for the value of a particular semaphore to become greater than its current value
GETZCNT	return the number of processes waiting for the value of a particular semaphore to be equal to zero

GETALL   return the value for all semaphores in a semaphore set

SETALL   set all semaphore values in a semaphore set

IPC_STAT   return the status information contained in the associated data structure for the specified semid, and place it in the data structure pointed to by the buf pointer in the user memory area; arg.buf is the union member that contains pointer

IPC_SET   for the specified semaphore set (semid), set the effective user/group identification and operation permissions

IPC_RMID   remove the specified semaphore set (semid) along with its associated data structure.

A process must have an effective user identification of OWNER/CREATOR or superuser to perform an IPC_SET or IPC_RMID control command. Read/alter permission is required as applicable for the other control commands.

The arg argument is used to pass the system call the appropriate union member for the control command to be performed. For some of the control commands, the arg argument is not required and is simply ignored.

- arg.val required: SETVAL

- arg.buf required: IPC_STAT, IPC_SET

- arg.array required: GETALL, SETALL

- arg ignored: GETVAL, GETPID, GETNCNT, GETZCNT, IPC_RMID

The details of this system call are discussed in the following program. If you need more information on the logic manipulations in this program, read "Using semget". It goes into more detail than would be practical to do for every system call.

Example Program

Figure 4-8 is a menu-driven program. It allows all possible combinations of using the semctl system call to be exercised.

From studying this program, you can observe the method of passing arguments and receiving return values. The user-written program requirements are pointed out.

This program begins (lines 5-9) by including the required header files as specified by the semctl(2) entry in the *Programmer's Reference Manual*. Note that in this program errno is declared as an external variable, and therefore the <sys/errno.h> header file does not have to be included.

Variable, structure, and union names have been chosen to be as close as possible to those in the synopsis. Their declarations are self explanatory. These names make the program more readable and are perfectly legal since they are local to the program. Those declared for this program and what they are used for are as follows:

semid_ds	used to receive the specified semaphore set identifier's data structure when an IPC_STAT control command is performed
c	used to receive the input values from the scanf function (line 119) when performing a SETALL control command
i	used as a counter to increment through the union arg.array when displaying the semaphore values for a GETALL (lines 98-100) control command, and when initializing the arg.array when performing a SETALL (lines 117-121) control command
length	used as a variable to test for the number of semaphores in a set against the i counter variable (lines 98, 117)
uid	used to store the IPC_SET value for the user identification
gid	used to store the IPC_SET value for the group identification
mode	used to store the IPC_SET value for the operation permissions
retrn	used to store the return value from the system call
semid	used to store and pass the semaphore set identifier to the system call
semnum	used to store and pass the semaphore number to the system call
cmd	used to store the code for the desired control command so that subsequent processing can be performed on it

`choice`	used to determine which member (`uid`, `gid`, `mode`) for the `IPC_SET` control command is to be changed
`semvals[]`	used to store the set of semaphore values when getting (`GETALL`) or initializing (`SETALL`)
`arg.val`	used to pass the system call a value to set, or to store a value returned from the system call, for a single semaphore (union member)
`arg.buf`	a pointer passed to the system call which locates the data structure in the user memory area where the `IPC_STAT` control command is to place its return values, or where the `IPC_SET` command gets the values to set (union member)
`arg.array`	a pointer passed to the system call which locates the array in the user memory where the `GETALL` control command is to place its return values, or when the `SETALL` command gets the values to set (union member)

Note that the `semid_ds` data structure in this program (line 14) uses the data structure located in the `<sys/sem.h>` header file of the same name as a template for its declaration.

Note that the `semvals` array is declared to have 25 elements (0 through 24). This number corresponds to the maximum number of semaphores allowed per set (`SEMMSL`), a system-tunable parameter.

Now that all of the required declarations have been presented for this program, this is how it works.

First, the program prompts for a valid semaphore set identifier, which is stored in the `semid` variable (lines 24-26). This is required for all `semctl` system calls.

Then, the code for the desired control command must be entered (lines 17-42), and the code is stored in the `cmd` variable. The code is tested to determine the control command for subsequent processing.

If the `GETVAL` control command is selected (code 1), a message prompting for a semaphore number is displayed (lines 48, 49). When it is entered, it is stored in the `semnum` variable (line 50). Then, the system call is performed, and the semaphore value is displayed (lines 51-54). Note that the `arg` argument is not required in this case, and the system call will simply ignore it. If the system call is successful, a message indicates this along with the semaphore set identifier used (lines 197, 198); if the system call is unsuccessful, an error message is displayed along with the value of the external errno variable (lines 194, 195).

If the SETVAL control command is selected (code 2), a message prompting for a semaphore number is displayed (lines 55, 56). When it is entered, it is stored in the semnum variable (line 57). Next, a message prompts for the value to which the semaphore is to be set; it is stored as the arg.val member of the union (lines 58, 59). Then, the system call is performed (lines 60, 62). Depending upon success or failure, the program returns the same messages as for GETVAL above.

If the GETPID control command is selected (code 3), the system call is made immediately since all required arguments are known (lines 63-66), and the PID of the process performing the last operation is displayed. Note that the arg argument is not required in this case, and the system call will simply ignore it. Depending upon success or failure, the program returns the same messages as for GETVAL above.

If the GETNCNT control command is selected (code 4), a message prompting for a semaphore number is displayed (lines 67-71). When entered, it is stored in the semnum variable (line 73). Then, the system call is performed and the number of processes waiting for the semaphore to become greater than its current value is displayed (lines 73-76). Note that the arg argument is not required in this case, and the system call will simply ignore it. Depending upon success or failure, the program returns the same messages as for GETVAL above.

If the GETZCNT control command is selected (code 5), a message prompting for a semaphore number is displayed (lines 77-80). When it is entered, it is stored in the semnum variable (line 81). Then the system call is performed and the number of processes waiting for the semaphore value to become equal to zero is displayed (lines 82-85). Depending upon success or failure, the program returns the same messages as for GETVAL above.

If the GETALL control command is selected (code 6), the program first performs an IPC_STAT control command to determine the number of semaphores in the set (lines 87-93). The length variable is set to the number of semaphores in the set (line 93). The arg.array union member is set to point to the semvals array where the system call is to store the values of the semaphore set (line 96). Now, a loop is entered which displays each element of the arg.array from zero to one less than the value of length (lines 98-104). The semaphores in the set are displayed on a single line, separated by a space. Depending upon success or failure, the program returns the same messages as for GETVAL above.

If the SETALL control command is selected (code 7), the program first performs an IPC_STAT control command to determine the number of semaphores in the set (lines 107-110). The length variable is set to the number of semaphores in the set (line 113). Next, the program prompts for the values to be set and enters a loop which takes values from the keyboard and initializes the semvals array to contain the desired values of the semaphore set (lines 115-121). The loop puts the first entry into the array position for semaphore number zero and ends when the semaphore number that is filled in the array equals one less than the value of length. The arg.array union member is set to point to the semvals array from which the system call is to obtain the semaphore values. The system call is then made (lines 122-125). Depending upon success or failure, the program returns the same messages as for GETVAL above.

If the IPC_STAT control command is selected (code 8), the system call is performed (line 129), and the status information returned is printed out (lines 130-141); only the members that can be set are printed out in this program. Note that if the system call is unsuccessful, the status information of the last successful one is printed out. In addition, an error message is displayed, and the errno variable is printed out (line 194).

If the IPC_SET control command is selected (code 9), the program gets the current status information for the semaphore set identifier specified (lines 145-149). This is necessary because this example program provides for changing only one member at a time, and the semctl system call changes all of them. Also, if an invalid value happened to be stored in the user memory area for one of these members, it would cause repetitive failures for this control command until corrected. The next thing the program does is to prompt for a code corresponding to the member to be changed (lines 150-156). This code is stored in the choice variable (line 157). Now, depending upon the member picked, the program prompts for the new value (lines 158-181). The value is placed into the appropriate member in the user memory area data structure, and the system call is made (line 184). Depending upon success or failure, the program returns the same messages as for GETVAL above.

If the IPC_RMID control command (code 10) is selected, the system call is performed (lines 186-188). The semaphore set identifier along with its associated data structure and semaphore set is removed from the UNIX operating system. Depending upon success or failure, the program returns the same messages as for the other control commands.

The example program for the semctl system call follows. We suggest that you name the source program file semctl.c and the executable file semctl.

Figure 4-8: semctl **System Call Example**

```
1       /*This is a program to illustrate
2       **the semaphore control, semctl(),
3       **system call capabilities.
4       */

5       /*Include necessary header files.*/
6       #include    <stdio.h>
7       #include    <sys/types.h>
8       #include    <sys/ipc.h>
9       #include    <sys/sem.h>

10      /*Start of main C language program*/
11      main()
12      {
13          extern int errno;
14          struct semid_ds semid_ds;
15          int c, i, length;
16          int uid, gid, mode;
17          int retrn, semid, semnum, cmd, choice;
18          ushort semvals[25];
19          union semun {
20              int val;
21              struct semid_ds *buf;
22              ushort *array;
23          } arg;

24          /*Enter the semaphore ID.*/
25          printf("Enter the semid = ");
26          scanf("%d", &semid);

27          /*Choose the desired command.*/
28          printf("\nEnter the number for\n");
29          printf("the desired cmd:\n");
30          printf("GETVAL      =  1\n");
31          printf("SETVAL      =  2\n");
32          printf("GETPID      =  3\n");
33          printf("GETNCNT     =  4\n");
34          printf("GETZCNT     =  5\n");
35          printf("GETALL      =  6\n");
36          printf("SETALL      =  7\n");
```

(continued on next page)

Figure 4-8: `semctl` **System Call Example** (continued)

```
37          printf("IPC_STAT    = 8\n");
38          printf("IPC_SET     = 9\n");
39          printf("IPC_RMID    = 10\n");
40          printf("Entry       = ");
41          scanf("%d", &cmd);

42          /*Check entries.*/
43          printf ("\nsemid =%d, cmd = %d\n\n",
44              semid, cmd);

45          /*Set the command and do the call.*/
46          switch (cmd)
47          {

48          case 1: /*Get a specified value.*/
49              printf("\nEnter the semnum = ");
50              scanf("%d", &semnum);
51              /*Do the system call.*/
52              retrn = semctl(semid, semnum, GETVAL, arg);
53              printf("\nThe semval = %d", retrn);
54              break;
55          case 2: /*Set a specified value.*/
56              printf("\nEnter the semnum = ");
57              scanf("%d", &semnum);
58              printf("\nEnter the value = ");
59              scanf("%d", &arg.val);
60              /*Do the system call.*/
61              retrn = semctl(semid, semnum, SETVAL, arg);
62              break;
63          case 3: /*Get the process ID.*/
64              retrn = semctl(semid, 0, GETPID, arg);
65              printf("\nThe sempid = %d", retrn);
66              break;
67          case 4: /*Get the number of processes
68              waiting for the semaphore to
69              become greater than its current
70              value.*/
71              printf("\nEnter the semnum = ");
72              scanf("%d", &semnum);
73              /*Do the system call.*/
74              retrn = semctl(semid, semnum, GETNCNT, arg);
75              printf("\nThe semncnt = %d", retrn);
76              break;
```

(continued on next page)

Figure 4-8: `semctl` **System Call Example** (continued)

```
77        case 5: /*Get the number of processes
78            waiting for the semaphore
79            value to become zero.*/
80            printf("\nEnter the semnum = ");
81            scanf("%d", &semnum);
82            /*Do the system call.*/
83            retrn = semctl(semid, semnum, GETZCNT, arg);
84            printf("\nThe semzcnt = %d", retrn);
85            break;

86        case 6: /*Get all of the semaphores.*/
87            /*Get the number of semaphores in
88              the semaphore set.*/
89            arg.buf = &semid_ds;
90            retrn = semctl(semid, 0, IPC_STAT, arg);
91            if(retrn == -1)
92                goto ERROR;
93            length = arg.buf->sem_nsems;
94            /*Get and print all semaphores in the
95              specified set.*/
96            arg.array = semvals;
97            retrn = semctl(semid, 0, GETALL, arg);
98            for (i = 0; i < length; i++)
99            {
100                printf("%d", semvals[i]);
101                /*Separate each
102                  semaphore.*/
103                printf(" ");
104            }
105            break;

106       case 7: /*Set all semaphores in the set.*/
107            /*Get the number of semaphores in
108              the set.*/
109            arg.buf = &semid_ds;
110            retrn = semctl(semid, 0, IPC_STAT, arg);
111            if(retrn == -1)
112                goto ERROR;
113            length = arg.buf->sem_nsems;
114            printf("Length = %d\n", length);
115            /*Set the semaphore set values.*/
116            printf("\nEnter each value:\n");
117            for(i = 0; i < length ; i++)
118            {
```

(continued on next page)

Figure 4-8: semctl **System Call Example** (continued)

```
119                scanf("%d", &c);
120                semvals[i] = c;
121            }
122        /*Do the system call.*/
123        arg.array = semvals;
124        retrn = semctl(semid, 0, SETALL, arg);
125        break;

126    case 8: /*Get the status for the semaphore set.*/
127        /*Get and print the current status values.*/
128        arg.buf = &semid_ds;
129        retrn = semctl(semid, 0, IPC_STAT, arg);
130        printf ("\nThe USER ID = %d\n",
131            arg.buf->sem_perm.uid);
132        printf ("The GROUP ID = %d\n",
133            arg.buf->sem_perm.gid);
134        printf ("The operation permissions = 0%o\n",
135            arg.buf->sem_perm.mode);
136        printf ("The number of semaphores in set = %d\n",
137            arg.buf->sem_nsems);
138        printf ("The last semop time = %d\n",
139            arg.buf->sem_otime);
140        printf ("The last change time  = %d\n",
141            arg.buf->sem_ctime);
142        break;

143    case 9:    /*Select and change the desired
144                member of the data structure.*/
145        /*Get the current status values.*/
146        arg.buf = &semid_ds;
147        retrn = semctl(semid, 0, IPC_STAT, arg.buf);
148        if(retrn == -1)
149            goto ERROR;
150        /*Select the member to change.*/
151        printf("\nEnter the number for the\n");
152        printf("member to be changed:\n");
153        printf("sem_perm.uid   = 1\n");
154        printf("sem_perm.gid   = 2\n");
155        printf("sem_perm.mode  = 3\n");
156        printf("Entry          = ");
157        scanf("%d", &choice);
158        switch(choice){

159        case 1: /*Change the user ID.*/
```

(continued on next page)

System Services and Application Packaging Tools

Figure 4-8: `semctl` System Call Example (continued)

```
160              printf("\nEnter USER ID = ");
161              scanf ("%d", &uid);
162              arg.buf->sem_perm.uid = uid;
163              printf("\nUSER ID = %d\n",
164                  arg.buf->sem_perm.uid);
165              break;

166          case 2: /*Change the group ID.*/
167              printf("\nEnter GROUP ID = ");
168              scanf("%d", &gid);
169              arg.buf->sem_perm.gid = gid;
170              printf("\nGROUP ID = %d\n",
171                  arg.buf->sem_perm.gid);
172              break;

173          case 3: /*Change the mode portion of
174                  the operation
175                      permissions.*/
176              printf("\nEnter MODE in octal = ");
177              scanf("%o", &mode);
178              arg.buf->sem_perm.mode = mode;
179              printf("\nMODE = 0%o\n",
180                  arg.buf->sem_perm.mode);
181              break;
182          }
183          /*Do the change.*/
184          retrn = semctl(semid, 0, IPC_SET, arg);
185          break;
186      case 10:    /*Remove the semid along with its
187                  data structure.*/
188          retrn = semctl(semid, 0, IPC_RMID, arg);
189      }
190      /*Perform the following if the call is unsuccessful.*/
1911     if(retrn == -1)
192      {
193  ERROR:
194          printf ("\nThe semctl call failed!, error number = %d\n", errno);
195          exit(0);
196      }
197      printf ("\n\nThe semctl system call was successful\n");
198      printf ("for semid = %d\n", semid);
199      exit (0);
200  }
```

Operations on Semaphores

This section describes how to use the semop system call. The accompanying program illustrates its use.

Using semop

The synopsis found in the semop(2) entry in the *Programmer's Reference Manual* is as follows:

```
#include <sys/types.h>
#include <sys/ipc.h>
#include <sys/sem.h>

int semop (semid, sops, nsops)
int semid;
struct sembuf *sops;
unsigned nsops;
```

The semop system call requires three arguments to be passed to it and returns an integer value which will be zero for successful completion or -1 otherwise.

The semid argument must be a valid, non-negative, integer value. In other words, it must have already been created by using the semget system call.

The sops argument points to an array of structures in the user memory area that contains the following for each semaphore to be changed:

- the semaphore number (sem_num)
- the operation to be performed (sem_op)
- the control flags (sem_flg)

The *sops declaration means that either an array name (which is the address of the first element of the array) or a pointer to the array can be used. sembuf is the *tag* name of the data structure used as the template for the structure members in the array; it is located in the <sys/sem.h> header file.

The nsops argument specifies the length of the array (the number of structures in the array). The maximum size of this array is determined by the SEMOPM system-tunable parameter. Therefore, a maximum of SEMOPM operations can be performed for each semop system call.

The semaphore number (sem_num) determines the particular semaphore within the set on which the operation is to be performed.

The operation to be performed is determined by the following:

- if sem_op is positive, the semaphore value is incremented by the value of sem_op

- if sem_op is negative, the semaphore value is decremented by the absolute value of sem_op

- if sem_op is zero, the semaphore value is tested for equality to zero

The following operation commands (flags) can be used:

- IPC_NOWAIT—this operation command can be set for any operations in the array. The system call will return unsuccessfully without changing any semaphore values at all if any operation for which IPC_NOWAIT is set cannot be performed successfully. The system call will be unsuccessful when trying to decrement a semaphore more than its current value, or when testing for a semaphore to be equal to zero when it is not.

- SEM_UNDO—this operation command is used to tell the system to undo the process's semaphore changes automatically when the process exits; it allows processes to avoid deadlock problems. To implement this feature, the system maintains a table with an entry for every process in the system. Each entry points to a set of undo structures, one for each semaphore used by the process. The system records the net change.

Example Program

Figure 4-9 is a menu-driven program. It allows all possible combinations of using the semop system call to be exercised.

From studying this program, you can observe the method of passing arguments and receiving return values. The user-written program requirements are pointed out.

This program begins (lines 5-9) by including the required header files as specified by the shmop(2) entry in the *Programmer's Reference Manual*. Note that in this program errno is declared as an external variable; therefore, the <sys/errno.h> header file does not have to be included.

Variable and structure names have been chosen to be as close as possible to those in the synopsis. Their declarations are self explanatory. These names make the program more readable and are perfectly legal since the declarations are local to the program. The variables declared for this program and what they are used for are as follows:

sembuf[10]	used as an array buffer (line 14) to contain a maximum of ten sembuf type structures; ten is the standard value of the tunable parameter SEMOPM, the maximum number of operations on a semaphore set for each semop system call
sops	used as a pointer (line 14) to the sembuf array for the system call and for accessing the structure members within the array
string[8]	used as a character buffer to hold a number entered by the user
rtrn	used to store the return value from the system call
flags	used to store the code of the IPC_NOWAIT or SEM_UNDO flags for the semop system call (line 59)
sem_num	used to store the semaphore number entered by the user for each semaphore operation in the array
i	used as a counter (line 31) for initializing the structure members in the array, and used to print out each structure in the array (line 78)
semid	used to store the desired semaphore set identifier for the system call
nsops	used to specify the number of semaphore operations for the system call; must be less than or equal to SEMOPM

First, the program prompts for a semaphore set identifier that the system call is to perform operations on (lines 18-21). semid is stored in the semid variable (line 22).

A message is displayed requesting the number of operations to be performed on this set (lines 24-26). The number of operations is stored in the nsops variable (line 27).

Next, a loop is entered to initialize the array of structures (lines 29-76). The semaphore number, operation, and operation command (flags) are entered for each structure in the array. The number of structures equals the number of semaphore operations (nsops) to be performed for the system call, so nsops is tested against the i counter for loop control. Note that sops is used as a pointer to each element (structure) in the array, and sops is incremented just like i. sops is then used to point to each member in the structure for setting them.

After the array is initialized, all of its elements are printed out for feedback (lines 77-84).

The sops pointer is set to the address of the array (lines 85, 86). sembuf could be used directly, if desired, instead of sops in the system call.

The system call is made (line 88), and depending upon success or failure, a corresponding message is displayed. The results of the operation(s) can be viewed by using the semctl GETALL control command.

The example program for the semop system call follows. We suggest that you name the source program file semop.c and the executable file semop.

Figure 4-9: semop **System Call Example**

```
 1    /*This is a program to illustrate
 2    **the semaphore operations, semop(),
 3    **system call capabilities.
 4    */

 5    /*Include necessary header files.*/
 6    #include    <stdio.h>
 7    #include    <sys/types.h>
 8    #include    <sys/ipc.h>
 9    #include    <sys/sem.h>
10    /*Start of main C language program*/
11    main()
12    {
13        extern int errno;
14        struct sembuf sembuf[10], *sops;
15        char string[8];
16        int retrn, flags, sem_num, i, semid;
17        unsigned nsops;

18        /*Enter the semaphore ID.*/
19        printf("\nEnter the semid of\n");
20        printf("the semaphore set to\n");
21        printf("be operated on = ");
22        scanf("%d", &semid);
23        printf("\nsemid = %d", semid);

24        /*Enter the number of operations.*/
25        printf("\nEnter the number of semaphore\n");
26        printf("operations for this set = ");
27        scanf("%d", &nsops);
28        printf("\nnsops = %d", nsops);

29        /*Initialize the array for the
30         number of operations to be performed.*/
31        for(i = 0, sops = sembuf; i < nsops; i++, sops++)
32        {

33            /*This determines the semaphore in
34             the semaphore set.*/
35            printf("\nEnter the semaphore\n");
36            printf("number (sem_num) = ");
37            scanf("%d", &sem_num);
38            sops->sem_num = sem_num;
39            printf("\nThe sem_num = %d", sops->sem_num);
```

(continued on next page)

System Services and Application Packaging Tools

Figure 4-9: semop **System Call Example** (continued)

```
40            /*Enter a (-)number to decrement,
41              an unsigned number (no +) to increment,
42              or zero to test for zero.  These values
43              are entered into a string and converted
44              to integer values.*/
45            printf("\nEnter the operation for\n");
46            printf("the semaphore (sem_op) = ");
47            scanf("%s", string);
48            sops->sem_op = atoi(string);
49            printf("\nsem_op = %d\n", sops->sem_op);

50            /*Specify the desired flags.*/
51            printf("\nEnter the corresponding\n");
52            printf("number for the desired\n");
53            printf("flags:\n");
54            printf("No flags                 = 0\n");
55            printf("IPC_NOWAIT               = 1\n");
56            printf("SEM_UNDO                 = 2\n");
57            printf("IPC_NOWAIT and SEM_UNDO  = 3\n");
58            printf("              Flags      = ");
59            scanf("%d", &flags);

60            switch(flags)
61            {
62            case 0:
63                sops->sem_flg = 0;
64                break;
65            case 1:
66                sops->sem_flg = IPC_NOWAIT;
67                break;
68            case 2:
69                sops->sem_flg = SEM_UNDO;
70                break;
71            case 3:
72                sops->sem_flg = IPC_NOWAIT | SEM_UNDO;
73                break;
74            }
75            printf("\nFlags = 0%o\n", sops->sem_flg);
76        }

77        /*Print out each structure in the array.*/
78        for(i = 0; i < nsops; i++)
79        {
```

(continued on next page)

Figure 4-9: semop **System Call Example** (continued)

```
80          printf("\nsem_num = %d\n", sembuf[i].sem_num);
81          printf("sem_op = %d\n", sembuf[i].sem_op);
82          printf("sem_flg = 0%o\n", sembuf[i].sem_flg);
83          printf(" ");
84      }

85      sops = sembuf; /*Reset the pointer to
86                      sembuf[0].*/

87      /*Do the semop system call.*/
88      retrn = semop(semid, sops, nsops);
89      if(retrn == -1)  {
90          printf("\nSemop failed, error = %d\n", errno);
91      }
92      else {
93          printf ("\nSemop was successful\n");
94          printf("for semid = %d\n", semid);

95          printf("Value returned = %d\n", retrn);
96      }
97  }
```

System Services and Application Packaging Tools

Shared Memory

The shared memory type of IPC allows two or more processes (executing programs) to share memory and, consequently, the data contained there. This is done by allowing processes to set up access to a common virtual memory address space. This sharing occurs on a segment basis, which is memory management hardware-dependent.

This sharing of memory provides the fastest means of exchanging data between processes. However, processes that reference a shared memory segment must reside on one processor. Consequently, processes running on different processors (such as in an Remote File Sharing (RFS) network or a multiprocessing environment) may not be able to use shared memory segments.

A process initially creates a shared memory segment facility using the shmget system call. Upon creation, this process sets the overall operation permissions for the shared memory segment facility, sets its size in bytes, and can specify that the shared memory segment is for reference only (read-only) upon attachment. If the memory segment is not specified to be for reference only, all other processes with appropriate operation permissions can read from or write to the memory segment.

shmat (shared memory attach) and shmdt (shared memory detach) can be performed on a shared memory segment.

shmat allows processes to associate themselves with the shared memory segment if they have permission. They can then read or write as allowed.

shmdt allows processes to disassociate themselves from a shared memory segment. Therefore, they lose the ability to read from or write to the shared memory segment.

The original owner/creator of a shared memory segment can relinquish ownership to another process using the shmctl system call. However, the creating process remains the creator until the facility is removed or the system is reinitialized. Other processes with permission can perform other functions on the shared memory segment using the shmctl system call.

System calls (documented in the *Programmer's Reference Manual*) make these shared memory capabilities available to processes. The calling process passes arguments to a system call, and the system call either successfully or unsuccessfully performs its function. If the system call is successful, it performs its function and returns the appropriate information. Otherwise, a known error code (−1) is returned to the process, and the external variable errno is set accordingly.

Using Shared Memory

Sharing memory between processes occurs on a virtual segment basis. There is only one copy of each individual shared memory segment existing in the UNIX operating system at any point in time.

Before sharing of memory can be realized, a uniquely identified shared memory segment and data structure must be created. The unique identifier created is called the shared memory identifier (shmid); it is used to identify or refer to the associated data structure. The data structure includes the following for each shared memory segment:

- operation permissions
- segment size
- segment descriptor (for internal system use only)
- PID performing last operation
- PID of creator
- current number of processes attached
- last attach time
- last detach time
- last change time

The C programming language data structure definition for the shared memory segment data structure is located in the <sys/shm.h> header file. It is as follows:

```
/*
**      There is a shared mem id data structure for
**      each segment in the system.
*/

struct shmid_ds {
        struct ipc_perm    shm_perm;      /* operation permission struct */
        int                shm_segsz;     /* segment size */
        struct region      *shm_reg;      /* ptr to region structure */
        char               pad[4];        /* for swap compatibility */
        pid_t              shm_lpid;      /* pid of last shmop */
        pid_t              shm_cpid;      /* pid of creator */
        ushort             shm_nattch;    /* used only for shminfo */
        ushort             shm_cnattch;   /* used only for shminfo */
        time_t             shm_atime;     /* last shmat time */
        time_t             shm_dtime;     /* last shmdt time */
        time_t             shm_ctime;     /* last change time */
};
```

Note that the shm_perm member of this structure uses ipc_perm as a template.

The ipc_perm data structure is the same for all IPC facilities; is it located in the <sys/ipc.h> header file and shown in Figure 4-1.

The shmget system call performs two tasks:

- it gets a new shared memory identifier and creates an associated shared memory segment data structure for it

- it returns an existing shared memory identifier that already has an associated shared memory segment data structure

The task performed is determined by the value of the key argument passed to the shmget system call. For the first task, if the key is not already in use for an existing shared memory identifier and the IPC_CREAT flag is set in shmflg, a new identifier is returned with an associated shared memory segment data structure created for it provided no system-tunable parameters would be exceeded.

There is also a provision for specifying a key of value zero which is known as the private key (IPC_PRIVATE); when specified, a new shmid is always returned with an associated shared memory segment data structure created for it unless a system-tunable parameter would be exceeded. The ipcs command will show the key field for the shmid as all zeros.

For the second task, if a shmid exists for the key specified, the value of the existing shmid is returned. If it is not desired to have an existing shmid returned, a control command (IPC_EXCL) can be specified (set) in the shmflg argument passed to the system call. "Using shmget" discusses how to use this system call.

When performing the first task, the process that calls shmget becomes the owner/creator, and the associated data structure is initialized accordingly. Remember, ownership can be changed, but the creating process always remains the creator (see "Controlling Shared Memory"). The creator of the shared memory segment also determines the initial operation permissions for it.

Once a uniquely identified shared memory segment data structure is created, shmop (shared memory segment operations) and shmctl (shared memory control) can be used.

Shared memory segment operations consist of attaching and detaching shared memory segments. shmat and shmdt are provided for each of these operations (see "Operations for Shared Memory" for details on these system calls).

The shmctl system call permits you to control the shared memory facility in the following ways:

- by retrieving the data structure associated with a shared memory segment (IPC_STAT)

- by changing operation permissions for a shared memory segment (IPC_SET)

- by removing a particular shared memory segment from the UNIX operating system along with its associated shared memory segment data structure (IPC_RMID)

- by locking a shared memory segment in memory (SHM_LOCK)

- by unlocking a shared memory segment (SHM_UNLOCK)

See "Controlling Shared Memory" for details of the shmctl system call.

Getting Shared Memory Segments

This section describes how to use the shmget system call. The accompanying program illustrates its use.

Using shmget

The synopsis found in the shmget(2) entry in the *Programmer's Reference Manual* is as follows:

```
#include  <sys/types.h>
#include  <sys/ipc.h>
#include  <sys/shm.h>

int  shmget (key, size, shmflg)
key_t  key;
int size, shmflg;
```

All of these include files are located in the /usr/include/sys directory of the UNIX operating system. The following line in the synopsis:

```
int shmget (key, size, shmflg)
```

informs you that shmget is a function with three formal arguments that returns an integer-type value. The next two lines:

```
key_t  key;
int size, shmflg;
```

declare the types of the formal arguments. key_t is defined by a typedef in the <sys/types.h> header file to be an integer.

The integer returned from this function (upon successful completion) is the shared memory identifier (shmid) that was discussed earlier.

As declared, the process calling the shmget system call must supply three arguments to be passed to the formal key, size, and shmflg arguments.

A new shmid with an associated shared memory data structure is provided if either

- key is equal to IPC_PRIVATE,

or

- key is a unique integer and shmflg ANDed with IPC_CREAT is "true" (not zero).

The value passed to the shmflg argument must be an integer-type value and will specify the following:

- operations permissions
- control fields (commands)

Access permissions determine the read/write attributes and modes determine the user/group/other attributes of the shmflg argument. They are collectively referred to as "operation permissions." Figure 4-10 reflects the numeric values (expressed in octal notation) for the valid operation permissions codes.

Figure 4-10: Operation Permissions Codes

Operation Permissions	Octal Value
Read by User	00400
Write by User	00200
Read by Group	00040
Write by Group	00020
Read by Others	00004
Write by Others	00002

A specific octal value is derived by adding or bitwise ORing the octal values for the operation permissions desired. That is, if read by user and read/write by others is desired, the code value would be 00406 (00400 plus 00006). There are constants located in the <sys/shm.h> header file which can be used for the user (OWNER). They are:

```
SHM_R 0400
SHM_W 0200
```

Control flags are predefined constants (represented by all uppercase letters).
The flags that apply to the `shmget` system call are `IPC_CREAT` and `IPC_EXCL`
and are defined in the `<sys/ipc.h>` header file.

The value for `shmflg` is, therefore, a combination of operation permissions and
control commands. After determining the value for the operation permissions
as previously described, the desired flag(s) can be specified. This is accom-
plished by adding or bitwise ORing (|) them with the operation permissions;
the bit positions and values for the control commands in relation to those of the
operation permissions make this possible.

The `shmflg` value can easily be set by using the names of the flags in conjunction with the octal operation permissions value:

```
shmid = shmget (key, size, (IPC_CREAT | 0400));

shmid = shmget (key, size, (IPC_CREAT | IPC_EXCL | 0400));
```

As specified by the `shmget`(2) entry in the *Programmer's Reference Manual*, success or failure of this system call depends upon the argument values for `key`,
`size`, and `shmflg`, and system-tunable parameters. The system call will
attempt to return a new `shmid` if one of the following conditions is true:

- `key` is equal to `IPC_PRIVATE` .

- `key` does not already have a `shmid` associated with it and (`shmflg` &
  `IPC_CREAT`) is "true" (not zero).

The `key` argument can be set to `IPC_PRIVATE` like this:

```
shmid = shmget (IPC_PRIVATE, size, shmflg);
```

The `SHMMNI` system-tunable parameter determines the maximum number of
unique shared memory segments (`shmids`) that may be in use at any given
time. If the maximum number of shared memory segments is already in use, an
attempt to create an additional segment will fail.

`IPC_EXCL` is another control command used in conjunction with `IPC_CREAT`.

It will cause the system call to retrieve an error if a shared memory identifier
exists for the specified `key` provided. This is necessary to prevent the process

from thinking that it has received a new (unique) shmid when it has not. In other words, when both PC_CREAT and IPC_EXCL are specified, a unique shared memory identifier is returned if the system call is successful. Any value for shmflg returns a new identifier if the key equals zero (IPC_PRIVATE) and no system-tunable parameters are exceeded.

The system call will fail if the value for the size argument is less than SHMMIN or greater than SHMMAX. These tunable parameters specify the minimum and maximum shared memory segment sizes.

Refer to the shmget(2) manual page in the *Programmer's Reference Manual* for specific associated data structure initialization for successful completion. The specific failure conditions and their error names are contained there also.

Example Program

Figure 4-11 is a menu-driven program. It allows all possible combinations of using the shmget system call to be exercised.

From studying this program, you can observe the method of passing arguments and receiving return values. The user-written program requirements are pointed out.

This program begins (lines 4-7) by including the required header files as specified by the shmget(2) entry in the *Programmer's Reference Manual*. Note that the <sys/errno.h> header file is included as opposed to declaring errno as an external variable; either method will work.

Variable names have been chosen to be as close as possible to those in the synopsis for the system call. Their declarations are self explanatory. These names make the program more readable and are perfectly legal since they are local to the program. The variables declared for this program and what they are used for are as follows:

key	used to pass the value for the desired key
opperm	used to store the desired operation permissions
flags	used to store the desired control commands (flags)
shmid	used for returning the message queue identification number for a successful system call or the error code (−1) for an unsuccessful one

size   used to specify the shared memory segment size

opperm_flags   used to store the combination from the logical ORing of
the opperm and flags variables; it is then used in the
system call to pass the shmflg argument

The program begins by prompting for a hexadecimal key, an octal operation
permissions code, and finally for the control command combinations (flags)
which are selected from a menu (lines 14-31). All possible combinations are
allowed even though they might not be viable. This allows observing the errors
for illegal combinations.

Next, the menu selection for the flags is combined with the operation permissions; the result is stored in the opperm_flags variable (lines 35-50).

A display then prompts for the size of the shared memory segment; it is stored
in the size variable (lines 51-54).

The system call is made next; the result is stored in the shmid variable (line 56).

Since the shmid variable now contains a valid message queue identifier or the
error code (−1), it is tested to see if an error occurred (line 58). If shmid equals
−1, a message indicates that an error resulted and the external errno variable is
displayed (line 60).

If no error occurred, the returned shared memory segment identifier is
displayed (line 64).

The example program for the shmget system call follows. We suggest that you
name the source program file shmget.c and the executable file shmget.

Figure 4-11: shmget **System Call Example**

```
 1    /*This is a program to illustrate
 2    **the shared memory get, shmget(),
 3    **system call capabilities.*/
 4    #include    <sys/types.h>
 5    #include    <sys/ipc.h>
 6    #include    <sys/shm.h>
 7    #include    <errno.h>
 8    /*Start of main C language program*/
 9    main()
10    {
11        key_t key;                /*declare as long integer*/
12        int opperm, flags;
13        int shmid, size, opperm_flags;
14        /*Enter the desired key*/
15        printf("Enter the desired key in hex = ");
16        scanf("%x", &key);
17        /*Enter the desired octal operation
18          permissions.*/
19        printf("\nEnter the operation\n");
20        printf("permissions in octal = ");
21        scanf("%o", &opperm);
22        /*Set the desired flags.*/
23        printf("\nEnter corresponding number to\n");
24        printf("set the desired flags:\n");
25        printf("No flags                  = 0\n");
26        printf("IPC_CREAT                 = 1\n");
27        printf("IPC_EXCL                  = 2\n");
28        printf("IPC_CREAT and IPC_EXCL    = 3\n");
29        printf("            Flags         = ");
30        /*Get the flag(s) to be set.*/
31        scanf("%d", &flags);
32        /*Check the values.*/
33        printf ("\nkey =0x%x, opperm = 0%o, flags = %d\n",
34            key, opperm, flags);
35        /*Incorporate the control fields (flags) with
36          the operation permissions*/
37        switch (flags)
38        {
39        case 0:    /*No flags are to be set.*/
40            opperm_flags = (opperm | 0);
41            break;
42        case 1:    /*Set the IPC_CREAT flag.*/
```

(continued on next page)

Figure 4-11: shmget **System Call Example** (continued)

```
43            opperm_flags = (opperm | IPC_CREAT);
44            break;
45     case 2:    /*Set the IPC_EXCL flag.*/
46            opperm_flags = (opperm | IPC_EXCL);
47            break;
48     case 3:    /*Set the IPC_CREAT and IPC_EXCL flags.*/
49            opperm_flags = (opperm | IPC_CREAT | IPC_EXCL);
50     }
51     /*Get the size of the segment in bytes.*/
52     printf ("\nEnter the segment");
53     printf ("\nsize in bytes = ");
54     scanf ("%d", &size);
55     /*Call the shmget system call.*/
56     shmid = shmget (key, size, opperm_flags);
57     /*Perform the following if the call is unsuccessful.*/
58     if(shmid == -1)
59     {
60            printf ("\nThe shmget call failed, error number = %d\n", errno);
61     }
62     /*Return the shmid upon successful completion.*/
63     else
64            printf ("\nThe shmid = %d\n", shmid);
65     exit(0);
66     }
```

Controlling Shared Memory

This section describes how to use the shmctl system call. The accompanying program illustrates its use.

Using shmctl

The synopsis found in the shmctl(2) entry in the *Programmer's Reference Manual* is as follows:

```
#include <sys/types.h>
#include <sys/ipc.h>
#include <sys/shm.h>

int shmctl (shmid, cmd, buf)
int shmid, cmd;
struct shmid_ds *buf;
```

The shmctl system call requires three arguments to be passed to it. It returns an integer value which will be zero for successful completion or -1 otherwise.

The shmid variable must be a valid, non-negative, integer value. In other words, it must have already been created by using the shmget system call.

The cmd argument can be replaced by one of following values:

IPC_STAT   return the status information contained in the associated data structure for the specified shmid and place it in the data structure pointed to by the buf pointer in the user memory area

IPC_SET   for the specified shmid, set the effective user and group identification, and operation permissions

IPC_RMID   remove the specified shmid with its associated shared memory segment data structure

SHM_LOCK   lock the specified shared memory segment in memory; must be superuser to perform this operation

SHM_LOCK   lock the shared memory segment from memory; must be superuser to perform this operation

A process must have an effective user identification of OWNER/CREATOR or superuser to perform an IPC_SET or IPC_RMID control command. Only the superuser can perform a SHM_LOCK or SHM_UNLOCK control command. A process must have read permission to perform the IPC_STAT control command.

The details of this system call are discussed in the example program. If you need more information on the logic manipulations in this program, read "Using shmget". It goes into more detail than what would be practical for every system call.

Example Program

Figure 4-12 is a menu-driven program. It allows all possible combinations of using the shmctl system call to be exercised.

From studying this program, you can observe the method of passing arguments and receiving return values. The user-written program requirements are pointed out.

This program begins (lines 5-9) by including the required header files as specified by the shmctl(2) entry in the *Programmer's Reference Manual*. Note that in this program errno is declared as an external variable, and therefore, the <sys/errno.h> header file does not have to be included.

Variable and structure names have been chosen to be as close as possible to those in the synopsis for the system call. Their declarations are self explanatory. These names make the program more readable and are perfectly legal since they are local to the program. The variables declared for this program and what they are used for are as follows:

uid	used to store the IPC_SET value for the user identification
gid	used to store the IPC_SET value for the group identification
mode	used to store the IPC_SET value for the operation permissions
rtrn	used to store the return integer value from the system call
shmid	used to store and pass the shared memory segment identifier to the system call
command	used to store the code for the desired control command so that subsequent processing can be performed on it
choice	used to determine which member for the IPC_SET control command is to be changed

`shmid_ds`	used to receive the specified shared memory segment identifier's data structure when an `IPC_STAT` control command is performed
`buf`	a pointer passed to the system call which locates the data structure in the user memory area where the `IPC_STAT` control command is to place its return values or where the `IPC_SET` command gets the values to set.

Note that the `shmid_ds` data structure in this program (line 16) uses the data structure of the same name located in the `<sys/shm.h>` header file as a template for its declaration.

The next important thing to observe is that although the `buf` pointer is declared to be a pointer to a data structure of the `shmid_ds` type, it must also be initialized to contain the address of the user memory area data structure (line 17).

Now that all of the required declarations have been explained for this program, this is how it works.

First, the program prompts for a valid shared memory segment identifier which is stored in the `shmid` variable (lines 18-20). This is required for every `shmctl` system call.

Then, the code for the desired control command must be entered (lines 21-29); it is stored in the command variable. The code is tested to determine the control command for subsequent processing.

If the `IPC_STAT` control command is selected (code 1), the system call is performed (lines 39, 40) and the status information returned is printed out (lines 41-71). Note that if the system call is unsuccessful (line 139), the status information of the last successful call is printed out. In addition, an error message is displayed and the `errno` variable is printed out (lines 141). If the system call is successful, a message indicates this along with the shared memory segment identifier used (lines 143-147).

If the `IPC_SET` control command is selected (code 2), the first thing done is to get the current status information for the shared memory identifier specified (lines 88-90). This is necessary because this example program provides for changing only one member at a time, and the system call changes all of them. Also, if an invalid value happened to be stored in the user memory area for one of these members, it would cause repetitive failures for this control command until corrected. The next thing the program does is to prompt for a code corresponding to the member to be changed (lines 91-96). This code is stored in the choice variable (line 97). Now, depending upon the member picked, the program prompts for the new value (lines 98-120). The value is placed in the appropriate member in the user memory area data structure, and the system call is made (lines 121-128). Depending upon success or failure, the program returns the same messages as for IPC_STAT above.

If the IPC_RMID control command (code 3) is selected, the system call is performed (lines 125-128), and the shmid along with its associated message queue and data structure are removed from the UNIX operating system. Note that the buf pointer is ignored in performing this control command and its value can be zero or NULL. Depending upon the success or failure, the program returns the same messages as for the other control commands.

If the SHM_LOCK control command (code 4) is selected, the system call is performed (lines 130,131). Depending upon the success or failure, the program returns the same messages as for the other control commands.

If the SHM_UNLOCK control command (code 5) is selected, the system call is performed (lines 133-135). Depending upon the success or failure, the program returns the same messages as for the other control commands.

The example program for the shmctl system call follows. We suggest that you name the source program file shmctl.c and the executable file shmctl.

Figure 4-12: shmctl **System Call Example**

```
1     /*This is a program to illustrate
2     **the shared memory control, shmctl(),
3     **system call capabilities.
4     */

5     /*Include necessary header files.*/
6     #include    <stdio.h>
7     #include    <sys/types.h>
8     #include    <sys/ipc.h>
9     #include    <sys/shm.h>

10    /*Start of main C language program*/
11    main()
12    {
13        extern int errno;
14        int uid, gid, mode;
15        int rtrn, shmid, command, choice;
16        struct shmid_ds shmid_ds, *buf;
17        buf = &shmid_ds;

18        /*Get the shmid, and command.*/
19        printf("Enter the shmid = ");
20        scanf("%d", &shmid);
21        printf("\nEnter the number for\n");
22        printf("the desired command:\n");

23        printf("IPC_STAT    = 1\n");
24        printf("IPC_SET     = 2\n");
25        printf("IPC_RMID    = 3\n");
26        printf("SHM_LOCK    = 4\n");
27        printf("SHM_UNLOCK  = 5\n");
28        printf("Entry       = ");
29        scanf("%d", &command);

30        /*Check the values.*/
31        printf ("\nshmid =%d, command = %d\n",
32            shmid, command);

33        switch (command)
34        {
35        case 1:    /*Use shmctl() to get
36                   the data structure for
37                   shmid in the shmid_ds area pointed
38                   to by buf and then print it out.*/
```

(continued on next page)

Figure 4-12: shmctl **System Call Example** (continued)

```
39          rtrn = shmctl(shmid, IPC_STAT,
40              buf);
41          printf ("\nThe USER ID = %d\n",
42              buf->shm_perm.uid);
43          printf ("The GROUP ID = %d\n",
44              buf->shm_perm.gid);
45          printf ("The creator's ID = %d\n",
46              buf->shm_perm.cuid);
47          printf ("The creator's group ID = %d\n",
48              buf->shm_perm.cgid);
49          printf ("The operation permissions = 0%o\n",
50              buf->shm_perm.mode);
51          printf ("The slot usage sequence\n");
52          printf ("number = 0%x\n",
53              buf->shm_perm.seq);
54          printf ("The key= 0%x\n",
55              buf->shm_perm.key);
56          printf ("The segment size = %d\n",
57              buf->shm_segsz);
58          printf ("The pid of last shmop = %d\n",
59              buf->shm_lpid);
60          printf ("The pid of creator = %d\n",
61              buf->shm_cpid);
62          printf ("The current # attached = %d\n",
63              buf->shm_nattch);
64          printf("The last shmat time = %ld\n",
65              buf->shm_atime);
66          printf("The last shmdt time = %ld\n",
67              buf->shm_dtime);
68          printf("The last change time = %ld\n",
69              buf->shm_ctime);
70          break;

            /* Lines 71 - 85 deleted */

86      case 2:     /*Select and change the desired
87                      member(s) of the data structure.*/

88          /*Get the original data for this shmid
89              data structure first.*/
90          rtrn = shmctl(shmid, IPC_STAT, buf);

91          printf("\nEnter the number for the\n");
92          printf("member to be changed:\n");
```

(continued on next page)

Figure 4-12: shmctl System Call Example (continued)

```
93          printf("shm_perm.uid   = 1\n");
94          printf("shm_perm.gid   = 2\n");
95          printf("shm_perm.mode  = 3\n");
96          printf("Entry           = ");
97          scanf("%d", &choice);

98          switch(choice){
99          case 1:
100             printf("\nEnter USER ID = ");
101             scanf ("%d", &uid);
102             buf->shm_perm.uid = uid;
103             printf("\nUSER ID = %d\n",
104                 buf->shm_perm.uid);
105             break;

106         case 2:
107             printf("\nEnter GROUP ID = ");
108             scanf("%d", &gid);
109             buf->shm_perm.gid = gid;
110             printf("\nGROUP ID = %d\n",
111                 buf->shm_perm.gid);
112             break;

113         case 3:
114             printf("\nEnter MODE in octal = ");
115             scanf("%o", &mode);
116             buf->shm_perm.mode = mode;
117             printf("\nMODE = 0%o\n",
118                 buf->shm_perm.mode);
119             break;
120         }
121         /*Do the change.*/
122         rtrn = shmctl(shmid, IPC_SET,
123             buf);
124         break;

125     case 3:    /*Remove the shmid along with its
126                     associated
127                     data structure.*/
128         rtrn = shmctl(shmid, IPC_RMID, (struct shmid_ds *) NULL);
129         break;

130     case 4: /*Lock the shared memory segment*/
131         rtrn = shmctl(shmid, SHM_LOCK, (struct shmid_ds *) NULL);
```

(continued on next page)

Figure 4-12: shmctl **System Call Example** (continued)

```
132         break;
133     case 5: /*Unlock the shared memory
134             segment.*/
135         rtrn = shmctl(shmid, SHM_UNLOCK, (struct shmid_ds *) NULL);
136         break;
137     }
138     /*Perform the following if the call is unsuccessful.*/
139     if(rtrn == -1)
140     {
41          printf ("\nThe shmctl call failed, error number = %d\n", errno);
142     }
143     /*Return the shmid upon successful completion.*/
144     else
145         printf ("\nShmctl was successful for shmid = %d\n",
146             shmid);
147     exit (0);
148     }
```

Operations for Shared Memory

This section describes how to use the shmat and shmdt system calls. The accompanying program illustrates their use.

Using shmop

The synopsis found in the shmop(2) entry in the *Programmer's Reference Manual* is as follows:

```
#include <sys/types.h>
#include <sys/ipc.h>
#include <sys/shm.h>

char *shmat (shmid, shmaddr, shmflg)
int shmid;
char *shmaddr;
int shmflg;

int shmdt (shmaddr)
char *shmaddr;
```

Attaching a Shared Memory Segment

The shmat system call requires three arguments to be passed to it. It returns a character pointer value. Upon successful completion, this value will be the address in memory where the process is attached to the shared memory segment and when unsuccessful the value will be −1.

The shmid argument must be a valid, non-negative, integer value. In other words, it must have already been created by using the shmget system call.

The shmaddr argument can be zero or user supplied when passed to the shmat system call. If it is zero, the UNIX operating system picks the address where the shared memory segment will be attached. If it is user supplied, the address must be a valid address that the UNIX operating system would pick. The following illustrates some typical address ranges.

    0xc00c0000
    0xc00e0000
    0xc0100000
    0xc0120000

Note that these addresses are in chunks of 20,000 hexadecimal. It would be wise to let the operating system pick addresses so as to improve portability.

The shmflg argument is used to pass the SHM_RND and SHM_RDONLY flags to the shmat system call.

Detaching Shared Memory Segments

The shmdt system call requires one argument to be passed to it. It returns an integer value which will be zero for successful completion or -1 otherwise.

Further details on shmat and shmdt are discussed in the example program. If you need more information on the logic manipulations in this program, read "Using shmget". It goes into more detail than would be practical to do for every system call.

Example Program

Figure 4-13 is a menu-driven program. It allows all possible combinations of using the shmat and shmdt system calls to be exercised.

From studying this program, you can observe the method of passing arguments and receiving return values. The user-written program requirements are pointed out.

This program begins (lines 5-9) by including the required header files as specified by the shmop(2) entry in the *Programmer's Reference Manual*. Note that in this program errno is declared as an external variable; therefore, the <sys/errno.h> header file does not have to be included.

Variable and structure names have been chosen to be as close as possible to those in the synopsis. Their declarations are self explanatory. These names make the program more readable and are perfectly legal since they are local to the program. The variables declared for this program and what they are used for are as follows:

addr — used to store the address of the shared memory segment for the shmat and shmdt system calls and to receive the return value from the shmat system call

laddr — used to store the desired attach/detach address entered by the user

flags — used to store the codes of the SHM_RND or SHM_RDONLY flags for the shmat system call

i — used as a loop counter for attaching and detaching

`attach`	used to store the desired number of attach operations
`shmid`	used to store and pass the desired shared memory segment identifier
`shmflg`	used to pass the value of flags to the `shmat` system call
`retrn`	used to store the return values from the `shmdt` system call
`detach`	used to store the desired number of detach operations

This example program combines both the `shmat` and `shmdt` system calls. The program prompts for the number of attachments and enters a loop until they are done for the specified shared memory identifiers. Then, the program prompts for the number of detachments to be performed and enters a loop until they are done for the specified shared memory segment addresses.

shmat

The program prompts for the number of attachments to be performed, and the value is stored at the address of the attach variable (lines 19-23).

A loop is entered using the attach variable and the i counter (lines 23-72) to perform the specified number of attachments.

In this loop, the program prompts for a shared memory segment identifier (lines 26-29); it is stored in the `shmid` variable (line 30). Next, the program prompts for the address where the segment is to be attached (lines 32-36); it is stored in the `laddr` variable (line 37) and converted to a pointer (line 39). Then, the program prompts for the desired flags to be used for the attachment (lines 40-47), and the code representing the flags is stored in the `flags` variable (line 48). The `flags` variable is tested to determine the code to be stored for the `shmflg` variable used to pass them to the `shmat` system call (lines 49-60). The system call is executed (line 63). If successful, a message stating so is displayed along with the attach address (lines 68-70). If unsuccessful, a message stating so is displayed and the error code is displayed (line 65). The loop then continues until it finishes.

shmdt

After the attach loop completes, the program prompts for the number of detach operations to be performed (lines 73-77) and the value is stored in the detach variable (line 76).

A loop is entered using the detach variable and the i counter (lines 80-98) to perform the specified number of detachments.

In this loop, the program prompts for the address of the shared memory segment to be detached (lines 81-85); it is stored in the laddr variable (line 86) and converted to a pointer (line 88). Then, the shmdt system call is performed (line 89). If successful, a message stating so is displayed along with the address that the segment was detached from (lines 95, 96). If unsuccessful, the error number is displayed (line 92). The loop continues until it finishes.

The example program for the shmop system calls follows. We suggest that you name the source program file shmop.c and the executable file shmop.

Figure 4-13: shmop System Call Example

```
1      /*This is a program to illustrate
2      **the shared memory operations, shmop(),
3      **system call capabilities.
4      */

5      /*Include necessary header files.*/
6      #include    <stdio.h>
7      #include    <sys/types.h>
8      #include    <sys/ipc.h>
9      #include    <sys/shm.h>
10     /*Start of main C language program*/
11     main()
12     {
13         extern int errno;
14         char *addr;
15         long laddr;
16         int flags, i, attach;
17         int shmid, shmflg, retrn, detach;

18         /*Loop for attachments by this process.*/
19         printf("Enter the number of\n");
20         printf("attachments for this\n");
21         printf("process (1-4).\n");
22         printf("      Attachments = ");

23         scanf("%d", &attach);
24         printf("Number of attaches = %d\n", attach);
```

(continued on next page)

Figure 4-13: shmop **System Call Example** (continued)

```
25        for(i = 1; i <= attach; i++) {
26            /*Enter the shared memory ID.*/
27            printf("\nEnter the shmid of\n");
28            printf("the shared memory segment to\n");
29            printf("be operated on = ");
30            scanf("%d", &shmid);
31            printf("\nshmid = %d\n", shmid);


32            /*Enter the value for shmaddr.*/
33            printf("\nEnter the value for\n");
34            printf("the shared memory address\n");
35            printf("in hexadecimal:\n");
36            printf("          Shmaddr = ");
37            scanf("%lx", &laddr);
38            addr = (char*) laddr;
39            printf("The desired address = 0x%lx\n", (long)addr);

40            /*Specify the desired flags.*/
41            printf("\nEnter the corresponding\n");
422           printf("number for the desired\n");
43            printf("flags:\n");
44            printf("SHM_RND              = 1\n");
45            printf("SHM_RDONLY           = 2\n");
46            printf("SHM_RND and SHM_RDONLY = 3\n");
47            printf("          Flags    = ");
48            scanf("%d", &flags);

49            switch(flags)
50            {
51            case 1:
52                shmflg = SHM_RND;
53                break;
54            case 2:
55                shmflg = SHM_RDONLY;
56                break;
57            case 3:
58                shmflg = SHM_RND | SHM_RDONLY;
59                break;
60            }
61            printf("\nFlags = 0%o\n", shmflg);

62            /*Do the shmat system call.*/
63            addr = shmat(shmid, addr, shmflg);
```

(continued on next page)

Figure 4-13: shmop **System Call Example** (continued)

```
64              if(addr == (char*) -1) {
65                  printf("\nShmat failed, error = %d\n", errno);
66              }
67              else {
68                  printf ("\nShmat was successful\n");
69                  printf("for shmid = %d\n", shmid);
70                  printf("The address = 0x%lx\n", (long)addr);
71              }
72          }

73          /*Loop for detachments by this process.*/
74          printf("Enter the number of\n");
75          printf("detachments for this\n");
76          printf("process (1-4).\n");
77          printf("        Detachments = ");

78          scanf("%d", &detach);
79          printf("Number of attaches = %d\n", detach);
80          for(i = 1; i <= detach; i++) {

81              /*Enter the value for shmaddr.*/
82              printf("\nEnter the value for\n");
83              printf("the shared memory address\n");
84              printf("in hexadecimal:\n");
85              printf("        Shmaddr = ");
86              scanf("%lx", &laddr);
87              addr = (char*)laddr;
88              printf("The desired address = 0x%lx\n", (long)addr);

89              /*Do the shmdt system call.*/
90              retrn = shmdt(addr);
91              if(retrn == -1) {
92                  printf("Error = %d\n", errno);
93              }
94              else {
95                  printf ("\nShmdt was successful\n");
96                  printf("for address  = 0x%lx\n", (long)addr);

97              }
98          }
99      }
```

5 Process Scheduler

Introduction

The UNIX system scheduler determines when processes run. It maintains process priorities based on configuration parameters, process behavior, and user requests; it uses these priorities to assign processes to the CPU.

System V Release 4 gives users absolute control over the order in which certain processes run and the amount of time each process may use the CPU before another process gets a chance.

By default, the Release 4 scheduler uses a time-sharing policy like the policy used in previous releases. A time-sharing policy adjusts process priorities dynamically in an attempt to provide good response time to interactive processes and good throughput to processes that use a lot of CPU time.

The System V Release 4 scheduler offers a real-time scheduling policy as well as a time-sharing policy. Real-time scheduling allows users to set fixed priorities on a per-process basis. The highest-priority real-time user process always gets the CPU as soon as it is runnable, even if system processes are runnable. An application can therefore specify the exact order in which processes run. An application may also be written so that its real-time processes have a guaranteed response time from the system.

For most UNIX environments, the default scheduler configuration works well and no real-time processes are needed: administrators should not change configuration parameters and users should not change scheduler properties of their processes. However, when the requirements for an application include strict timing constraints, real-time processes sometimes provide the only way to satisfy those constraints..

 NOTE Real-time processes used carelessly can have a dramatic negative effect on the performance of time-sharing processes.

This chapter is addressed to programmers who need more control over order of process execution than they get using default scheduler parameters.

Because changes in scheduler administration can affect scheduler behavior, programmers may also need to know something about scheduler administration. For administrative information on the scheduler, see the *System Administrator's Guide*. There are also a few reference manual entries with information on scheduler administration:

- dispadmin(1M) tells how to change scheduler configuration in a running system.

- ts_dptbl(4) and rt_dptbl(4) describe the time-sharing and real-time parameter tables that are used to configure the scheduler.

The rest of this chapter is organized as follows:

- The "Overview of the Process Scheduler" tells what the scheduler does and how it does it. It also introduces scheduler classes.

- The "Commands and Function Calls" section describes and gives examples of the priocntl(1) command and the priocntl(2) and priocntlset(2) system calls, the user interface to scheduler services. The priocntl functions allow you to retrieve scheduler configuration information and to get or set scheduler parameters for a process or a set of processes.

- "Interaction with Other Functions" describes the interactions between the scheduler and related functions.

- The "Performance" section discusses scheduler latencies that some applications must be aware of and mentions some considerations other than the scheduler that application designers must take into account to ensure that their requirements are met.

Overview of the Process Scheduler

The following figure shows how the System V Release 4 process scheduler works:

Figure 5-1: The System V Release 4 Process Scheduler

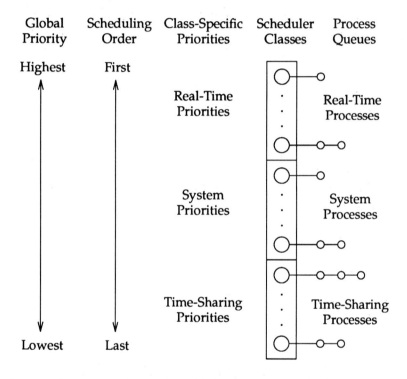

When a process is created, it inherits its scheduler parameters, including scheduler class and a priority within that class. A process changes class only as a result of a user request. The system manages the priority of a process based on user requests and a policy associated with the scheduler class of the process.

In the default configuration, the initialization process belongs to the time-sharing class. Because processes inherit their scheduler parameters, all user login shells begin as time-sharing processes in the default configuration.

The scheduler converts class-specific priorities into global priorities. The global priority of a process determines when it runs—the scheduler always runs the runnable process with highest global priority. Numerically higher priorities run first. Once the scheduler assigns a process to the CPU, the process runs until it uses up its time slice, sleeps, or is preempted by a higher-priority process. Processes with the same priority run round-robin.

Administrators specify default time slices in the configuration tables, but users may assign per-process time slices to real-time processes.

You can display the global priority of a process with the −cl options of the ps(1) command. You can display configuration information about class-specific priorities with the priocntl(1) command and the dispadmin(1M) command.

By default, all real-time processes have higher priorities than any kernel process, and all kernel processes have higher priorities than any time-sharing process.

 NOTE As long as there is a runnable real-time process, no kernel process and no time-sharing process runs.

The following sections describe the scheduling policies of the three default classes.

Time-Sharing Class

The goal of the time-sharing policy is to provide good response time to interactive processes and good throughput to CPU-bound processes. The scheduler switches CPU allocation frequently enough to provide good response time, but not so frequently that it spends too much time doing the switching. Time slices are typically on the order of a few hundred milliseconds.

The time-sharing policy changes priorities dynamically and assigns time slices of different lengths. The scheduler raises the priority of a process that sleeps after only a little CPU use (a process sleeps, for example, when it starts an I/O operation such as a terminal read or a disk read); frequent sleeps are characteristic of interactive tasks such as editing and running simple shell commands. On the other hand, the time-sharing policy lowers the priority of a process that uses the CPU for long periods without sleeping.

The default time-sharing policy gives larger time slices to processes with lower priorities. A process with a low priority is likely to be CPU-bound. Other processes get the CPU first, but when a low-priority process finally gets the CPU, it gets a bigger chunk of time. If a higher-priority process becomes runnable during a time slice, however, it preempts the running process.

The scheduler manages time-sharing processes using configurable parameters in the time-sharing parameter table `ts_dptbl`. This table contains information specific to the time-sharing class.

System Class

The system class uses a fixed-priority policy to run kernel processes such as servers and housekeeping processes like the paging demon. The system class is reserved for use by the kernel; users may neither add nor remove a process from the system class. Priorities for system class processes are set up in the kernel code for those processes; once established, the priorities of system processes do not change. (User processes running in kernel mode are not in the system class.)

Real-Time Class

The real-time class uses a fixed-priority scheduling policy so that critical processes can run in predetermined order. Real-time priorities never change except when a user requests a change. Contrast this fixed-priority policy with the time-sharing policy, in which the system changes priorities in order to provide good interactive response time.

Privileged users can use the `priocntl` command or the `priocntl` system call to assign real-time priorities.

The scheduler manages real-time processes using configurable parameters in the real-time parameter table `rt_dptbl`. This table contains information specific to the real-time class.

Commands and Function Calls

Here is a programmer's view of default process priorities:

Figure 5-2: Process Priorities (Programmer View)

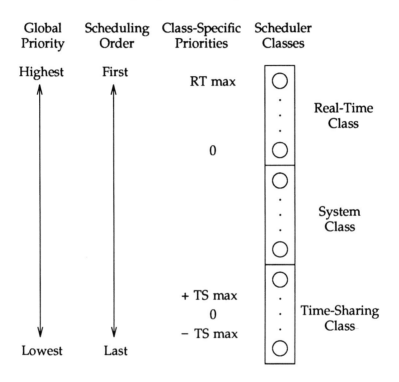

From a user or programmer's point of view, a process priority has meaning only in the context of a scheduler class. You specify a process priority by specifying a class and a class-specific priority value. The class and class-specific value are mapped by the system into a global priority that the system uses to schedule processes.

- Real-time priorities run from zero to a configuration-dependent maximum. The system maps them directly into global priorities. They never change except when a user changes them.

■ System priorities are controlled entirely in the kernel. Users cannot affect them.

■ Time-sharing priorities have a user-controlled component (the "user priority") and a component controlled by the system. The system does not change the user priority except as the result of a user request. The system changes the system-controlled component dynamically on a per-process basis in order to provide good overall system performance; users cannot affect the system-controlled component. The scheduler combines these two components to get the process global priority.

The user priority runs from the negative of a configuration-dependent maximum to the positive of that maximum. A process inherits its user priority. Zero is the default initial user priority.

The "user priority limit" is the configuration-dependent maximum value of the user priority. You may set a user priority to any value below the user priority limit. With appropriate permission, you may raise the user priority limit. Zero is the default user priority limit.

You may lower the user priority of a process to give the process reduced access to the CPU or, with the appropriate permission, raise the user priority to get better service. Because you cannot set the user priority above the user priority limit, you must raise the user priority limit before you raise the user priority if both have their default values of zero.

An administrator configures the maximum user priority independent of global time-sharing priorities. In the default configuration, for example, a user may set a user priority only in the range from −20 to +20, but 60 time-sharing global priorities are configured.

A system administrator's view of priorities is different from that of a user or programmer. When configuring scheduler classes, an administrator deals directly with global priorities. The system maps priorities supplied by users into these global priorities. See the *System Administrator's Guide.*

The ps −cel command reports global priorities for all active processes. The priocntl command reports the class-specific priorities that users and programmers use.

Global process priorities and user-supplied priorities are in ascending order: numerically higher priorities run first.

The `priocntl(1)` command and the `priocntl(2)` and `priocntlset(2)` system calls set or retrieve scheduler parameters for processes. The basic idea for setting priorities is the same for all three functions:

- Specify the target processes.

- Specify the scheduler parameters you want for those processes.

- Do the command or system call to set the parameters for the processes.

You specify the target processes using an ID type and an ID. The ID type tells how to interpret the ID. [This concept of a set of processes applies to signals as well as to the scheduler; see `sigsend(2)`.] The following table lists the valid ID types that you may specify.

`priocntl` ID types
process ID
parent process ID
process group ID
session ID
class ID
effective user ID
effective group ID
all processes

These IDs are basic properties of UNIX processes. [See `intro(2)`.] The class ID refers to the scheduler class of the process. `priocntl` works only for the time-sharing and the real-time classes, not for the system class. Processes in the system class have fixed priorities assigned when they are started by the kernel.

The priocntl command

The priocntl command comes in four forms:

■ priocntl -l displays configuration information.

■ priocntl -d displays the scheduler parameters of processes.

■ priocntl -s sets the scheduler parameters of processes.

■ priocntl -e executes a command with the specified scheduler parameters.

1. Here is the output of the -l option for the default configuration.

```
$ priocntl -l
CONFIGURED CLASSES


SYS (System Class)

TS (Time Sharing)
        Configured TS User Priority Range: -20 through 20

RT (Real Time)
        Maximum Configured RT Priority: 59
```

2. The -d option displays the scheduler parameters of a process or a set of processes. The syntax for this option is

    priocntl -d -i *idtype* *idlist*

idtype tells what kind of IDs are in *idlist*. *idlist* is a list of IDs separated by white space. Here are the valid values for *idtype* and their corresponding ID types in *idlist*:

idtype	*idlist*
pid	process IDs
ppid	parent process IDs
pgid	process group IDs
sid	session IDs
class	class names (TS or RT)
uid	effective user IDs
gid	effective group IDs
all	

Here are some examples of the −d option of priocntl:

```
$ # display info on all processes
$ priocntl -d -i all
       .
       .
       .
$ # display info on all time-sharing processes:
$ priocntl -d -i class TS
       .
       .
       .
$ # display info on all processes with user ID 103 or 6626
$ priocntl -d -i uid 103 6626
       .
       .
       .
```

3. The −s option sets scheduler parameters for a process or a set of processes. The syntax for this option is

> priocntl −s −c *class class_options* −i *idtype idlist*

idtype and *idlist* are the same as for the −d option described above.

class is TS for time-sharing or RT for real-time. You must be superuser to create a real-time process, to raise a time-sharing user priority above a per-process limit, or to raise the per-process limit above zero. Class options are class-specific:

Class-specific options for `priocntl`			
class	−c *class*	options	meaning
real-time	RT	−p *pri*	priority
		−t *tslc*	time slice
		−r *res*	resolution
time-sharing	TS	−p *upri*	user priority
		−m *uprilim*	user priority limit

For a real-time process you may assign a priority and a time slice.

■ The priority is a number from 0 to the real-time maximum as reported by `priocntl −1`; the default maximum is 59.

■ You specify the time slice as a number of clock intervals and the resolution of the interval. Resolution is specified in intervals per second. The time slice, therefore, is *tslc/res* seconds. To specify a time slice of one-tenth of a second, for example, you could specify a *tslc* of 1 and a *res* of 10. If you specify a time slice without specifying a resolution, millisecond resolution (a *res* of 1000) is assumed.

If you change a time-sharing process into a real-time process, it gets a default priority and time slice if you don't specify one. If you wish to change only the priority of a real-time process and leave its time slice unchanged, omit the −t option. If you wish to change only the time slice of a real-time process and leave its priority unchanged, omit the −p option.

For a time-sharing process you may assign a user priority and a user priority limit.

■ The user priority is the user-controlled component of a time-sharing priority. The scheduler calculates the global priority of a time-sharing process by combining this user priority with a system-controlled component that depends on process behavior. The user priority has the same effect as a value set by `nice` (except that `nice` uses higher numbers for lower priority).

■ The user priority limit is the maximum user priority a process may set for itself without being superuser. By default, the user priority limit is 0; you must be superuser to set a user priority limit above 0.

Both the user priority and the user priority limit must be within the user priority range reported by the `priocntl -l` command. The default range is −20 to +20.

A process may lower and raise its user priority as often as it wishes, as long as the value is below its user priority limit. It is a courtesy to other users to lower your user priority for big chunks of low-priority work. On the other hand, if you lower your user priority limit, you must be superuser to raise it. A typical use of the user priority limit is to reduce permanently the priority of child processes or of some other set of low-priority processes.

The user priority can never be greater than the user priority limit. If you set the user priority limit below the user priority, the user priority is lowered to the new user priority limit. If you attempt to set the user priority above the user priority limit, the user priority is set to the user priority limit.

Here are some examples of the −s option of `priocntl`:

```
# # make process with ID 24668 a real-time process with default parameters:
# priocntl -s -c RT -i pid 24668

# # make 3608 RT with priority 55 and a one-fifth second time slice:
# priocntl -s -c RT -p 55 -t 1 -r 5 -i pid 3608

# # change all processes into time-sharing processes:
# priocntl -s -c TS -i all

# # for uid 1122, reduce TS user priority and user priority limit to -10:
# priocntl -s -c TS -p -10 -m -10 -i uid 1122
```

4. The −e option sets scheduler parameters for a specified command and executes the command. The syntax for this option is

       `priocntl -e -c` *class class_options command [command arguments]*

The class and class options are the same as for the −s option described above.

```
# # start a real-time shell with default real-time priority:
# priocntl -e -c RT /bin/sh

$ # run make with a time-sharing  user priority of -10:
$ priocntl -e -c TS -p -10 make bigprog
```

The `priocntl` command subsumes the function of `nice`, which continues to work as in previous releases. `nice` works only on time-sharing processes and uses higher numbers to assign lower priorities. The final example above is equivalent to using `nice` to set an "increment" of 10:

```
nice -10 make bigprog
```

The priocntl system call

```
#include      <sys/types.h>
#include      <sys/procset.h>
#include      <sys/priocntl.h>
#include      <sys/rtpriocntl.h>
#include      <sys/tspriocntl.h>

long priocntl(idtype_t idtype, id_t id, int cmd,
     cmd_struct arg);
```

The `priocntl` system call gets or sets scheduler parameters of a set of processes. The input arguments:

- `idtype` is the type of ID you are specifying.
- `id` is the ID.
- `cmd` specifies which `priocntl` function to perform. The functions are listed in the table below.
- `arg` is a pointer to a structure that depends on cmd.

Here are the valid values for *idtype*, which are defined in `priocntl.h`, and their corresponding ID types in *id*:

idtype	Interpretation of id
P_PID	process ID (of a single process)
P_PPID	parent process ID
P_PGID	process group ID
P_SID	session ID
P_CID	class ID
P_UID	effective user ID
P_GID	effective group ID
P_ALL	all processes

Here are the valid values for `cmd`, their meanings, and the type of `arg`:

priocntl Commands		
cmd	arg Type	Function
PC_GETCID	pcinfo_t	get class ID and attributes
PC_GETCLINFO	pcinfo_t	get class name and attributes
PC_SETPARMS	pcparms_t	set class and scheduling parameters
PC_GETPARMS	pcparms_t	get class and scheduling parameters

Here are the values `priocntl` returns on success:

- The GETCID and GETCLINFO commands return the number of configured scheduler classes.

- PC_SETPARMS returns 0.

- PC_GETPARMS returns the process ID of the process whose scheduler properties it is returning.

On failure, `priocntl` returns −1 and sets `errno` to indicate the reason for the failure. See `priocntl`(2) for the complete list of error conditions.

PC_GETCID, PC_GETCLINFO

The PC_GETCID and PC_GETCLINFO commands retrieve scheduler parameters for a class based on the class ID or class name. Both commands use the pcinfo structure to send arguments and receive return values:

```
typedef struct pcinfo {
    id_t  pc_cid;                  /* class id */
    char  pc_clname[PC_CLNMSZ];    /* class name */
    long  pc_clinfo[PC_CLINFOSZ];  /* class information */
} pcinfo_t;
```

The PC_GETCID command gets scheduler class ID and parameters given the class name. The class ID is used in some of the other priocntl commands to specify a scheduler class. The valid class names are TS for time-sharing and RT for real-time.

For the real-time class, pc_clinfo contains an rtinfo structure, which holds rt_maxpri, the maximum valid real-time priority; in the default configuration, this is the highest priority any process can have. The minimum valid real-time priority is zero. rt_maxpri is a configurable value; the *System Administrator's Guide* tells how to configure process priorities.

```
typedef struct rtinfo {
    short  rt_maxpri;  /* maximum real-time priority */
} rtinfo_t;
```

For the time-sharing class, pc_clinfo contains a tsinfo structure, which holds ts_maxupri, the maximum time-sharing user priority. The minimum time-sharing user priority is −ts_maxupri. ts_maxupri is also a configurable value.

```
typedef struct tsinfo {
    short  ts_maxupri;  /* limits of user priority range */
} tsinfo_t;
```

The following program is a cheap substitute for priocntl −l; it gets and prints the range of valid priorities for the time-sharing and real-time scheduler classes.

```
/*
 * Get scheduler class IDs and priority ranges.
 */

#include <sys/types.h>
#include <sys/priocntl.h>
#include <sys/rtpriocntl.h>
#include <sys/tspriocntl.h>
#include <stdio.h>
#include <string.h>
#include <stdlib.h>
#include <errno.h>

main ()
{
        pcinfo_t        pcinfo;
        tsinfo_t        *tsinfop;
        rtinfo_t        *rtinfop;
        short           maxtsupri, maxrtpri;

    /* time sharing */
        (void) strcpy (pcinfo.pc_clname, "TS");
        if (priocntl (0L, 0L, PC_GETCID, &pcinfo) == -1L) {
                perror ("PC_GETCID failed for time-sharing class");
                exit (1);
        }
        tsinfop = (struct tsinfo *) pcinfo.pc_clinfo;
        maxtsupri = tsinfop->ts_maxupri;
        (void) printf("Time sharing: ID %ld, priority range -%d through %d\n",
                pcinfo.pc_cid, maxtsupri, maxtsupri);

    /* real time */
        (void) strcpy(pcinfo.pc_clname, "RT");
        if (priocntl (0L, 0L, PC_GETCID, &pcinfo) == -1L) {
                perror ("PC_GETCID failed for real-time class");
                exit (2);
        }
        rtinfop = (struct rtinfo *) pcinfo.pc_clinfo;
        maxrtpri = rtinfop->rt_maxpri;
        (void) printf("Real time:    ID %ld, priority range 0 through %d\n",
                pcinfo.pc_cid, maxrtpri);
        return (0);
}
```

The following screen shows the output of this program, called getcid in this example.

```
$ getcid
Time sharing: ID 1, priority range -20 through 20
Real time:    ID 2, priority range 0 through 59
```

The following function is useful in the examples below. Given a class name, it uses PC_GETCID to return the class ID and maximum priority in the class.

 NOTE All the following examples omit the lines that include header files. The examples compile with the same header files as in the first example above.

```
/*
 *  Return class ID and maximum priority.
 *  Input argument name is class name.
 *  Maximum priority is returned in *maxpri.
 */

id_t
schedinfo (name, maxpri)
        char *name;
        short *maxpri;
{
        pcinfo_t        info;
        tsinfo_t        *tsinfop;
        rtinfo_t        *rtinfop;

        (void) strcpy(info.pc_clname, name);
        if (priocntl (0L, 0L, PC_GETCID, &info) == -1L) {
                return (-1);
        }
        if (strcmp(name, "TS") == 0) {
                tsinfop = (struct tsinfo *) info.pc_clinfo;
                *maxpri = tsinfop->ts_maxupri;
        } else if (strcmp(name, "RT") == 0) {
                rtinfop = (struct rtinfo *) info.pc_clinfo;
                *maxpri = rtinfop->rt_maxpri;
        } else {
                return (-1);
        }
        return (info.pc_cid);
}
```

The PC_GETCLINFO command gets a scheduler class name and parameters
given the class ID. This command makes it easy to write applications that make
no assumptions about what classes are configured.

The following program uses PC_GETCLINFO to get the class name of a process
based on the process ID. This program assumes the existence of a function
getclassID, which retrieves the class ID of a process given the process ID; this
function is given in the following section.

```
/* Get scheduler class name given process ID. */

main (argc, argv)
        int argc;
        char *argv[];
{
        pcinfo_t        pcinfo;
        id_t            pid, classID;
        id_t            getclassID();

        if ((pid = atoi(argv[1])) <= 0) {
                perror ("bad pid");
                exit (1);
        }
        if ((classID = getclassID(pid)) == -1) {
                perror ("unknown class ID");
                exit (2);
        }
        pcinfo.pc_cid = classID;
        if (priocntl (0L, 0L, PC_GETCLINFO, &pcinfo) == -1L) {
                perror ("PC_GETCLINFO failed");
                exit (3);
        }
        (void) printf("process ID %d, class %s\n", pid, pcinfo.pc_clname);
}
```

PC_GETPARMS, PC_SETPARMS

The PC_GETPARMS command gets and the PC_SETPARMS command sets
scheduler parameters for processes. Both commands use the pcparms structure
to send arguments or receive return values:

```
typedef struct pcparms {
    id_t  pc_cid;                    /* process class */
    long  pc_clparms[PC_CLPARMSZ];   /* class specific */
} pcparms_t;
```

Ignoring class-specific information for the moment, we can write a simple function for returning the scheduler class ID of a process, as promised in the previous section.

```
/*
 * Return scheduler class ID of process with ID pid.
 */

getclassID (pid)
        id_t pid;
{

        pcparms_t        pcparms;

        pcparms.pc_cid = PC_CLNULL;
        if (priocntl(P_PID, pid, PC_GETPARMS, &pcparms) == -1) {
                return (-1);
        }
        return (pcparms.pc_cid);
}
```

For the real-time class, pc_clparms contains an rtparms structure. rtparms
holds scheduler parameters specific to the real-time class:

```
typedef struct rtparms {
    short   rt_pri;         /* real-time priority */
    ulong   rt_tqsecs;      /* seconds in time quantum */
    long    rt_tqnsecs;     /* additional nsecs in quantum */
} rtparms_t;
```

rt_pri is the real-time priority; rt_tqsecs is the number of seconds and
rt_tqnsecs is the number of additional nanoseconds in a time slice. That is,
rt_tqsecs seconds plus rt_tqnsecs nanoseconds is the interval a process
may use the CPU without sleeping before the scheduler gives another process a
chance at the CPU.

For the time-sharing class, pc_clparms contains a tsparms structure.
tsparms holds the scheduler parameter specific to the time-sharing class:

```
typedef struct tsparms {
    short   ts_uprilim;     /* user priority limit */
    short   ts_upri;        /* user priority */
} tsparms_t;
```

ts_upri is the user priority, the user-controlled component of a time-sharing priority. ts_uprilim is the user priority limit, the maximum user priority a process may set for itself without being superuser. These values are described above in the discussion of the −s option of the priocntl command. Both the user priority and the user priority limit must be within the range reported by the priocntl −1 command; this range is also reported by the PC_GETCID and PC_GETCLINFO commands to the priocntl system call.

The PC_GETPARMS command gets the scheduler class and parameters of a single process. The return value of the priocntl is the process ID of the process whose parameters are returned in the pcparms structure. The process chosen depends on the idtype and id arguments to priocntl and on the value of pcparms.pc_cid, which contains PC_CLNULL or a class ID returned by PC_GETCID:

Figure 5-3: What Gets Returned by PC_GETPARMS

Number of Processes Selected by idtype and id	pc_cid		
	RT class ID	TS class ID	PC_CLNULL
1	RT parameters of process selected	TS parameters of process selected	class and parameters of process selected
More than 1	RT parameters of highest-priority RT process	TS parameters of process with highest user priority	(error)

If idtype and id select a single process and pc_cid does not conflict with the class of that process, priocntl returns the scheduler parameters of the process. If they select more than one process of a single scheduler class, priocntl returns parameters using class-specific criteria as shown in the table. priocntl returns an error in the following cases:

- idtype and id select one or more processes and none is in the class specified by pc_cid.

- `idtype` and `id` select more than one process process and `pc_cid` is `PC_CLNULL`.

- `idtype` and `id` select no processes.

The following program takes a process ID as its input and prints the scheduler class and class-specific parameters of that process:

```
/*
 *   Get scheduler class and parameters of
 *   process whose pid is input argument.
 */

main (argc, argv)
        int argc;
        char *argv[];
{
        pcparms_t       pcparms;
        rtparms_t       *rtparmsp;
        tsparms_t       *tsparmsp;
        id_t            pid, rtID, tsID;
        id_t            schedinfo();
        short           priority, tsmaxpri, rtmaxpri;
        ulong           secs;
        long            nsecs;

        pcparms.pc_cid = PC_CLNULL;
        rtparmsp = (rtparms_t *) pcparms.pc_clparms;
        tsparmsp = (tsparms_t *) pcparms.pc_clparms;
        if ((pid = atoi(argv[1])) <= 0) {
                perror ("bad pid");
                exit (1);
        }

    /* get scheduler properties for this pid */
        if (priocntl(P_PID, pid, PC_GETPARMS, &pcparms) == -1) {
                perror ("GETPARMS failed");
                exit (2);
        }

    /* get class IDs and maximum priorities for TS and RT */
        if ((tsID = schedinfo ("TS", &tsmaxpri)) == -1) {
                perror ("schedinfo failed for TS");
                exit (3);
        }
```

(continued on next page)

```
            if ((rtID = schedinfo ("RT", &rtmaxpri)) == -1) {
                perror ("schedinfo failed for RT");
                exit (4);
            }

    /* print results */
            if (pcparms.pc_cid == rtID) {
                priority = rtparmsp->rt_pri;
                secs = rtparmsp->rt_tqsecs;
                nsecs = rtparmsp->rt_tqnsecs;
                (void) printf ("process %d: RT priority %d\n",
                        pid, priority);
                (void) printf ("  time slice %ld secs, %ld nsecs\n",
                        secs, nsecs);
            } else if (pcparms.pc_cid == tsID) {
                priority = tsparmsp->ts_upri;
                (void) printf ("process %d: TS priority %d\n",
                        pid, priority);
            } else {
                printf ("Unknown scheduler class %d\n",
                        pcparms.pc_cid);
                exit (5);
            }
            return (0);
    }
```

The PC_SETPARMS command sets the scheduler class and parameters of a set of processes. The idtype and id input arguments specify the processes to be changed. The pcparms structure contains the new parameters: pc_cid contains the ID of the scheduler class to which the processes are to be assigned, as returned by PC_GETCID; pc_clparms contains the class-specific parameters:

- If pc_cid is the real-time class ID, pc_clparms contains an rtparms structure in which rt_pri contains the real-time priority and rt_tqsecs plus rt_tqnsecs contains the time slice to be assigned to the processes.

- If pc_cid is the time-sharing class ID, pc_clparms contains a tsparms structure in which ts_uprilim contains the user priority limit and ts_upri contains the user priority to be assigned to the processes.

The following program takes a process ID as input, makes the process a real-time process with the highest valid priority minus 1, and gives it the default time slice for that priority. The program calls the schedinfo function listed above to get the real-time class ID and maximum priority.

```
/*
 * Input arg is proc ID.  Make process a real-time
 * process with highest priority minus 1.
 */

main (argc, argv)
        int argc;
        char *argv[];
{
        pcparms_t        pcparms;
        rtparms_t        *rtparmsp;
        id_t             pid, rtID;
        id_t             schedinfo();
        short            maxrtpri;

        if ((pid = atoi(argv[1])) <= 0) {
                perror ("bad pid");
                exit (1);
        }

    /* Get highest valid RT priority. */
        if ((rtID = schedinfo ("RT", &maxrtpri)) == -1) {
                perror ("schedinfo failed for RT");
                exit (2);
        }

    /* Change proc to RT, highest prio - 1, default time slice */
        pcparms.pc_cid = rtID;
        rtparmsp = (struct rtparms *) pcparms.pc_clparms;
        rtparmsp->rt_pri = maxrtpri - 1;
        rtparmsp->rt_tqnsecs = RT_TQDEF;

        if (priocntl(P_PID, pid, PC_SETPARMS, &pcparms) == -1) {
                perror ("PC_SETPARMS failed");
                exit (3);
        }

}
```

The following table lists the special values rt_tqnsecs can take when
PC_SETPARMS is used on real-time processes. When any of these is used,
rt_tqsecs is ignored. These values are defined in the header file
rtpriocntl.h:

rt_tqnsecs	Time Slice
RT_TQINF	infinite
RT_TQDEF	default
RT_NOCHANGE	unchanged

RT_TQINF specifies an infinite time slice. RT_TQDEF specifies the default time
slice configured for the real-time priority being set with the SETPARMS call.
RT_NOCHANGE specifies no change from the current time slice; this value is useful, for example, when you change process priority but do not wish to change
the time slice. (You can also use RT_NOCHANGE in the rt_pri field to change a
time slice without changing the priority.)

The priocntlset system call

```
#include     <sys/types.h>
#include     <sys/signal.h>
#include     <sys/procset.h>
#include     <sys/priocntl.h>
#include     <sys/rtpriocntl.h>
#include     <sys/tspriocntl.h>

long priocntlset (procset_t *psp, int cmd,
        cmd_struct arg) ;
```

The priocntlset system call changes scheduler parameters of a set of
processes, just like priocntl. priocntlset has the same command set as
priocntl; the cmd and arg input arguments are the same. But while
priocntl applies to a set of processes specified by a single idtype/id pair,
priocntlset applies to a set of processes that results from a logical combination of two idtype/id pairs. The input argument psp points to a procset
structure that specifies the two idtype/id pairs and the logical operation to

perform. This structure is defined in `procset.h`:

```
typedef struct procset {
        idop_t    p_op;            /* operator connecting */
                                   /* left and right sets */
    /* left set:  */
        idtype_t  p_lidtype;       /* left ID type */
        id_t      p_lid;           /* left ID */

    /* right set:  */
        idtype_t  p_ridtype;       /* right ID type */
        id_t      p_rid;           /* right ID */
} procset_t;
```

`p_lidtype` and `p_lid` specify the ID type and ID of one ("left") set of processes; `p_ridtype` and `p_rid` specify the ID type and ID of a second ("right") set of processes. `p_op` specifies the operation to perform on the two sets of processes to get the set of processes to operate on. The valid values for `p_op` and the processes they specify are:

- `POP_DIFF`: set difference—processes in left set and not in right set

- `POP_AND`: set intersection—processes in both left and right sets

- `POP_OR`: set union—processes in either left or right sets or both

- `POP_XOR`: set exclusive-or—processes in left or right set but not in both

The following macro, also defined in `procset.h`, offers a convenient way to initialize a `procset` structure :

```
#define setprocset(psp, op, ltype, lid, rtype, rid) \
            (psp)->p_op       = (op); \
            (psp)->p_lidtype  = (ltype); \
            (psp)->p_lid      = (lid); \
            (psp)->p_ridtype  = (rtype); \
            (psp)->p_rid      = (rid);
```

Here is a situation where `priocntlset` would be useful: suppose an application had both real-time and time-sharing processes that ran under a single user ID. If the application wanted to change the priority of only its real-time processes without changing the time-sharing processes to real-time processes, it could do so as follows. (This example uses the function `schedinfo`, which is defined above in the section on `PC_GETCID`.)

```
/*
 * Change real-time priorities of this uid
 * to highest real-time priority minus 1.
 */
main (argc, argv)
        int argc;
        char *argv[];
{
        procset_t       procset;
        pcparms_t       pcparms;
        struct rtparms  *rtparmsp;
        id_t            rtclassID;
        id_t            schedinfo();
        short           maxrtpri;
    /* left set: select processes with same uid as this process */
        procset.p_lidtype = P_UID;
        procset.p_lid = getuid();
    /* get info on real-time class */
        if ((rtclassID = schedinfo ("RT", &maxrtpri)) == -1) {
                perror ("schedinfo failed");
                exit (1);
        }
    /* right set: select real-time processes */
        procset.p_ridtype = P_CID;
        procset.p_rid = rtclassID;
    /* select only my RT processes */
        procset.p_op = POP_AND;
    /* specify new scheduler parameters */
        pcparms.pc_cid = rtclassID;
        rtparmsp = (struct rtparms *) pcparms.pc_clparms;
        rtparmsp->rt_pri = maxrtpri - 1;
        rtparmsp->rt_tqnsecs = RT_NOCHANGE;
        if (priocntlset (&procset, PC_SETPARMS, &pcparms) == -1) {
                perror ("priocntlset failed");
                exit (2);
        }
}
```

priocntl offers a simple scheduler interface that is adequate for many applications; applications that need a more powerful way to specify sets of processes can use priocntlset.

Interaction with Other Functions

Kernel Processes

The kernel assigns its demon and housekeeping processes to the system scheduler class. Users may neither add processes to nor remove processes from this class, nor may they change the priorities of these processes. The command `ps -cel` lists the scheduler class of all processes. Processes in the system class are identified by a `SYS` entry in the `CLS` column.

If the workload on a machine contains real-time processes that use too much CPU, they can lock out system processes, which can lead to all sorts of trouble. Real-time applications must ensure that they leave some CPU time for system and other processes.

fork, exec

Scheduler class, priority, and other scheduler parameters are inherited across the `fork(2)` and `exec(2)` system calls.

nice

The `nice(1)` command and the `nice(2)` system call work as in previous versions of the UNIX system. They allow you to change the priority of only a time-sharing process. You still use use lower numeric values to assign higher time-sharing priorities with these functions.

To change the scheduler class of a process or to specify a real-time priority, you must use one of the `priocntl` functions. You use higher numeric values to assign higher priorities with the `priocntl` functions.

init

The init process is treated as a special case by the scheduler. To change the scheduler properties of init, init must be the only process specified by idtype and id or by the procset structure.

Performance

Because the scheduler determines when and for how long processes run, it has an overriding importance in the performance and perceived performance of a system.

By default, all processes are time-sharing processes. A process changes class only as a result of one of the priocntl functions.

In the default configuration, all real-time process priorities are above any time-sharing process priority. This implies that as long as any real-time process is runnable, no time-sharing process or system process ever runs. So if a real-time application is not written carefully, it can completely lock out users and essential kernel housekeeping.

Besides controlling process class and priorities, a real-time application must also control several other factors that influence its performance. The most important factors in performance are CPU power, amount of primary memory, and I/O throughput. These factors interact in complex ways. For more information, see the chapter on performance management in the *System Administrator's Guide*. In particular, the sar(1) command has options for reporting on all the factors discussed in this section.

Process State Transition

Applications that have strict real-time constraints may need to prevent processes from being swapped or paged out to secondary memory. Here's a simplified overview of UNIX process states and the transitions between states:

Figure 5-4: Process State Transition Diagram

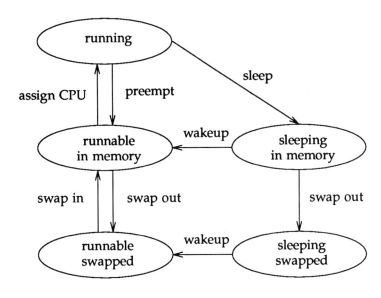

An active process is normally in one of the five states in the diagram. The arrows show how it changes states.

- A process is running if it is assigned to a CPU. A process is preempted—that is, removed from the running state—by the scheduler if a process with a higher priority becomes runnable. A process is also preempted if it consumes its entire time slice and a process of equal priority is runnable.

- A process is runnable in memory if it is in primary memory and ready to run, but is not assigned to a CPU.

- A process is sleeping in memory if it is in primary memory but is waiting for a specific event before it can continue execution. For example, a process is sleeping if it is waiting for an I/O operation to complete, for a locked resource to be unlocked, or for a timer to expire. When the event occurs, the process is sent a wakeup; if the reason for its sleep is gone, the process becomes runnable.

■ A process is runnable and swapped if it is not waiting for a specific event but has had its whole address space written to secondary memory to make room in primary memory for other processes.

■ A process is sleeping and swapped if it is both waiting for a specific event and has had its whole address space written to secondary memory to make room in primary memory for other processes.

If a machine does not have enough primary memory to hold all its active processes, it must page or swap some address space to secondary memory:

■ When the system is short of primary memory, it writes individual pages of some processes to secondary memory but still leaves those processes runnable. When a process runs, if it accesses those pages, it must sleep while the pages are read back into primary memory.

■ When the system gets into a more serious shortage of primary memory, it writes all the pages of some processes to secondary memory and marks those processes as swapped. Such processes get back into a schedulable state only by being chosen by the system scheduler demon process, then read back into memory.

Both paging and swapping, and especially swapping, introduce delay when a process is ready to run again. For processes that have strict timing requirements, this delay can be unacceptable. To avoid swapping delays, real-time processes are never swapped, though parts of them may be paged. An application can prevent paging and swapping by locking its text and data into primary memory. For more information see memcntl(2) in the *Programmer's Reference Manual*. Of course, how much can be locked is limited by how much memory is configured. Also, locking too much can cause intolerable delays to processes that do not have their text and data locked into memory. Tradeoffs between performance of real-time processes and performance of other processes depend on local needs. On some systems, process locking may be required to guarantee the necessary real-time response.

Software Latencies

Designers of some real-time applications must have information on software latencies to analyze the performance characteristics of their applications and to predict whether performance constraints can be met. These latencies depend on kernel implementation and on system hardware, so it is not practical to list the latencies. It is useful, however, to describe some of the most important latencies. Consider the following time-line:

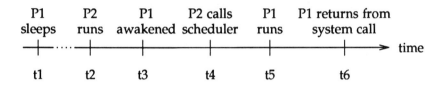

P1 and P2 represent processes; t1 through t6 represent points in time. Suppose that P1 has a higher priority than all other active processes, including P2. P1 runs and does a system call that causes it to sleep at time t1, waiting for I/O. P2 runs. The I/O device interrupts, resulting in a wakeup at time t3 that makes P1 runnable. If P2 is running in user mode at time t3, it is preempted immediately and the interval (t4 − t3) is, for practical purposes, zero. If P2 is running in kernel mode at time t3, it is preempted as soon as it gets to a kernel preemption point, a point in kernel code where data structures are in a consistent state and where the state of the current process (P2 in this example) may be saved and a different process run. Therefore, if P2 is running in kernel mode at time t3, the interval (t4 − t3) depends on kernel preemption points, which are spread throughout the kernel. It is useful to know both a typical time to preemption and a maximum time to preemption; these times depend on kernel implementation and on hardware. Eventually, the scheduler runs (at time t4), finds that a higher-priority process P1 is runnable, and runs it. We refer to the interval (t5 − t4) as the software switch latency of the system. This latency is, for practical purposes, a constant; again it is an implementation-dependent value. At time t6, P1 returns to the user program from the system call that put it to sleep at time t1. For simplicity, suppose that the program is getting only a few bytes of data from the I/O device. In this simple case, the interval (t6 − t5) consists basically of the overhead of getting out of the system call. We refer to the interval (t6 − t3) as the software wakeup latency of the system; this is the interval from the I/O device interrupt until the user process returns to application level to deal with the interrupt (assuming that it is the highest priority process). So the software wakeup latency is composed of a preemption latency, context-switch time, and a part of system call overhead. Of course, the latency increases as the system call asks for more data.

This discussion of latencies assumes that the text and data of the processes are in primary memory. An application may have to use process locking to guarantee that its processes do not get swapped or paged out of primary memory. See the discussion in the previous section.

Primary Memory for Real-Time U-Blocks

A process u-block contains per-process information that is not needed when the process is swapped out. The u-block is contained in the user structure defined in user.h. Normally u-blocks themselves may be swapped or paged. To guarantee software latencies, however, the UNIX kernel always keeps the u-blocks of real-time processes in primary memory—it never swaps them. (Time sharing u-blocks may be swapped.) Designers of real-time applications should realize that each real-time process has a 6 Kbyte u-area always in primary memory.

6 Symbolic Links

Introduction

A symbolic link is a special type of file that represents another file. The data in a symbolic link consists of the path name of a file or directory to which the symbolic link file is linked. The link that is formed is called symbolic to distinguish it from a regular (also called a hard) link such as can be created by using the ln(1) command. A symbolic link differs functionally from a regular link in three major ways: files from different file systems may be linked together; directories as well as regular files may be symbolically linked by any user; and a symbolic link can be created even if the file it represents does not exist.

In order to understand how a symbolic link works, it is necessary to understand how the UNIX operating system views files. (The following description pertains to files that belong to the standard System V file system type.) The internal representation of a file is contained in an inode, which contains a description of the layout of the file data on disk as well as information about the file, such as the file owner, the access permissions, and the access times. Every file has one inode, but a file may have several names, all of which point to the inode. Each name is called a regular (or hard) link.

When a file is created, an inode is allocated for it, the file contents are stored in data blocks, and an entry is created in a directory. A directory is a file whose data is a sequence of entries, each consisting of an inode number and the name of a file. The inode initially has a link count of one, which means that this file has one name (or one link to it).

We are now in a position to understand the difference between the creation of a regular and a symbolic link. When a user creates a regular link to a file with the ln(1) command, a new directory entry is created containing a new file name and the inode number of an existing file. The link count of the file is incremented.

In contrast, when a user creates a symbolic link both a new directory entry and a new inode are created. A data block is allocated to contain the path name of the file to which the symbolic link refers. The link count of the referenced file is not incremented.

Symbolic links can be used to solve a variety of common problems. For example, it frequently happens that a disk partition (such as root) runs out of disk space. With symbolic links, an administrator can create a link from a directory on that file system to a directory on another file system. Such a link provides extra disk space and is, in most cases, transparent to both users and programs.

Symbolic links can also help deal with the built-in path names that appear in the code of many commands. Changing the path names would require changing the programs and recompiling them. With symbolic links, the path names can effectively be changed by making the original files symbolic links that point to new files.

In a shared resource environment like RFS, symbolic links can be very useful. For example, if it is important to have a single copy of certain administrative files, symbolic links can be used to help share them. Symbolic links can also be used to share resources selectively. Suppose a system administrator wants to do a remote mount of a directory that contains sharable devices. These devices must be in /dev on the client system, but this system has devices of its own so the administrator does not want to mount the directory onto /dev. Rather than do this, the administrator can mount the directory at a location other than /dev and then use symbolic links in the /dev directory to refer to these remote devices. (This is similar to the problem of built-in path names since it is normally assumed that devices reside in the /dev directory.)

Finally, symbolic links can be valuable within the context of the virtual file system (VFS) architecture. With VFS new services, such as higher performance files, events, and network IPC, may be provided on a file system basis. Symbolic links can be used to link these services to home directories or to places that make more sense to the application or user. Thus one might create a database index file in a RAM-based file system type and symbolically link it to the place where the database server expects it and manages it.

Using Symbolic Links

 NOTE The phrases "following symbolic links" and "not following symbolic links" as they are used in this document refer to the evaluation of the last component of a path name. In the evaluation of a path name, if any component other than the last is a symbolic link, the symbolic link is followed and the referenced file is used in the path name evaluation. However, if the last component of a path name is a symbolic link, the link may or may not be followed.

Properties of Symbolic Links

This section summarizes some of the essential characteristics of symbolic links. Succeeding sections describe how symbolic links may be used, based on the characteristics outlined here.

As we have seen above, a symbolic link is a new type of file that represents another file. The file to which it refers may be of any type; a regular file, a directory, a character-special, block-special, or FIFO-special file, or another symbolic link. The file may be on the local system or on a remote system. In fact, the file to which a symbolic link refers does not even have to exist. In particular, the file does not have to exist when the symbolic link is created or when it is removed.

Creation and removal of a symbolic link follow the same rules that apply to any file. To do either, the user must have write permission in the directory that contains the symbolic link.

The ownership and the access permissions (mode) of the symbolic link are ignored for all accesses of the symbolic link. It is the ownership and access permissions of the referenced file that are used. A symbolic link cannot be opened or closed and its contents cannot be changed once it has been created.

If the file /usr/jan/junk is a symbolic link to the file /etc/passwd, in effect the file name /etc/passwd is substituted for junk so that when the user executes

        cat /usr/jan/junk

it is the contents of the file /etc/passwd that are printed.

Similarly, if /usr/jan/junk is a symbolic link to the file ../junk2, executing

        cat /usr/jan/junk

is the same as executing

        cat /usr/jan/../junk2

or

        cat /usr/junk2

When a symbolic link is followed and brings a user to a different part of the file tree, we may distinguish between where the user really is (the physical path) and how the user got there (the virtual path). The behavior of /usr/bin/pwd, the shell built-in pwd, and . . are all based on the physical path. In practical terms this means that there is no way for the user to retrace the path which brought the user to the current position in the file tree.

 Other shells may use the virtual path. For example, by default the Korn shell pwd uses the virtual path, though there is an option allowing the user to make it use the physical path.

Consider the case shown in Figure 6-1 where /usr/include/sys is a symbolic link to /usr/src/uts/sys.

Figure 6-1: File Tree with Symbolic Link

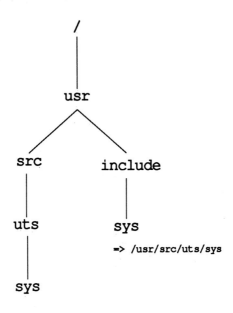

Here if a user enters

cd /usr/include/sys

and then enters pwd, the result is

/usr/src/uts/sys

If the user then enters   cd .. followed by pwd, the result is

/usr/src/uts

Creating Symbolic Links

Syntax and Semantics

To create a symbolic link, the new system call symlink(2) is used and the owner must have write permission in the directory where the link will reside. The file is created with the user's user-id and group-id but these are subsequently ignored. The mode of the file is created as 0777.

 No checking is done when a symbolic link is created. There is nothing to stop a user from creating a symbolic link that refers to itself or to an ancestor of itself or several links that loop around among themselves. Therefore, when evaluating a path name, it is important to put a limit on the number of symbolic links that may be encountered in case the evaluation encounters a loop. The variable MAXSYMLINKS is used to force the error ELOOP after MAXSYMLINKS symbolic links have been encountered. The value of MAXSYMLINKS should be at least 20.

To create a symbolic link, the ln(1) command is used with the −s option. If the −s option is not used and a user tries to create a link to a file on another file system, a symbolic link will not be created and the command will fail.

The syntax for creating symbolic links is as follows:

> ln −s *sourcefile1* [*sourcefile2* ...] *target*

With two arguments:

- *sourcefile1* may be any path name and need not exist.

- *target* may be an existing directory or a non-existent file.

- If *target* is an existing directory, a file is created in directory *target* whose name is the last component of *sourcefile1* ('basename *sourcefile1*'). This file is a symbolic link that references *sourcefile1*.

- If *target* does not exist, a file with name *target* is created and it is a symbolic link that references *sourcefile1*.

- If *target* already exists and is not a directory, an error is returned.

- *sourcefile1* and *target* may reside on different file systems.

With more than two arguments:

- For each *sourcefile*, a file is created in *target* whose name is *sourcefile* or its last component ('basename *sourcefile*') and is a symbolic link to *sourcefile*.

- If *target* is not an existing directory, an error is returned.

- Each *sourcefile* and *target* may reside on different file systems.

Examples

The following examples show how symbolic links may be created.

```
ln -s /usr/src/uts/sys  /usr/include/sys
```

In this example /usr/include is an existing directory. But file sys does not exist so it will be created as a symbolic link that refers to /usr/src/uts/sys. The result is that when file /usr/include/sys/x is accessed, the file /usr/src/uts/sys/x will actually be accessed.

This kind of symbolic link may be used when files exist in the directory /usr/src/uts/sys but programs often refer to files in /usr/include/sys. Rather than creating corresponding files in /usr/include/sys that are hard links to files in /usr/src/uts/sys, one symbolic link can be used to link the two directories. In this example /usr/include/sys becomes a symbolic link that links the former /usr/include/sys directory to the /usr/src/uts/sys directory.

```
ln -s  /etc/group  .
```

In this example the *target* is a directory (the current directory), so a file called group ('basename /etc/group') is created in the current directory that is a symbolic link to /etc/group.

```
ln -s  /fs1/jan/abc  /var/spool/abc
```

In this example we imagine that /fs1/jan/abc does not exist at the time the command is issued. Nevertheless, the file /var/spool/abc is created as a symbolic link to /fs1/jan/abc. Later, /fs1/jan/abc may be created as a directory, regular file, or any other file type.

The following example illustrates the use of more than two arguments:

```
ln -s  /etc/group  /etc/passwd  .
```

The user would like to have the `group` and `passwd` files in the current directory but cannot use hard links because `/etc` is a different file system. When more than two arguments are used, the last argument must be a directory; here it is the current directory. Two files, `group` and `passwd`, are created in the current directory, each a symbolic link to the associated file in `/etc`.

Removing Symbolic Links

Normally, when accessing a symbolic link, one follows the link and actually accesses the referenced file. However, this is not the case when one attempts to remove a symbolic link. When the `rm`(1) command is executed and the argument is a symbolic link, it is the symbolic link that is removed; the referenced file is not touched.

Accessing Symbolic Links

Suppose `abc` is a symbolic link to file `def`. When a user accesses the symbolic link `abc`, it is the file permissions (ownership and access) of file `def` that are actually used; the permissions of `abc` are always ignored. If file `def` is not accessible (i.e., either it does not exist or it exists but is not accessible to the user because of access permissions) and a user tries to access the symbolic link `abc`, the error message will refer to `abc`, not file `def`.

Copying Symbolic Links

This section describes the behavior of the `cp`(1) command when one or more arguments are symbolic links. With the `cp`(1) command, if any argument is a symbolic link, that link is followed. Then the semantics of the command are as described in the *User's Reference Manual*. Suppose the command line is

```
cp sym file3
```

where `sym` is a symbolic link that references a regular file `test1` and `file3` is a regular file. After execution of the command, `file3` gets overwritten with the contents of the file `test1`.

If the last argument is a symbolic link that references a directory, then files are copied to that directory. Suppose the command line is

```
cp file1 sym symd
```

where `file1` is a regular file, `sym` is a symbolic link that references a regular file `test1`, and `symd` is a symbolic link that references a directory `DIR`. After execution of the command, there will be two new files, `DIR/file1` and `DIR/sym` that have the same contents as `file1` and `test1`.

Linking Symbolic Links

This section describes the behavior of the `ln(1)` command when one or more arguments are symbolic links. To understand the difference in behavior between this and the `cp(1)` command, it is useful to think of a copy operation as dealing with the contents of a file while the link operation deals with the name of a file.

If the first argument to `ln(1)` is a symbolic link it is not followed, and a hard link is made to the symbolic link. With the last argument, a `stat(2)` is done to see if it is a directory; if it is, files are linked in that directory. Otherwise, if the last argument is an existing file, it is overwritten. This means that if the last argument is a symbolic link to a directory, it is followed but if it is a symbolic link to a regular file, the symbolic link is overwritten.

For example, if the command line is

```
ln sym file1
```

where `sym` is a symbolic link that references a regular file `foo`, and `file1` is a regular file, `file1` is overwritten and hard-linked to `sym`, i.e., `file1` becomes a symbolic link that references `foo`. Thus a hard link has been created to a symbolic link.

If the command is

```
ln file1 sym
```

where the files are the same as in the first example, `sym` is overwritten and hard-linked to `file1`.

When the last argument is a directory as in

```
ln file1 sym symd
```

where symd is a symbolic link to a directory DIR, the file DIR/file1 is hard-linked to file1 and DIR/sym is hard-linked to sym.

Moving Symbolic Links

This section describes the behavior of the mv(1) command. Like the ln(1) command, mv(1) deals with file names rather than file contents. With two arguments, a user invokes the mv(1) command to rename a file. Therefore, one would not want to follow the first argument if it is a symbolic link because it is the name of the file that is to be changed rather than the file contents. Suppose that sym is a symbolic link to /etc/passwd and abc is a regular file. If the command

```
mv sym abc
```

is executed, the file sym is renamed abc and is still a symbolic link to /etc/passwd. If abc existed (as a regular file or a symbolic link to a regular file) before the command was executed, it is overwritten.

Suppose the command is

```
mv sym1 file1 symd
```

where sym1 is a symbolic link to a regular file foo, file1 is a regular file, and symd is a symbolic link that references a directory DIR. When the command is executed, the files sym1 and file1 are moved from the current directory to the DIR directory so that there are two new files, DIR/sym1, which is still a symbolic link to foo, and DIR/file1.

In SVR4.0, the rename(2) system call will be used by the mv(1) command. If the first argument to rename(2) is a symbolic link, rename(2) does not follow it; instead it renames the symbolic link itself. Prior to SVR4.0 a file was moved using the link(2) system call followed by the unlink(2) system call. Since link(2) and unlink(2) do not follow symbolic links, the result of those two operations is the same as the result of a call to rename(2).

Archiving Commands

The cpio(1) command is used to copy file archives usually to or from a storage medium such as a tape, disk, or diskette. By default, cpio(1) does not follow symbolic links. However, a new −L option may be used with the −o and −p options to indicate that symbolic links should be followed. Note that this option is not valid with the −i option.

Normally, a user invokes the find(1) command to produce a list of filenames and pipes this into the cpio(1) command to create an archive of the files listed. The find(1) command also has a new option −follow to indicate that symbolic links should be followed. If a user invokes find(1) with the −follow option, then cpio(1) must also be invoked with its new option −L to indicate that it too should follow symbolic links.

When evaluating the output from find(1), following or not following symbolic links only makes a difference when a symbolic link to a directory is encountered. For example, if /usr/jan/symd is a symbolic link to the directory ../joe/test and files test1 and test2 are in directory /usr/joe/test, the output of a find command starting from /usr/jan will include the file /usr/jan/symd if symbolic links are not followed but will include the files /usr/jan/symd, /usr/jan/symd/test1, and /usr/jan/syd/test2 when symbolic links are followed.

If the user wants to preserve the structure of the directories being archived, it is recommended that symbolic links not be followed on both commands. (This is the default.) When this is done symbolic links will be preserved and the directory hierarchy will be duplicated as it was.

If the user is more concerned that the contents of the files be saved, then the user should use the −L option to cpio(1) and the −follow option to find(1) to follow symbolic links.

 The user should take care not to mix modes, that is, the user should either follow or not follow symbolic links for both cpio(1) and find(1). If modes are mixed, an archive will be created but the resulting hierarchy created by cpio −i may exhibit unexpected and undesirable results.

When copying in using the −i option to cpio(1), symbolic links will be copied as is. It should be noted that systems prior to SVR4.0 do not understand symbolic links and the result of copying in a symbolic link will be a regular file whose contents are the path name of the referenced file. So if a user is creating an archive to be read in on a pre-SVR4.0 system, it may be more useful to follow symbolic links.

File Ownership and Permissions

The commands chmod(1), chown(1), and chgrp(1), and their corresponding system calls are used to change the mode and ownership of a file. If the argument to chmod(1), chown(1), or chgrp(1) is a symbolic link, the mode and ownership of the referenced file rather than of the symbolic link itself will be changed. In such cases, the link is followed.

Once a symbolic link has been created, its permissions cannot be changed. By default, the chown(1) and chgrp(1) commands change the owner and group of the referenced file. However, a new −h option enables the user to change the owner and group of the symbolic link itself. This is useful for removing files from sticky directories.

Using Symbolic Links with RFS

 To use symbolic links on two systems running RFS, both systems must be running SVR4.0. In cases where the server is an SVR4.0 system but the client is not, errors will be generated when the client encounters a symbolic link.

When using symbolic links in an RFS environment, it is important to understand how pathnames are evaluated. The rule by which evaluations are performed is simple. Symbolic links that a client encounters on the server are interpreted in accordance with the client's view of the file tree.

Users on a server system must keep this rule in mind when they create symbolic links in order to avoid problems. The examples that follow illustrate situations in which failure to consider the client's view of the file tree can lead to problems.

System Services and Application Packaging Tools

Figure 6-2: Symbolic Links with RFS: Example 1

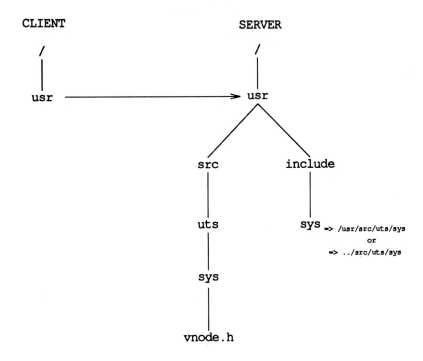

In the example shown in Figure 6-2, the server advertises its /usr file system as USR. If the server creates the symbolic link /usr/include/sys as an absolute pathname to /usr/src/uts/sys, evaluation of the link will work as intended as long as a client mounts USR as /usr. Another way of saying this is that if the file tree naming conventions are the same on the client and the server, things will work as intended.

However, if the client mounts USR as /mnt/usr, when the symbolic link /usr/src/uts/sys is evaluated, the evaluation will be done with respect to the client's view of the file tree and will not cross the mount point back to the server but will remain on the client. Thus the client will not access the file intended.

In this situation the server should create the symbolic link as a relative path name, `../src/uts/sys`, so that evaluation will produce the desired results regardless of where the client mounts USR.

Figure 6-3: Symbolic Links with RFS: Example 2

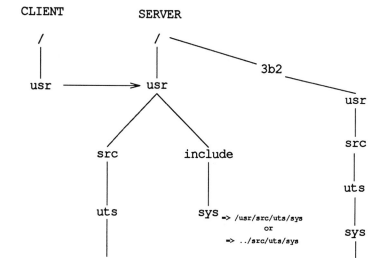

Another example of a situation that could cause problems is shown in Figure 6-3. Here again the server advertises its /usr file system as USR. But in this case the server has a symbolic link from /usr/src/uts/sys/new.h to /3b2/usr/src/uts/sys/new.h. Because the referenced file, /3b2/usr/src/uts/sys/new.h, is outside of the advertised resource, users on the server can access this file but users on the client cannot. In this example, it would make no difference if the symbolic link was a relative rather than an absolute pathname, because the directory /3b2 on the server is not part of the client's name space. When the symbolic link is evaluated, the system will look for the file on the client and will not follow the link as intended.

System Services and Application Packaging Tools

7 Memory Management

Overview of the Virtual Memory System

The UNIX system provides a complete set of memory management mechanisms, providing applications complete control over the construction of their address space and permitting a wide variety of operations on both process address spaces and the variety of memory objects in the system. Process address spaces are composed of a vector of memory pages, each of which can be independently mapped and manipulated. Typically, the system presents the user with mappings that simulate the traditional UNIX process memory environment, but other views of memory are useful as well.

The UNIX memory-management facilities:

- Unify the system's operations on memory.

- Provide a set of kernel mechanisms powerful and general enough to support the implementation of fundamental system services without special-purpose kernel support.

- Maintain consistency with the existing environment, in particular using the UNIX file system as the name space for named virtual-memory objects.

Virtual Memory, Address Spaces and Mapping

The system's virtual memory (VM) consists of all available physical memory resources. Examples include local and remote file systems, processor primary memory, swap space, and other random-access devices. Named objects in the virtual memory are referenced though the UNIX file system. However, not all file system objects are in the virtual memory; devices that cannot be treated as storage, such as terminal and network device files, are not in the virtual memory. Some virtual memory objects, such as private process memory and shared memory segments, do not have names.

A process's address space is defined by mappings onto objects in the system's virtual memory (usually files). Each mapping is constrained to be sized and aligned with the page boundaries of the system on which the process is executing. Each page may be mapped (or not) independently. Only process addresses which are mapped to some system object are valid, for there is no memory associated with processes themselves—all memory is represented by objects in the system's virtual memory.

Each object in the virtual memory has an object address space defined by some physical storage. A reference to an object address accesses the physical storage that implements the address within the object. The virtual memory's associated physical storage is thus accessed by transforming process addresses to object addresses, and then to the physical store.

A given process page may map to only one object, although a given object address may be the subject of many process mappings. An important characteristic of a mapping is that the object to which the mapping is made is not affected by the mere existence of the mapping. Thus, it cannot, in general, be expected that an object has an "awareness" of having been mapped, or of which portions of its address space are accessed by mappings; in particular, the notion of a "page" is not a property of the object. Establishing a mapping to an object simply provides the potential for a process to access or change the object's contents.

The establishment of mappings provides an access method that renders an object directly addressable by a process. Applications may find it advantageous to access the storage resources they use directly rather than indirectly through read and write. Potential advantages include efficiency (elimination of unnecessary data copying) and reduced complexity (single-step updates rather than the read, modify buffer, write cycle). The ability to access an object and have it retain its identity over the course of the access is unique to this access method, and facilitates the sharing of common code and data.

Networking, Heterogeneity and Coherence

VM is designed to fit well with the larger UNIX heterogeneous environment. This environment makes extensive use of networking to access file systems—file systems that are now part of the system's virtual memory. Networks are not constrained to consist of similar hardware or to be based upon a common operating system; in fact, the opposite is encouraged, for such constraints create serious barriers to accommodating heterogeneity. While a given set of processes may apply a set of mechanisms to establish and maintain the properties of various system objects—properties such as page sizes and the ability of objects to synchronize their own use—a given operating system should not impose such mechanisms on the rest of the network.

As it stands, the access method view of a virtual memory maintains the potential for a given object (say a text file) to be mapped by systems running the UNIX memory management system and also to be accessed by systems for which virtual memory and storage management techniques such as paging are totally foreign, such as PC-DOS. Such systems can continue to share access to the object, each using and providing its programs with the access method appropriate to that system. The unacceptable alternative would be to prohibit access to the object by less capable systems.

Another consideration arises when applications use an object as a communications channel, or otherwise attempt to access it simultaneously. In both of these cases, the object is being shared, and thus the applications must use some synchronization mechanism to guarantee the coherence of their transactions with it. The scope and nature of the synchronization mechanism is best left to the application to decide. For example, file access on systems which do not support virtual memory access methods must be indirect, by way of read and write. Applications sharing files on such systems must coordinate their access using semaphores, file locking, or some application-specific protocols. What is required in an environment where mapping replaces read and write as the access method is an operation, such as fsync, that supports atomic update operations.

The nature and scope of synchronization over shared objects is application-defined from the outset. If the system attempted to impose any automatic semantics for sharing, it might prohibit other useful forms of mapped access that have nothing whatsoever to do with communication or sharing. By providing the mechanism to support coherency, and leaving it to cooperating applications to apply the mechanism, the needs of applications are met without erecting barriers to heterogeneity. Note that this design does not prohibit the creation of libraries that provide coherent abstractions for common application needs. Not all abstractions on which an application builds need be supplied by the "operating system."

Memory Management Interfaces

The applications programmer gains access to the facilities of the VM system through several sets of system calls. This section summarizes these calls, and provides examples of their use. For details, see the *Programmer's Reference Manual*.

Creating and Using Mappings

```
caddr_t
mmap(caddr_t addr, size_t len, int prot, int flags, int fd, off_t off);
```

mmap establishes a mapping between a process's address space and an object in the system's virtual memory. It is the system's most fundamental function for defining the contents of an address space — all other system functions that contribute to the definition of an address space are built from mmap. The format of an mmap call is:

        paddr = mmap(addr, len, prot, flags, fd, off);

mmap establishes a mapping from the process's address space at an address *paddr* for *len* bytes to the object specified by *fd* at offset *off* for *len* bytes. The value returned by mmap is an implementation-dependent function of the parameter *addr* and the setting of the MAP_FIXED bit of *flags*, as described below. A successful call to mmap returns *paddr* as its result. The address range *[paddr, paddr + len)* must be valid for the address space of the process and the range *[off, off + len)* must be valid for the virtual memory object. (The notation *[start, end)* refers to the interval from *start* to *end*, including *start* but not including *end*.)

 NOTE The mapping established by mmap replaces any previous mappings for the process's pages in the range *[paddr, paddr + len)*.

The parameter *prot* determines whether read, execute, write or some combination of accesses are permitted to the pages being mapped. To deny all access, set *prot* to `PROT_NONE`. Otherwise, specify permissions by an OR of `PROT_READ`, `PROT_EXECUTE`, and `PROT_WRITE`. A write access must fail if `PROT_WRITE` has not been set, though the behavior of the write can be influenced by setting `MAP_PRIVATE` in the *flags* parameter, as described below.

The *flags* parameter provides other information about the handling of mapped pages:

- `MAP_SHARED` and `MAP_PRIVATE` specify the mapping type, and one of them must be specified. The mapping type describes the disposition of store operations made by this process into the address range defined by the mapping operation. If `MAP_SHARED` is specified, write references will modify the mapped object. No further operations on the object are necessary to effect a change — the act of storing into a `MAP_SHARED` mapping is equivalent to doing a `write` system call.

  On the other hand, if `MAP_PRIVATE` is specified, an initial write reference to a page in the mapped area will create a copy of that page and redirect the initial and successive write references to that copy. This operation is sometimes referred to as copy-on-write and occurs invisibly to the process causing the store. Only pages actually modified have copies made in this manner. `MAP_PRIVATE` mappings are used by system functions such as `exec`(2) when mapping files containing programs for execution. This permits operations by programs such as debuggers to modify the "text" (code) of the program without affecting the file from which the program is obtained.

  The mapping type is retained across a `fork`.

NOTE The private copy is not created until the first write; until then, other users who have the object mapped `MAP_SHARED` can change the object. That is, if one user has an object mapped `MAP_PRIVATE` and another user has the same object mapped `MAP_SHARED`, and the `MAP_SHARED` user changes the object before the `MAP_PRIVATE` user does the first write, then the changes appear in the `MAP_PRIVATE` user's copy that the system makes on the first write. If an application needs isolation from changes made by other processes, it should use `read` to make a copy of the data it wishes to keep isolated.

■ MAP_FIXED informs the system that the value returned by mmap must be
addr, exactly. The use of MAP_FIXED is discouraged, as it may prevent an
implementation from making the most effective use of system resources.
When MAP_FIXED is not set, the system uses *addr* as a hint to arrive at
paddr. The *paddr* so chosen is an area of the address space that the system
deems suitable for a mapping of *len* bytes to the specified object. An *addr*
value of zero grants the system complete freedom in selecting *paddr*, subject to constraints described below. A non-zero value of *addr* is taken as a
suggestion of a process address near which the mapping should be
placed. When the system selects a value for *paddr*, it never places a mapping at address 0, nor replaces any extant mapping, nor maps into areas
considered part of the potential data or stack "segments." The system
strives to choose alignments for mappings that maximize the performance
of the its hardware resources.

The file descriptor used in a mmap call need not be kept open after the mapping
is established. If it is closed, the mapping will remain until such time as it is
replaced by another call to mmap that explicitly specifies the addresses occupied
by this mapping; or until the mapping is removed either by process termination
or a call to munmap. Although the mapping endures independent of the
existence of a file descriptor, changes to the file can influence accesses to the
mapped area, even if they do not affect the mapping itself. For instance, should
a file be shortened by a call to truncate, such that the mapping now
"overhangs" the end of the file, then accesses to that area of the file which
"does not exist" will result in SIGBUS signals. It is possible to create the mapping in the first place such that it "overhangs" the end of the file — the only
requirement when creating a mapping is that the addresses, lengths, and offsets
specified in the operation be possible (i.e., within the range permitted for the
object in question), not that they exist at the time the mapping is created (or
subsequently.)

Similarly, if a program accesses an address in a manner inconsistently with how
it has been mapped (for instance, by attempting a store operation into a mapping that was established with only PROT_READ access), then a SIGSEGV signal
will result. SIGSEGV signals will also result on any attempt to reference an
address not defined by any mapping.

In general, if a program makes a reference to an address that is inconsistent
with the mapping (or lack of a mapping) established at that address, the system
will respond with a SIGSEGV violation. However, if a program makes a reference to an address consistent with how the address is mapped, but that address

does not evaluate at the time of the access to allocated storage in the object being mapped, then the system will respond with a SIGBUS violation. In this manner a program (or user) can distinguish between whether it is the mapping or the object that is inconsistent with the access, and take appropriate remedial action.

Using mmap to access system memory objects can simplify programs in a variety of ways. Keeping in mind that mmap can really be viewed as just a means to access memory objects, it is possible to program using mmap in many cases where you might program with read or write. However, it is important to realize that mmap can only be used to gain access to memory objects — those objects that can be thought of as randomly accessible storage. Thus, terminals and network connections cannot be accessed with mmap because they are not "memory." Magnetic tapes, even though they are memory devices, can not be accessed with mmap because storage locations on the tape can only be addressed sequentially. Some examples of situations which can be thought of as candidates for use of mmap over more traditional methods of file access include:

- Random access operations — either map the entire file into memory or, if the address space can not accommodate the file or if the file size is variable, create "windows" of mappings to the object.

- Efficiency — even in situations where access is sequential, if the object being accessed can be accessed via mmap, an efficiency gain may be obtained by avoiding the copying operations inherent in accesses via read or write.

- Structured storage — if the storage being accessed is collected as tables or data structures, algorithms can be more conveniently written if access to the file is treated just as though the tables were in memory. Previously, programs could not simply make storage or table alterations in memory and save them for access in subsequent runs; however, when the addresses of the table are defined by mappings to a file, then changes to the storage are changes to the file, and are thus automatically recorded in it.

- Scattered storage — if a program requires scattered regions of storage, such as multiple heaps or stack areas, such areas can be defined by mapping operations during program operation.

The remainder of this section will illustrate some other concepts surrounding mapping creation and use.

Mapping /dev/zero gives the calling program a block of zero-filled virtual memory of the size specified in the call to mmap. /dev/zero is a special device, that responds to read as an infinite source of bytes with the value 0, but when mapped creates an unnamed object to back the mapped region of memory. The following code fragment demonstrates a use of this to create a block of scratch storage in a program, at an address of the system's choosing.

```
/*
 * Function to allocate a block of zeroed storage.  Parameter
 * is the number of bytes desired.  The storage is mapped as
 * MAP_SHARED, so that if a fork occurs, the child process
 * will be able to access and modify the storage.  If we wished
 * to cause the child's modifications (as well as those by the
 * parent) to be invisible to the ancestry of processes, we
 * would use MAP_PRIVATE.
 */
caddr_t
get_zero_storage(int len);
{
        int fd;
        caddr_t result;

        if ((fd = open("/dev/zero", O_RDWR)) == -1)
                return ((caddr_t)-1);
        result = mmap(0, len, PROT_READ|PROT_WRITE, MAP_SHARED, fd, 0);
        (void) close(fd);
        return (result);
}
```

As written, this function permits a hierarchy of processes to use the area of allocated storage as a region of communication (for implicit interprocess communication purposes). Later in this chapter we will describe a set of system facilities that provide a similar function packaged for accomplishing the same purpose without requiring that the processes be in a parent-child hierarchy.

In some cases, devices or files are only useful if accessed via mapping. An example of this is frame buffer devices used to support bit-mapped displays, where display management algorithms function best if they can operate randomly on the addresses of the display directly.

Finally, it is important to remember that mappings can be operated upon at the granularity of a single page. Even though a mapping operation may define multiple pages of an address space, there is absolutely no restriction that subsequent operations on those addresses must operate on the same number of pages. For instance, an mmap operation defining ten pages of an address space may be followed by subsequent munmap (see below) operations that remove every other page from the address space, leaving five mapped pages each followed by an unmapped page. Those unmapped pages may subsequently be mapped to different locations in the same or different objects, or the whole range of pages (or any partition, superset, or subset of the pages) used in other mmap or other memory management operations. Further, it must be noted that any mapping operation that operates on more than a single page can "partially succeed" in that some parts of the address range can be affected even though the call returns a failure. Thus, an mmap operation that replaces another mapping, if it fails, may have deleted the previous mapping and failed to replace it. Similarly, other operations (unless specifically stated otherwise) may process some pages in the range successfully before operating on a page where the operation fails.

Not all device drivers support memory mapping. mmap fails if you try to map a device that does not support mapping.

Removing Mappings

```
int
munmap(caddr_t addr, size_t len);
```

munmap removes all mappings for pages in the range *[addr, addr + len)* from the address space of the calling process. It is not an error to remove mappings from addresses that do not have them, and any mapping, no matter how it was established, can be removed with munmap. munmap does not in any way affect the objects that were mapped at those addresses.

Cache Control

The UNIX memory management system can be thought of as a form of "cache management", in which a processor's primary memory is used as a cache for pages from objects from the system's virtual memory. Thus, there are a number of operations which control or interrogate the status of this "cache", as described in this section.

```
int
mincore(caddr_t addr, size_t len, char *vec);
```

mincore determines the residency of the memory pages in the address space covered by mappings in the range *[addr, addr + len)*. Using the "cache concept" described earlier, this function can be viewed as an operation that interrogates the status of the cache, and returns an indication of what is currently resident in the cache. The status is returned as a char-per-page in the character array referenced by *vec* (which the system assumes to be large enough to encompass all the pages in the address range). Each character contains either a "1" (indicating that the page is resident in the system's primary storage), or a "0" (indicating that the page is not resident in primary storage.) Other bits in the character are reserved for possible future expansion — therefore, programs testing residency should test only the least significant bit of each character.

mincore returns residency information that is accurate at an instant in time. Because the system may frequently adjust the set of pages in memory, this information may quickly be outdated. Only locked pages are guaranteed to remain in memory.

```
int
memcntl(caddr_t addr, size_t len, int cmd, caddr_t arg, int attr, int mask);
```

memcntl provides several control operations over mappings in the range *[addr, addr + len)*, including locking pages into physical memory, unlocking them, and writing pages to secondary storage. The functions described in the rest of this section offer simplified interfaces to the memcntl operations.

```
int
mlock(caddr_t addr, size_t len);

int
munlock(caddr_t addr, size_t len);
```

mlock causes the pages referenced by the mapping in the range *[addr, addr + len)* to be locked in physical memory. References to those pages (through other mappings in this or other processes) will not result in page faults that require an I/O operation to obtain the data needed to satisfy the reference. Because this operation ties up physical system resources, and has the potential to disrupt normal system operation, use of this facility is restricted to the superuser. The system will not permit more than a configuration-dependent limit of pages to be locked in memory simultaneously, the call to mlock will fail if this limit is exceeded.

munlock releases the locks on physical pages. Note that if multiple mlock calls are made through the same mapping, only a single munlock call will be required to release the locks (in other words, locks on a given mapping do not nest.) However, if different mappings to the same pages are processed with mlock, then the pages will not be unlocked until the locks on all the mappings are released.

Locks are also released when a mapping is removed, either through being replaced with an mmap operation or removed explicitly with munmap. A lock will be transferred between pages on the "copy-on-write" event associated with a MAP_PRIVATE mapping, thus locks on an address range that includes MAP_PRIVATE mappings will be retained transparently along with the copy-on-write redirection (see mmap above for a discussion of this redirection).

```
int
mlockall(int flags);

int
munlockall(void);
```

mlockall and munlockall are similar in purpose and restriction to mlock and munlock, except that they operate on entire address spaces. mlockall accepts a *flags* argument built as a bit-field of values from the set:

MCL_CURRENT   Current mappings
MCL_FUTURE   Future mappings

If *flags* is MCL_CURRENT, the lock is to affect everything currently in the address space. If *flags* is MCL_FUTURE, the lock is to affect everything added in the future. If *flags* is (MCL_CURRENT | MCL_FUTURE), the lock is to affect both current and future mappings.

munlockall removes all locks on all pages in the address space, whether established by mlock or mlockall.

```
int
msync(caddr_t addr, size_t len, int flags);
```

msync supports applications which require assertions about the integrity of data in the storage backing their mapping, either for correctness or for coherent communications in a distributed environment. msync causes all modified copies of pages over the range *[addr, addr + len)* to be flushed to the objects mapped by those addresses. In the cache analogy discussed previously, msync is the cache "write-back," or flush, operation. It is similar in purpose to the fsync operation for files.

msync optionally invalidates such cache entries so that further references to the pages cause the system to obtain them from their permanent storage locations.

The *flags* argument provides a bit-field of values that influences the behavior of msync. The bit names and their interpretations are:

MS_SYNC	synchronized write
MS_ASYNC	return immediately
MS_INVALIDATE	invalidate caches

MS_SYNC causes msync to return only after all I/O operations are complete. MS_ASYNC causes msync to return immediately once all I/O operations are scheduled. MS_INVALIDATE causes all cached copies of data from mapped objects to be invalidated, requiring them to be reobtained from the object's storage upon the next reference.

Other Mapping Functions

```
long
sysconf(PAGESIZE);
```

sysconf returns the system-dependent size of a memory page. For portability, applications should not embed any constants specifying the size of a page, and instead should make use of sysconf to obtain that information. Note that it is not unusual for page sizes to vary even among implementations of the same instruction set, increasing the importance of using this function for portability.

```
int
mprotect(caddr_t addr, size_t len, int prot);
```

mprotect has the effect of assigning protection *prot* to all pages in the range *[addr, addr + len)*. The protection assigned can not exceed the permissions allowed on the underlying object. For instance, a read-only mapping to a file that was opened for read-only access can not be set to be writable with mprotect (unless the mapping is of the MAP_PRIVATE type, in which case the write access is permitted since the writes will modify copies of pages from the object, and not the object itself).

Address Space Layout

Traditionally, the address space of a UNIX process has consisted of exactly three segments: one each for write-protected program code (text), a heap of dynamically allocated storage (data), and the process's stack. Text is read-only and shared, while the data and stack segments are private to the process.

System V Release 4 still uses text, data, and stack segments, though these should be thought of as constructs provided by the programming environment rather than by the operating system. As such, it is possible to construct processes that have multiple segments of each "type," or of types of arbitrary semantic value — no longer are programs restricted to being built only from objects the system was capable of representing directly. For instance, a process's address space may contain multiple text and data segments, some belonging to specific programs and some shared among multiple programs. Text segments from shared libraries, for example, typically appear in the address spaces of many processes. A process's address space is simply a vector of pages, and there is no necessary division between different address-space segments. Process text and data spaces are simply groups of pages mapped in ways appropriate to the function they provide the program.

A process's address space is usually sparsely populated, with data and text pages intermingled. The precise mechanics of the management of stack space is machine-dependent. By convention, page 0 is not used. Process address spaces are often constructed through dynamic linking when a program is exec'ed. Operations such as exec and dynamic linking build upon the mapping operations described previously. Dynamic linking is described further in the *Programmer's Guide: ANSI C and Programming Support Tools*.

While the system may have multiple areas that can be considered "data" segments, for programming convenience the system maintains operations to operate on an area of storage associated with a process's initial "heap storage area." A process can manipulate this area by calling brk and sbrk:

```
caddr_t
brk(caddr_t addr);

caddr_t
sbrk(int incr);
```

brk sets the system's idea of the lowest data segment location not used by the caller to *addr* (rounded up to the next multiple of the system's page size).

sbrk, the alternate function, adds *incr* bytes to the caller's data space and returns a pointer to the start of the new data area.

8 Packaging Application Software

An Overview of Software Packaging

This chapter describes how to package software that will be installed on a computer running UNIX System V Release 4. The approach to packaging in a Release 4 environment differs from a pre-Release 4 environment. Pre-Release 4 packages deliver information to the system through script actions but a Release 4 package does this through package information files. A packaging tool, the pkgmk command, is provided to help automate package creation. It gathers the components of a package on the development machine, copies them onto the installation medium, and places them into a structure that pkgadd recognizes.

This chapter also describes the installation tool, the pkgadd command, which copies the package from the installation medium onto a system and performs system housekeeping routines that concern the package. This tool is primarily for the installer but is described here to provide you with a background on the environment into which your packages will be placed and to help you test-install your packages.

The next two sections describe what a package consists of and gives an overview of the structural life cycle of a package (how its structure on your development machine relates to its structure on the installation medium and on the installation machine).

The remaining sections familiarize you with all of the tools, files, and scripts involved in creating a package, provide suggestions for how to approach software packaging, and describe some specific procedures. After reading this chapter, you should study Appendix C, which provides case studies using the tools and techniques described in this chapter.

All of the commands, files, and functions mentioned in this chapter have manual entries in Appendix B.

Contents of a Package

A software package is made up of a group of components that together create the software. These components naturally include the executables that comprise the software, but they also include at least two information files and can optionally include other information files and scripts.

As shown in Figure 8-1, a package's contents fall into three categories:

- required components (the pkginfo file, the prototype file, package objects)

- optional package information files

- optional packaging scripts

Figure 8-1: The Contents of a Package

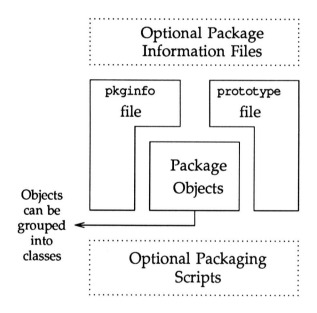

Required Components

At the very least, a package must contain the following components:

- Package Objects

  These are the objects that make up the software. They can be files (executable or data), directories, or named pipes. Objects can be manipulated in groups during installation by placing them into classes. You will learn more about classes when reading the section "Placing Objects into Classes."

- The pkginfo File

  The pkginfo file is a required package information file defining parameter values that describe a package. For example, this file defines values for the package abbreviation, the full package name, and the package architecture.

- The prototype File

  The prototype file is a required package information file that lists the contents of the package. There is one entry for each deliverable object and this entry consists of several fields of information describing the object. All package components, including the pkginfo file, must be listed in the prototype file.

Both required package information files are described further in "The Package Information Files" section and on their respective manual entries in Appendix B.

Optional Package Information Files

There are four optional package information files that you can add to your package:

- The compver File

  Defines previous versions of the package that are compatible with this version.

- The depend File

  Defines any software dependencies associated with this package.

- The space File

  Defines disk space requirements for the target environment beyond that used by objects defined in the prototype file (for example, files that will be dynamically created at installation time).

- The copyright File

  Defines the text for a copyright message that will be printed on the terminal at the time of package installation or removal.

Every package information file used must have an entry in the prototype file. All of these files are described further in the "The Package Information Files" section and on their respective manual entries in Appendix B.

Optional Installation Scripts

Your package can use three types of installation scripts, although no scripts are required. Many of the tasks executed in a pre-Release 4 installation script are now accomplished automatically by pkgadd. However, you may deliver scripts with a Release 4 package to perform customized actions. An installation script must be executable by sh (for example, a shell script or executable program). The three script types are the request script (solicits installer input), class action script (defines a set of actions to perform on a group of objects), and the procedure script (defines actions that will occur at particular points during installation).

Packaging scripts are described in detail in "The Installation Scripts" section. Example scripts can be found in Appendix C.

The Structural Life Cycle of a Package

The material covered in this chapter talks about package object pathnames. You should keep in mind while reading that a package object will reside in three places while being packaged and installed. To help you avoid confusion, consider which of the three possible locations are being discussed:

- On a development machine

  Packages originate on a development machine. They can be in the same directory structure on your machine as they will be placed on the installation machine. Or pkgmk can locate components on the development machine and give them different pathnames on the installation machine.

- On the installation media

  When pkgmk copies the package components from the development machine to the installation medium, it places them into the structure you have defined in your prototype file and a format that pkgadd recognizes.

- On the installation machine

  pkgadd copies a package from the installation medium and places it in the structure defined in your prototype file. Package objects can be defined as relocatable, meaning the installer can define the actual location of these package objects on the installation machine during installation. Objects with fixed locations are copied to their predefined path.

The Packaging Tools

The packaging tools are provided to automate package creation and to remove the burden of packaging from the developer. There are three packaging tools:

- pkgmk copies the components of a package from the development machine to the installation medium and performs all necessary formatting. It creates a fixed directory structure.

- pkgtrans translates an installable package from one package format to another. The two format types are directory structure and datastream. For example, pkgmk creates a directory structure. You would use pkgtrans to translate a package already formatted as a directory structure into a datastream format.

- pkgproto generates a prototype file based on the directory structure of your development area.

Each of these commands is described in the following text and has a manual entry in Appendix B.

The pkgmk Command

This command takes all of the package objects residing on the development machine, copies them onto the installation medium, and places them into a fixed directory structure. You are not required to know the details of the fixed directory structure since pkgmk takes care of the formatting. However, for your information, Appendix D describes the two types of package formats supported by these tools: a fixed directory structure and a datastream structure.

Files can be unstructured on the development machine and pkgmk will structure them correctly on the medium based on information supplied in the prototype file. The installation medium onto which a package is formatted can be what is typically thought of as a medium (a diskette, for example) or it can be a directory on a machine.

pkgmk requires the presence of two information files on the development machine, the prototype and the pkginfo file (other package information files may be present). The pkginfo file defines the values for a number of package parameters, such as the package abbreviation and the package name. The prototype file provides a complete list of the package contents. pkgmk creates the pkgmap file, which is the package contents file on the installation medium, by processing the prototype file and then adding three fields to each entry.

pkgmk follows these steps when processing a package:

1. Processes all of the command lines in the input prototype file. (proto-type command lines can tell pkgmk where to look for package objects, to merge another prototype into this one, define a default mode owner group for package objects, and can place a parameter value in the packaging environment.)

2. Copies the objects of a package onto the installation medium, using the prototype file as a listing of contents.

3. Puts the package objects into the proper format.

4. Divides a package into pieces and distributes those pieces on multiple volumes, if necessary.

5. Creates the pkgmap file (the content listing file that is placed on the installation medium). It looks like the prototype file except that all command lines are processed, and the volno, size, cksum, and modtime fields are added to each entry.

The pkgtrans Command

This command translates a package already created with pkgmk from one package format to another. It can make the following translations:

- a fixed directory structure to a datastream

- a datastream to a fixed directory structure

- a fixed directory structure to a fixed directory structure

Note that a package in a fixed directory structure can be in a directory on disk (for example, in a spooling directory) or on a removable device such as a diskette. A datastream can be on any device; for example, on a diskette or a tape.

The pkgproto Command

This command generates a prototype file. It scans the paths specified on the command line and creates description line entries for these paths. If the pathname is a directory, an entry for each object in the directory is generated. You can use the −c option of the pkgproto command to place objects into classes.

When you create a prototype file with an editor, it does not matter how package components are organized on your development machine. You use the *path1=path2* pathname format to define where the files reside on your development machine and where they should be placed on the installation machine. However, when you use pkgproto to create your file, your development area must be structured exactly as you wish your package to be structured.

The Installation Tools

The installation tools place the burden of installation on the system rather than on the package being installed. These tools are introduced to you here so that you can understand the environment into which your package will be placed. Manual pages for these tools are provided in Appendix B so that you can use them to test your package installation. The installation tools are:

- pkgadd installs a package.

- pkgrm removes a package.

- pkgask creates a file that contains an installer's response to prompts in the request script. This file is named on the pkgadd command line when a package is installed in noninteractive mode. It replaces the output of the request script.

- pkgchk checks the content and attribute information for an installed package to ensure that it was not corrupted during installation.

- pkginfo and pkgparam display information about packages.

The system administrator can set parameters that control various aspects of installation in an administration file called the admin file. Refer to the manual entries in Appendix B for more information on these commands and on the admin file.

The Package Information Files

Each of the six package information files will be described in the following pages. All of these files can be created using any editor. File formats are described in the following text and in full detail on the respective manual entry in Appendix B. The six package information files are:

- the pkginfo file
- the prototype file
- the compver file
- the copyright file
- the depend file
- the space file

This section also describes the system-generated pkgmap file, which pkgmk creates and places on the installation medium. It is similar to the prototype file.

The pkginfo File

This required package information file describes characteristics of the package, such as the package abbreviation, full package name, package version, and package architecture. The definitions in this file can set values for all of the installation parameters defined in the pkginfo manual entry found in Appendix B.

Each entry in the file uses the following format to establish the value of a parameter:

> *PARAM="value"*

Figure 8-2 shows an example pkginfo file.

Figure 8-2: Sample pkginfo **File**

```
PKG="pkgA"
NAME="My Package A"
ARCH="3B2"
RELEASE="4.0"
VERSION="2"
VENDOR="MYCOMPANY"
HOTLINE="1-800-677-BUGS"
VSTOCK="0122c3f5566"
CATEGORY="application"
ISTATES="S 2"
RSTATES="S 2"
```

The pkginfo and pkgparam commands can be used to access information in a
pkginfo file.

NOTE   Before defining the PKG, ARCH, and VERSION parameters, you need to know
how pkgadd defines a package instance and the rules associated with naming a package. Refer to the section "Defining a Package Instance" before
assigning values to these parameters.

The prototype File

This required package information file contains a list of the package contents.
The pkgmk command uses the prototype file to identify the contents of a
package and their location on the development machine when building the
package.

You can create this file in two ways. As with all the package information files,
you can use an editor to create a file named prototype. It should contain
entries following the description given later in this chapter. You can also use
the pkgproto command to automatically generate the file. To make use of the
second method, you must have a copy of your package on your development
machine that is structured exactly as you want it structured on the installation
machine and all modes and permissions must be correct. If you are not going
to use pkgproto, you do not need a structured copy of your package.

There are two types of entries in the prototype file: description lines and command lines.

The Description Lines

You must create one description line for each deliverable object that consists of several fields describing the object. This entry describes such information as mode, owner, and group for the object. You can also use this entry to accomplish the tasks listed below.

- You can override pkgmk's placement of an object on a multiple-part package. (Refer to the section "Distributing Packages over Multiple Volumes" for more details.)

- You can place objects into classes. (Refer to the section "Placing Your Objects into Classes" for details.)

- You can tell pkgmk where to find an object in your development directory structure and map that name to the correct placement on the installation machine. (Refer to the section "Mapping Development Pathnames to Installation Pathnames" for details.)

- You can define an object as relocatable. (Refer to the section "Setting Package Objects as Relocatable" for details.)

- You can define links. (Refer to the section "Creating the prototype File" for details.)

The generic format of the descriptive line is:

[part] ftype class pathname [major minor] [mode owner group]

Definitions for each field are as follows:

part   Designates the part in which an object should be placed. A package can be divided into a number of parts. A part is a collection of files and is the atomic unit by which a package is processed. A developer can choose the criteria for grouping files into a part (for example, by class). If not defined, pkgmk decides in which part the object will be placed.

ftype

Designates the file type of an object. Example file types are f (a standard executable or data file), d (a directory), l (a linked file), and i (a package information file). (Refer to the prototype manual entry in Appendix B for a complete list of file types.)

class

Defines the class to which an object belongs. All objects must belong to a class. If the object belongs to no special class, this field should be defined as none.

pathname

Defines the pathname which an object should have on the installation machine. If you do not begin this name with a slash, the object is considered to be relocatable. You can use the form path1=path2 to map the location of an object on your development machine to the pathname it should have on the installation machine.

major/minor

Defines the major and minor numbers for a block or character special device.

mode/owner/group

Defines the mode, owner, and group for an object. If not defined, the defaults defined with the default command are assigned. If not defined and there are not defaults, the values 644 root other are used.

Figure 8-3 shows an example of this file with only description lines.

Figure 8-3: Sample #1 prototype File

```
i pkginfo
i request
d bin ncmpbin 0755 root other
f bin ncmpbin/dired=/usr/ncmp/bin/dired 0755 root other
f bin ncmpbin/less=/usr/ncmp/bin/less 0755 root other
f bin ncmpbin/ttype=/usr/ncmp/bin/ttype 0755 root other
```

The Command Lines

There are four types of commands that can be embedded in the prototype file. They are:

search *pathnames*
: Specifies a list of directories (separated by white space) in which pkgmk should search when looking for package objects. *pathnames* is prepended to the basename of each object in the prototype file until the object is located.

include *filename*
: Specifies the pathname of another prototype file that should be merged into this one during processing. (Note that search requests do not span include files. Each prototype file should have its own search command defined, if one is needed.)

default *mode owner group*
: Defines the default *mode owner group* that should be used if this information is not supplied in a prototype entry that requires the information. (The defaults do not apply to entries in any include files. Each prototype should have its own default command defined, if one is needed.)

param=value
: Places the indicated parameter in the packaging environment. This allows you to expand a variable pathname so that pkgmk can locate the object without changing the actual object pathname. (This assignment will not be available in the installation environment.)

A command line must always begin with an exclamation point (!). Commands may have variable substitutions embedded within them.

Figure 8-4 shows an example prototype file with both description and command lines.

System Services and Application Packaging Tools

Figure 8-4: Sample #2 prototype **File**

```
!PROJDIR=/usr/myname
!search /usr/myname/bin /usr/myname/src /usr/myname/hdrs
!include $PROJDIR/src/prototype
i pkginfo
i request
d bin ncmpbin 0755 root other
f bin ncmpbin/dired=/usr/ncmp/bin/dired 0755 root other
f bin ncmpbin/less=/usr/ncmp/bin/less 0755 root other
f bin ncmpbin/ttype=/usr/ncmp/bin/ttype 0755 root other
!default 755 root bin
```

The compver File

This package information file defines previous (or future) versions of the package that are compatible with this version. Each line in the file consists of a string defining a version of the package with which the current version is compatible. The string must match the definition of the VERSION parameter in the pkginfo file of the package considered to be compatible. Figure 8-5 shows an example of this file.

Figure 8-5: Sample compver **File**

```
Version 1.3
Version 1.0
```

The copyright File

This package information file contains the text of a copyright message that will be printed on the terminal at the time of package installation or removal. The display is exactly as shown in the file. Figure 8-6 shows an example of this file.

Figure 8-6: Sample copyright **File**

```
Copyright (c) 1989 AT&T
All Rights Reserved.


THIS PACKAGE CONTAINS UNPUBLISHED PROPRIETARY SOURCE CODE OF AT&T.

The copyright notice above does not evidence any
actual or intended publication of such source code.
```

The depend File

This package information file defines software dependencies associated with the package. You can define three types of package dependencies with this file:

- a prerequisite package (meaning this package depends on the existence of another package)

- a reverse dependency (meaning another package depends on the existence of this package)

- an incompatible package (meaning your package is incompatible with this one)

The generic format of a line in this file is:

```
type pkg name
          (arch) version
          (arch) version
```

Definitions for each field are as follows:

type	Defines the dependency type. P indicates the named package is a prerequisite for installation. I indicates the named package is incompatible. R indicates a reverse dependency, that is, the named package requires that this package be on the system. This last type should only be used when a pre-Release 4 package (that cannot deliver a depend file) relies on the newer package.
pkg	Indicates the package abbreviation for the package.
name	Specifies the full package name (used for display purposes only).
(arch) version	Defines a particular instance of a package by defining the architecture and version. If (arch) version is not supplied, it means the entry refers to any instance of the package.

Figure 8-7 shows an example of this file.

Figure 8-7: Sample depend **File**

```
P acu     Advanced C Utilities
          Issue 4 Version 1
P cc      C Programming Language
          Issue 4 Version 1 (3B2)
R vpkg    Another Vendor Package
```

The space File

This package information file defines disk space requirements for the target environment beyond that which is used by objects defined in the prototype file—for example, files that will be dynamically created at installation time. It should define the maximum amount of additional space that a package will require.

The generic format of a line in this file is:

pathname blocks inodes

Definitions for each field are as follows:

name   Names a directory in which there are objects that will
            require additional space. The name may be the mount
            point for a filesystem. Names that do not begin with a
            slash (/) indicate relocatable directories.

blocks   Defines the number of 512 byte disk blocks required
            for installation of the files and directory entries con-
            tained in the pathname. (Do not include file system
            dependent disk usage.)

inodes   Defines the number of inodes required for installation
            of the files and directory entries contained in name.

Figure 8-8 shows an example of this file.

Figure 8-8: Sample space File

```
# extra space required by config data which is
# dynamically loaded onto the system
data  500  1
```

The pkgmap File

The pkgmk command creates the pkgmap file when it processes the prototype
file. This new file contains all of the information in the prototype file plus
three new fields for each entry. These fields are size (file size in bytes), cksum
(checksum of file), and modtime (last time of modification). All command lines
defined in the prototype file are executed as pkgmk creates the pkgmap file.
The pkgmap file is placed on the installation medium. The prototype file is
not. Refer to the pkgmap manual entry in Appendix B for more details about
this file.

The Installation Scripts

The pkgadd command automatically performs all of the actions necessary to install a package, using the package information files as input. As a result, you do not have to supply any packaging scripts. However, if you want to customize the installation procedures for your package needs, the following three types of scripts can be used:

request script
: Solicits administrator interaction during package installation for the purpose of assigning or redefining environment parameter assignments.

class action scripts
: Define an action or set of actions that should be applied to a class of files during installation or removal. You define your own classes or you can use one of three standard classes (sed, awk, and build). See the ''Placing Objects into Classes'' section for details on how to define a class.

procedure scripts
: Specifies a procedure to be invoked before or after the installation or removal of a package. The four procedure scripts are preinstall, postinstall, preremove, and postremove.

You decide which type of script to use based on when you want the script to execute. To help you with this assessment, script processing is discussed next, followed by a description of parameters available to packaging scripts, how to get information about a package for your scripts, and script exit codes. After that, each type of script is described in detail.

 NOTE All installation scripts must be executable by sh (for example, a shell script or a program executable).

Script Processing

You can customize the actions taken during installation by delivering installation scripts with your package. The decision on which type of script to use to meet a need depends upon when the action of the script is needed during the installation process. As a package is installed, pkgadd performs the following steps:

- Executes the request script.

  This is the only point at which your package can solicit input from the installer.

- Executes the preinstall script.

- Installs the package objects.

  Installation occurs class-by-class and class action scripts are executed accordingly. The list of classes operated upon and the order in which they should be installed is initially defined with the CLASSES parameter in your pkginfo file. However, your request script can change the value of CLASSES.

- Executes the postinstall script.

When a package is being removed, pkgrm performs these steps:

- Executes the preremove script.

- Executes the removal class action scripts.

  Removal also occurs class-by-class. As with the installation class action scripts, if more than one removal script exists, they are processed in the reverse order in which the classes were listed in the CLASSES parameter at the time of installation.

- Executes the postremove script.

The request script is not processed at the time of package removal. However, its output (a list of parameter values) is saved and so is available to removal scripts.

Installation Parameters

These following four groups of parameters are available to all installation scripts. Some of the parameters can be modified by a request script, others cannot be modified at all.

- The four system parameters that are part of the installation software (see below for a description of these). None of these parameters can be modified by a package.

- The 20 standard installation parameters defined in the pkginfo file. Of these, a package can only modify the CLASSES parameter. (The standard installation parameters are described in detail in the pkginfo manual entry in Appendix B.)

- You can define your own installation parameters by assigning a value to them in the pkginfo file. Such a parameter must be alphanumeric with an initial capital letter. Any of these parameters can be changed by a request script.

- Your request script can define new parameters by assigning values to them and placing them into the installation environment, as shown in Figure 8-9.

The four installation parameters that can be accessed by installation scripts are described below:

PATH   Specifies the search list used by sh to find commands;
                on script invocation, PATH is set to
                /sbin:/usr/sbin:/usr/bin:/usr/sadm/install/bin.

UPDATE   Indicates that the current installation is intended to
                update the system. Automatically set to true if the
                package being installed is overwriting a version of
                itself.

PKGINST   Specifies the instance identifier of the package being
                installed. If another instance of the package is not
                already installed, the value will be the package abbre-
                viation. Otherwise, it is the package abbreviation fol-
                lowed by a suffix, such as pkg.1.

(Multiple variations of the same package can reside simultaneously on the installation medium, as well as on the installation machine. Each variation is known as a package instance and assigned an instance identifier. See "Defining a Package Instance" for more details.)

PKGSAV   Specifies the directory where files can be saved for use by removal scripts or where previously saved files may be found.

Getting Package Information for a Script

There are two commands that can be used from your scripts to solicit information about a package.

The pkginfo command returns information about software packages, such as the instance identifier and package name.

The pkgparam command returns values only for the parameters requested.

The pkginfo and pkgparam [(1) and (4)] manual entries in Appendix B give details for these tools.

Exit Codes for Scripts

Each script must exit with one of the following exit codes:

0   Successful completion of script.

1   Fatal error. Installation process is terminated at this point.

2   Warning or possible error condition. Installation will continue. A warning message will be displayed at the time of completion.

3   Script was interrupted and possibly left unfinished. Installation terminates at this point.

10   System should be rebooted when installation of all selected packages is completed. (This value should be added to one of the single-digit exit codes described above.)

20   The system should be rebooted immediately upon completing installation of the current package. (This value should be added to one of the single-digit exit codes described above.)

See Appendix C for examples of exit codes in installation scripts.

The Request Script

The request script solicits interaction during installation and is the only place where your package can interact directly with the installer. It can be used, for example, to ask the installer if optional pieces of a package should be installed.

The output of a request script must be a list of parameters and their values. This list can include any of the parameters you created in the pkginfo file and the CLASSES parameter. The list can also introduce parameters that have not been defined elsewhere.

When your request script assigns values to a parameter, it must then make those values available to the installation environment for use by pkgadd and also by other packaging scripts. The following example shows a request script segment that performs this task for the four parameters CLASSES, NCMPBIN, EMACS, and NCMPMAN.

Figure 8-9: Placing Parameters Into the Installation Environment

```
# make parameters available to installation service
# and any other packaging script we might have
cat >$1 <<!
CLASSES='$CLASSES'
NCMPBIN='$NCMPBIN'
EMACS='$EMACS'
NCMPMAN='$NCMPMAN'
!
```

Request Script Naming Conventions

There can only be one request script per package and it must be named
request.

Request Script Usage Rules

1. The request script can not modify any files. It is intended only to interact
   with users and to create a list of parameter assignments based upon that
   interaction. (To enforce this restriction, the request script is executed as
   the nonprivileged user install.)

2. pkgadd calls the request script with one argument that names the file to
   which the output of this script will be written.

3. The parameter assignments should be added to the installation environment for use by pkgadd and other packaging scripts (as shown in Figure
   8-9).

4. System parameters and standard installation parameters, except for the
   CLASSES parameter, cannot be modified by a request script. Any of the
   other parameters available can be changed.

5. The format of the output list should be *PARAMETER="value"*. For example:

   ```
   CLASSES="none class1"
   ```

6. The list should be written to the file named as the argument to the request script.

7. The user's terminal is defined as standard input to the request script.

8. The request script is not executed during package removal. However, the parameter values assigned in the script are saved and are available during removal.

The Class Action Script

The class action script defines a set of actions to be executed during installation or removal of a package. The actions are performed on a group of pathnames based on their class definition. (See Appendix C for examples of class action scripts.)

Class Action Script Naming Conventions

The name of a class action script is based on which class it should operate and whether those actions should occur during package installation or removal. The two name formats are:

- i.*class* (operates on pathnames in the indicated class during package installation)

- r.*class* (operates on pathnames in the indicated class during package removal)

For example, the name of the installation script for a class named class1 would be i.class1 and the removal script would be named r.class1.

Class Action Script Usage Rules

1. Class action scripts are executed as uid=root and gid=other.

2. If a package spans more than one volume, the class action script will be executed once for each volume that contains at least one file belonging to the class. Consequently, each script must be "multiply executable." This means that executing a script any number of times with the same input must produce the same results as executing the script only once.

NOTE The installation service relies upon this condition being met.

3. The script is not executed if no files in the given class exist on the current volume.

4. pkgadd (and pkgrm) creates a list of all objects listed in the pkgmap file that belong to the class. As a result, a class action script can only act upon pathnames defined in the pkgmap and belonging to a particular class.

5. A class action script should never add, remove, or modify a pathname or system attribute that does not appear in the list generated by pkgadd unless by use of the installf or removef command. (See the manual entries in Appendix B for details on these two commands and the case studies in Appendix C for examples of them in use.)

6. When the class action script executes for the last time (meaning the input pathname is the last path on the last volume containing a file of this class), it is executed with the keyword argument ENDOFCLASS. This flag allows you to include post-processing actions into your script.

Installation of Classes

The following steps outline the system actions that occur when a class is installed. The actions are repeated once for each volume of a package as that volume is being installed.

1. pkgadd creates a pathname list.

   pkgadd creates a list of pathnames upon which the action script will operate. Each line of this list consists of source and destination pathnames, separated by white space. The source pathname indicates where the object to be installed resides on the installation volume and the destination pathname indicates the location on the installation machine where the object should be installed. The contents of the list is restricted by the following criteria:

- The list contains only pathnames belonging to the associated class.

- Directories, named pipes, character/block devices, and symbolic links are included in the list with the source pathname set to /dev/null. They are automatically created by pkgadd (if not already in existence) and given proper attributes (mode, owner, group) as defined in the pkgmap file.

- Linked files are not included in the list, that is, files where ftype is l. (ftype defines the file type and is defined in the prototype file. Links in the given class are created in Step 4.)

- If a pathname already exists on the target machine and its contents are no different from the one being installed, the pathname will not be included in the list.

  To determine this, pkgadd compares the cksum, modtime, and size fields in the installation software database with the values for those fields in your pkgmap file. If they are the same, it then checks the actually file on the installation machine to be certain it really has those values. If the field values are the same and are correct, the pathname for this object will not be included in the list.

2. If there is no class action script, the pathnames are copied to the target machine.

   If no class action script is provided for installation of a particular class, the pathnames in the generated list will simply be copied from the volume to the appropriate target location.

3. If there is a class action script, the script is executed.

   The class action script is invoked with standard input containing the list generated in Step 1. If this is the last volume of the package and there are no more objects in this class, the script is executed with the single argument of ENDOFCLASS.

4. pkgadd performs a content and attribute audit and creates links.

   After successfully executing Step 2 or 3, an audit of both content and attribute information is performed on the list of pathnames. pkgadd creates the links associated with the class automatically. Detected attribute inconsistencies are corrected for all pathnames in the generated list.

Removal of Classes

Objects are removed class-by-class. Classes that exist for a package, but are not listed in the CLASSES parameter are removed first (for example, an object installed with the installf command). Classes that are listed in the CLASSES parameter are removed in reverse order. The following steps outline the system actions that occur when a class is removed:

1. pkgrm creates a pathname list.

   pkgrm creates a list of installed pathnames that belong to the indicated class. Pathnames referenced by another package are excluded from the list unless their ftype is e (meaning the file should be edited upon installation or removal).

   If a pathname is referenced by another package, it will not be removed from the system. However, it may be modified to remove information placed in it by the package being removed.

2. If there is no class action script, the pathnames are removed.

   If your package has no removal class action script for the class, all of the pathnames in the list generated by pkgrm will be removed.

    NOTE You should always assign a class for files with an ftype of e (editable) and have an associated class action script for that class. Otherwise, they will be removed at this point, even if the pathname is shared with other packages.

3. If there is a class action script, the script is executed.

   pkgrm invokes the class action script with standard input containing the list generated in Step 1.

4. pkgrm performs an audit.

   Upon successful execution of the class action script, knowledge of the pathnames is removed from the system unless a pathname is referenced by another package.

The Special System Classes

The system provides three special classes. They are:

- The sed class (provides a method for using sed instructions to edit files upon installation and removal).
- The awk class (provides a method for using awk instructions to edit files upon installation and removal).
- The build class (provides a method to dynamically construct a file during installation).

The sed Class Script

The sed installation class provides a method of installing and removing objects that require modification to an existing object on the target machine. A sed class action script delivers sed instructions in the format shown in Figure 8-10. You can give instructions that will be executed during either installation or removal. Two commands indicate when instructions should be executed. sed instructions that follow the !install command are executed during package installation and those that follow the !remove command are executed during package removal. It does not matter in which order the commands are used in the file.

The sed class action script executes automatically at installation time if a file belonging to class sed exists. The name of the sed class file should be the same as the name of the file upon which the instructions will be executed.

Figure 8-10: sed Script Format

```
# comment, which may appear on any line in the file
!install
# sed(1) instructions which are to be invoked during
# installation of the object
[address [,address]] function [arguments]
   . . .

!remove
# sed(1) instructions to be invoked during the removal process
[address [,address]] function [arguments]
   . . .
```

address, function, and *arguments* are as defined in the manual entry sed(1) in the *User's Reference Manual.* See Case Studies 5a and 5b in Appendix C for examples of sed class action scripts.

The awk Class Script

The awk installation class provides a method of installing and removing objects that require modification to an existing object on the target machine. Modifications are delivered as awk instructions in an awk class action script.

The awk class action script executes automatically at the time of installation if a file belonging to class awk exists. Such a file contains instructions for the awk class script in the format shown in Figure 8-11. Two commands indicate when instructions should be executed. awk instructions that follow the !install command are executed during package installation and those that follow the !remove command are executed during package removal. It does not matter in which order the commands are used in the file.

The name of the awk class file should be the same as the name of the file upon which the instructions will be executed.

Figure 8-11: awk **Script Format**

```
# comment, which may appear on any line in the file
!install
# awk(1) program to install changes
    . . . (awk program)

!remove
# awk1(1) program to remove changes
    . . . (awk program)
```

The file to be modified is used as input to awk and the output of the script ulti-mately replaces the original object. Parameters may not be passed to awk using this syntax.

See Case Study 5a in Appendix C for example awk class action scripts.

The build Class Script

The build class installs or removes objects by executing instructions that create or modify the object file. These instructions are delivered as a build class action script.

The name of the instruction file should conform to standard UNIX system nam-ing conventions.

The build class action script executes automatically at installation time if a file belonging to class build exists.

A build script must be executable by sh. The script's output becomes the new version of the file as it is built.

See Case Study 5c in Appendix C for an example build class action script.

The Procedure Script

The procedure script gives a set of instructions that are performed at particular points in installation or removal. Four possible procedure scripts are described below. (Appendix C shows examples of procedure scripts.)

Naming Conventions for Procedure Scripts

The four procedure scripts must use one of the names listed below, depending on when these instructions are to be executed.

- `preinstall` (executes before class installation begins)
- `postinstall` (executes after all volumes have been installed)
- `preremove` (executes before class removal begins)
- `postremove` (executes after all classes have been removed)

Procedure Script Usage Rules

1. Procedure scripts are executed as `uid=root` and `gid=other`.

2. Each script should be multiply executable since it will be executed once for each volume in a package. This means that executing a script any number of times with the same input will produce the same results as executing the script only once.

3. Each installation procedure script must use the `installf` command to notify `pkgadd` that it will add or modify a pathname. After all additions or modifications are complete, this command should be invoked with the −`f` option to indicate all additions and modifications are complete. (See the manual entry for the `installf` command in Appendix B and the case studies in Appendix C for details and examples.)

4. Each removal procedure script must use the `removef` command to notify `pkgrm` that it will remove a pathname. After removal is complete, this command should be invoked with the −`f` option to indicate all removals have been completed. (See the manual entry for the `removef` command in Appendix B and the case studies in Appendix C for details and examples.)

The `installf` and `removef` commands must be used because procedure scripts are not automatically associated with any pathnames listed in the `pkgmap` file.

Basic Steps of Packaging

Since what steps you take to create a package depends on how customized your package will be, it is difficult to give you a step-by-step guide on how to proceed. Your first step should be to plan your packaging. For example you must decide on which package information files and scripts your package needs.

The following list presents an overview of some of the steps you might use in a packaging scenario. Not all of these steps are required and there exists no mandated order for their execution (although you must have all of your package objects together before executing pkgmk). The remainder of this chapter gives procedural information for each step.

 This list, and the following procedures, are intended as a guideline and
NOTE should not replace reading the rest of this chapter to learn what options are available to your package or replace your own individualized planning.

- Assign a package abbreviation.

    Every package installed in the Release 4 environment must have a package abbreviation.

- Define a package instance.

    You must decide on values for the three package parameters that will make each package instance unique. (You need to understand what a package instance is, how it is defined, what the instance identifier is, and how to use that identifier. All of this is covered in the procedure "Defining a Package Instance.")

- Place your objects into classes.

    You must decide on what installation classes you are going to use before you can create the prototype file and also before you can write your class action scripts.

- Set up a package and its objects as relocatable.

    Package objects can be delivered with either fixed locations, meaning that their location is defined by the package and cannot be changed, or with relocatable locations, meaning that they have no absolute location requirements. All of a package or parts of a package can be defined as relocatable. You should decide if package objects will have fixed locations or be relocatable before you write any installation scripts and before you create the prototype file.

- Decide which installation scripts your package needs.

  You must assess the needs of your package beyond the actions provided by pkgadd and decide on which type of installation scripts will allow you to deliver your customized actions.

- Define package dependencies

  You must decide if your package has dependencies on other packages and if any other packages depend on yours.

- Write a copyright message.

  You must decide if your package requires a copyright message to appear as it is being installed (and removed) and, if so, you must write that message.

- Create the pkginfo file.

  You must create a pkginfo file before executing pkgmk. It defines basic information concerning the package and can be created with any editor as long as it follows the format described earlier in this chapter and in the pkginfo manual entry in Appendix B.

- Create the prototype file.

  This file is required and must be created before you execute pkgmk. It lists all of the objects that belong to a package and information about each object (such as its file type and to which class it belongs). You can create it using any editor and you must follow the format described earlier in this chapter and in the prototype manual entry in Appendix B. You can also use the pkgproto command to generate a prototype file.

- Distribute packages over multiple volumes.

  pkgmk automatically distributes packages over multiple volumes. You must decide if you want to leave those calculations up to pkgmk or customize package placement on multiple volumes.

- Create the package.

  Create the package using the pkgmk command, which copies objects from the development machine to the installation medium, puts them into the proper structure, and automatically spans them across multiple volumes, if necessary.

  This is always the last step of packaging, unless you want to create a datastream structure for your package. If so, you must execute pkgtrans after creating a package with pkgmk.

Assigning a Package Abbreviation

Each package installed on a Release 4 machine must have a package abbreviation assigned to it. This abbreviation is defined with the PKG parameter in the pkginfo file.

A valid package abbreviation must meet the criteria defined below:

- It must start with an alphabetic character.

- Additional characters may be alphanumeric and contain the two special characters + and −.

- It cannot be longer than nine characters.

- Reserved names are install, new, and all.

Defining a Package Instance

The same software package can differ by version or architecture or both. Multiple variations of the same package can reside simultaneously on the same machine. Each variation is known as a package instance. pkgadd assigns a package identifier to each package instance at the time of installation. The package identifier is the package abbreviation with a numerical suffix. This identifier distinguishes an instance from any other package, including other instances of the same package.

Identifying a Package Instance

Three parameters defined in the pkginfo file combine to uniquely identify each instance. You cannot assign identical values for all three parameters for two instances of the same package installed in the same target environment. These parameters are:

- PKG (defines the software package abbreviation and remains constant for every instance of a package)
- VERSION (defines the software package version)
- ARCH (defines the software package architecture)

For example, you might identify two identical versions of a package that run on different hardware as:

Instance #1	Instance #2
PKG="*abbr*"	PKG="*abbr*"
VERSION="release 1"	VERSION="release 1"
ARCH="3B20"	ARCH="3B2"

Two different versions of a package that run on the same hardware might be identified as:

Instance #1   Instance #2

```
PKG="abbr"                     PKG="abbr"
VERSION="release 1"            VERSION="release 2"
ARCH="3B2"                     ARCH="3B2"
```

The instance identifier, assigned by pkgadd, maps the three pieces of information that identify an instance to one name consisting of the package abbreviation plus a suffix. The first instance of a package installed on a system does not have a suffix and so its instance identifier will be the package abbreviation. Subsequent instances receive a suffix, beginning with .2. An instance is given the lowest integer extension available and so may not correspond to the order in which a package was installed. For example, if mypkg.2 was deleted after mypkg.3 was installed, the next instance to be added will be named mypkg.2. Because the number of instances of a particular package can vary from machine to machine, the instance identifier can also vary.

 NOTE pkgmk also assigns an instance identifier to a package as it places it on the installation medium if one or more instances of a package already exists. That identifier bears no relationship to the identifier assigned to the same package on the installation machine.

Accessing the Instance Identifier in Your Scripts

Because the instance identifier is assigned at the time of installation and will differ from machine to machine, you should use the PKGINST system parameter to reference your package in your installation scripts.

Writing Your Installation Scripts

You should read the section "The Installation Scripts" to learn what types of scripts you can write and how to write them. You can also look at the case studies in Appendix C to see how the various scripts can be utilized and to see examples.

Remember, you are not required to write any installation scripts for a Release 4 package. The pkgadd command performs all of the actions necessary to install your package, using the information you supply with the package information files. Any installation script that you write will be used to perform customized actions beyond those executed by pkgadd.

 Be certain that every installation script being delivered with your package has an entry in the prototype file. The file type should be i.

Making Package Objects Relocatable

Package objects can be delivered either with fixed locations, meaning that their location on the installation machine is defined by the package and cannot be changed, or as relocatable, meaning that they have no absolute location requirements on the installation machine. The location for relocatable package objects is determined during the installation process.

You can define two types of relocatable objects: collectively relocatable and individually relocatable. All collectively relocatable objects are placed relative to the same directory once the relocatable root directory is established. Individually relocatable objects are not restricted to the same directory location as collectively relocatable objects.

Defining Collectively Relocatable Objects

Follow these steps to define package objects as collectively relocatable:

1. Define a value for the BASEDIR parameter.

   Put a definition for the BASEDIR parameter in your pkginfo file. This parameter names a directory where relocatable objects will be placed by default. If you supply no value for BASEDIR, no package objects will be considered as collectively relocatable.

2. Define objects as collectively relocatable in the prototype file.

   An object is defined as collectively relocatable by using a relative pathname in its entry in the prototype file. A relative pathname does not begin with a slash. For example, src/myfile is a relative pathname, while /src/myfile is a fixed pathname.

 NOTE A package can deliver some objects with relocatable locations and others with fixed locations.

All objects defined as collectively relocatable will be put under the same root directory on the installation machine. The root directory value will be one of the following (and in this order):

- the installer's response to pkgadd when asked where relocatable objects should be installed

- the value of BASEDIR as it is defined in the installer's admin file (the BASEDIR value assigned in the admin file overrides the value in the pkginfo file)

- the value of BASEDIR as it is defined in your pkginfo file (this value is used only as a default in case the other two possibilities have not supplied a value)

Defining Individually Relocatable Objects

A package object is defined as individually relocatable by using a variable in its pathname definition in the prototype file. Your request script must query the installer on where such an object should be placed and assign the response value to the variable. pkgadd will expand the pathname based on the output of your request script at the time of installation. Case Study 1 in Appendix C shows an example of the use of variable pathnames and the request script needed to solicit a value for the base directory.

Placing Objects into Classes

Installation classes allow a series of actions to be performed on a group of package objects at the time of their installation or removal. You place objects into a class in the prototype file. All package objects must be given a class, although the class of none may be used for objects that require no special action.

The installation parameter CLASSES, defined in the pkginfo file, is a list of classes to be installed (including the none class). Objects defined in the prototype file that belong to a class not listed in this parameter will not be installed. The actions to be performed on a class (other than simply copying the components to the installation machine) are defined in a class action script. These scripts are named after the class itself.

For example, to define and install a group of objects belonging to a class named class1, follow these steps:

1. Define the objects belonging to class1 as such in their prototype file entry. For example,

   ```
   f class1 /usr/src/myfile
   f class1 /usr/src/myfile2
   ```

2. Ensure that the CLASSES parameter in the pkginfo file has an entry for class1. For example,

   ```
   CLASSES="class1 class2 none"
   ```

3. Ensure that a class action script exists for this class. An installation script for a class named class1 would be named i.class1 and a removal script would be named r.class1.

   If you define a class but do not deliver a class action script, the only action taken for that class will be to copy components from the installation medium to the installation machine.

In addition to the classes that you can define, the system provides three standard classes for your use. The sed class provides a method for using sed instructions to edit files upon package installation and removal. The awk class provides a method for using awk instructions to edit files upon package installation and removal. The build class provides a method to dynamically construct a file during package installation.

Defining Package Dependencies

Package dependencies and incompatibilities can be defined with two of the optional package information files. Delivering a compver file lets you name versions of your package that are compatible with the one being installed. Delivering a depend file lets you define three types of dependencies associated with your package. These dependency types are:

- a prerequisite package (meaning your package depends on the existence of another package)

- a reverse dependency (meaning another package depends on the existence of your package)

 NOTE This type should only be used when a pre-Release 4 package (that cannot deliver a depend file) relies on the newer package.

- an incompatible package (meaning your package is incompatible with this one)

Refer to the sections "The depend File" and "The compver File" earlier in this chapter, or the manual entries depend and compver in Appendix B, for details on the formats of these files.

 NOTE Be certain that your depend and compver files have entries in the proto-type file. The file type should be i (for package information file).

Writing a Copyright Message

To deliver a copyright message, you must create a copyright file named copy-right. The message will be displayed exactly as it appears in the file (no formatting) as the package is being installed and as it is being removed. Refer to the section "The copyright File" earlier in this chapter or the copyright manual entry in Appendix B for more detail.

 NOTE Be certain that your copyright file has an entry in the prototype file. Its file type should be i (for package information file).

Reserving Additional Space on the Installation Machine

pkgadd assures that there is enough disk space to install your package, based on the object definitions in the pkgmap file. However, sometimes your package will require additional disk space beyond that needed by the objects defined in the pkgmap file. For example, your package might create a file during installation. pkgadd checks for additional space when you deliver a space file with your package. Refer to the section "The space File" earlier in this chapter or the space manual entry in Appendix B for details on the format of this file.

 NOTE Be certain that your space file has an entry in the prototype file. Its file type should be i (for package information file).

Creating the pkginfo File

The pkginfo file establishes values for parameters that describe the package and is a required package component. The format for an entry in this file is:

> *PARAM="value"*

PARAM can be any of the 19 standard parameters described in the pkginfo manual entry in Appendix B. You can also create your own package parameters simply by assigning a value to them in this file. Your parameter names must begin with a capital letter followed by either upper or lowercase letters.

The following five parameters are required:

- PKG (package abbreviation)
- NAME (full package name)
- ARCH (package architecture)
- VERSION (package version)
- CATEGORY (package category)

The CLASSES parameter dictates which classes are installed and the order of installation. Although the parameter is not required, no classes will be installed without it. Even if you have no class action scripts, the none class must be defined in the CLASSES parameter before objects belonging to that class will be installed.

 NOTE You can choose to define the value of CLASSES with a request script and not to deliver a value in the pkginfo file.

Creating the prototype File

The `prototype` file is a list of package contents and is a required package component.

You can create the `prototype` file by using any editor and following the format described in the section "The `prototype` File" and in the `prototype` manual entry in Appendix B. You can also use the `pkgproto` command to create one automatically.

Creating the File Manually

While creating the `prototype` file, you must at the very least supply the following three pieces of information about an object:

■ The object's type

All of the possible object types are defined in the `prototype` manual entry in Appendix B. `f` (for a data file), `l` (for a linked file), and `d` (for a directory) are examples of object types.

■ The object's class

All objects must be assigned a class. If no special handling is required, you can assign the class none.

■ The object's pathname

The pathname can define a fixed pathname such as `/mypkg/src/filename`, a collectively relocatable pathname such as `src/filename`, and an individually relocatable pathname such as `$BIN/filename` or `/opt/$PKGINST/filename`.

Creating Links

To define links you must do the following in the `prototype` entry for the linked object:

1. Define its `ftype` as `l` (a link) or `s` (a symbolic link).

2. Define its pathname with the format *path1=path2* where *path1* is the destination and *path2* is the source file.

Mapping Development Pathnames to Installation Pathnames

If your development area is in a different structure than you want the package to be in on the installation machine, you can use the prototype entry to map one pathname to the other. You use the *path1=path2* format for the pathname as is used to define links. However, if the ftype is not defined as l or s, *path1* is interpreted as the pathname you want the object to have on the installation machine and *path2* is interpreted as the pathname the object has on your development machine.

For example, your project might require a development structure that includes a project root directory and numerous src directories. However, on the installation machine you might want all files to go under a package root directory and for all src files to be in one directory. So, a file on your machine might be named /projdir/srcA/filename. If you want that file to be named /pkgroot/src/filename on the installation machine, your prototype entry for this file might look like this:

```
f class1 /pkgroot/src/filename=/projdir/srcA/filename
```

Defining Objects for pkgadd to Create

You can use the prototype file to define objects that are not actually delivered on the installation medium. pkgadd creates objects with the following ftypes if they do not already exist at the time of installation:

- d (directories)
- x (exclusive directories)
- l (linked files)
- s (symbolically linked files)
- p (named pipes)
- c (character special device)
- b (block special device)

To request that one of these objects be created on the installation machine, you should add an entry for it in the prototype file using the appropriate ftype.

For example, if you want a directory created on the installation machine, but do not want to deliver it on the installation medium, an entry for the directory in the prototype file is sufficient. An entry such as the one shown below will cause the directory to be created on the installation machine, even if it does not exist on the installation medium.

```
d none /directoryA 644 root other
```

Using the Command Lines

There are four types of commands that you can put into your prototype file. They allow you to do the following:

- Nest prototype files (the include command)

- Define directories for pkgmk to look in when attempting to locate objects as it creates the package (the search command)

- Set a default value for mode owner group (the default command). If all or most of your objects have the same values, using the default command will keep you from having to define these values for every entry in the prototype file.

- Assign a temporary value for variable pathnames to tell pkgmk where to locate these relocatable objects on your machine (with *param=value*)

Creating the File Using pkgproto

The pkgproto command scans your directories and generates a prototype file. pkgproto cannot assign ftypes of v (volatile files), e (editable files), or x (exclusive directories). You can edit the prototype file and add these ftypes, as well as perform any other fine-tuning you require (for example, adding command lines or classes).

pkgproto writes its output to the standard output. To create a file, you should redirect the output to a file. The examples shown in this section do not perform redirection in order to show you what the contents of the file would like.

Creating a Basic prototype

The standard format of pkgproto is

pkgproto *path* [...]

where *path* is the name of one or more paths to be included in the prototype file. If *path* is a directory, then entries are created for the contents of that directory as well.

With this form of the command, all objects are placed into the none class and are assigned the same mode owner group as exists on your machine. The following example shows pkgproto being executed to create a file for all objects in the directory /usr/bin:

```
$ pkgproto /usr/bin
d none /usr/bin 755 bin bin
f none /usr/bin/file1 755 bin bin
f none /usr/bin/file2 755 bin bin
f none /usr/bin/file3 755 bin bin
f none /usr/bin/file4 755 bin bin
f none /usr/bin/file5 755 bin bin
$
```

To create a prototype file that contains the output of the example above, you would execute pkgproto /usr/bin > prototype

NOTE If no pathnames are supplied when executing pkgproto, standard in (stdin) is assumed to be a list of paths. Refer to the pkgproto manual entry in Appendix B for details on this usage.

Assigning Objects to a Class

You can use the −c *class* option of pkgproto to assign objects to a class other than none. When using this option, you can only name one class. To define multiple classes in a prototype file created by pkgproto, you must edit the file after its creation.

The following example is the same as above except the objects have been assigned to class1.

```
$ pkgproto -c class1 /usr/bin
d class1 /usr/bin 755 bin bin
f class1 /usr/bin/file1 755 bin bin
f class1 /usr/bin/file2 755 bin bin
f class1 /usr/bin/file3 755 bin bin
f class1 /usr/bin/file4 755 bin bin
f class1 /usr/bin/file5 755 bin bin
$
```

Renaming Pathnames with pkgproto

You can use a *path1=path2* format on the pkgproto command line to give an object a different pathname in the prototype file than it has on your machine. You can, for example, use this format to define relocatable objects in a prototype file created by pkgproto.

The following example is like the others shown in this section, except that the objects are now defined as bin (instead of /usr/bin) and are thus relocatable.

```
$ pkgproto -c class1 /usr/bin=bin
d class1 bin 755 bin bin
f class1 bin/file1 755 bin bin
f class1 bin/file2 755 bin bin
f class1 bin/file3 755 bin bin
f class1 bin/file4 755 bin bin
f class1 bin/file5 755 bin bin
$
```

pkgproto and Links

pkgproto detects linked files and creates entries for them in the prototype file. If multiple files are linked together, it considers the first path encountered the source of the link.

If you have symbolic links established on your machine but want to generate an entry for that file with an ftype of f (file), then use the −i option of pkgproto. This option creates a file entry for all symbolic links.

Distributing Packages over Multiple Volumes

As packager, you no longer need to worry about placing package components on multiple volumes. pkgmk performs the calculations and actions necessary to organize a multiple volume package. As pkgmk creates your package, it will prompt you to insert a new volume as often as necessary to distribute the complete package over multiple volumes.

However, you can use the optional part field in the prototype file to define in which part you want an object to be placed. A number in this field overrides pkgmk and forces the placement of the component into the part given in the field. Note again that there is a one-to-one correspondence between parts and volumes for removable media formatted as file systems.

Creating a Package with pkgmk

pkgmk takes all of the objects on your machine (as defined in the prototype file), puts them in the fixed directory format and copies everything to the installation medium.

To package your software, execute

    pkgmk [-d *device*] [-f *filename*]

You must use the -d option to name the device onto which the package should be placed. *device* can be a directory pathname or the identifier for a disk. The default device is the installation spool directory.

pkgmk looks for a file named prototype. You can use the -f option to specify a package contents file named something other than prototype. This file must be in the prototype format.

For example, executing pkgmk -d /dev/diskette creates a package based on a file named prototype in your current working directory. The package will be formatted and copied to the diskette in the device /dev/diskette.

Creating a Package Instance

pkgmk will create a new instance of a package if one already exists on the device to which it is writing. It will assign the package an instance identifier. Use the -o option of pkgmk to overwrite an existing instance of a package rather than to create a new one.

Helping pkgmk Locate Package Contents

The following list describes situations that might require supplying pkgmk with extra information and an explanation of how to do so:

- Your development area is not structured in the same way that you want your package structured.

   You should use the *path1=path2* pathname format in your prototype file.

- You have relocatable objects in your package.

You can use the *path1=path2* pathname format in your `prototype` file, with *path1* as a relocatable name and *path2* a full pathname to that object on your machine.

You can use the `search` command in your `prototype` file to tell `pkgmk` where to look for objects.

You can use the −b *basedir* option of `pkgmk` to define a pathname to prepend to relocatable object names while creating the package. For example, executing

        pkgmk −d /dev/diskette −b usr2/myhome/reloc

would look in the directory `/usr2/myhome/reloc` for any relocatable object in your package.

■ You have variable object names.

You can use the `search` command in your `prototype` file to tell `pkgmk` where to look for objects.

You can use the *param="value"* command in your `prototype` file to give `pkgmk` a value to use for the object name variables as it creates your package.

You can use the *variable=value* option on the `pkgmk` command line to define a temporary value for variable names.

■ The root directory on your machine differs from the root directory described in the `prototype` file (and that will be used on the installation machine).

You can use the −r *rootpath* option to tell `pkgmk` to ignore the destination pathnames in the `prototype` file. Instead, `pkgmk` prepends *rootpath* to the source pathnames in order to find objects on your machine.

Creating a Package with pkgtrans

pkgtrans performs the following package translations:

- a fixed directory structure to a datastream
- a datastream to a fixed directory structure

To perform one of these translations, execute

pkgtrans *device1 device2* [*pkg1* [*, pkg2* [...]]]

where *device1* is the name of the device where the package currently resides, *device2* is the name of the device onto which the translated package will be placed, and *pkg1*(*pkg2* ...) is one or more package names. If no package names are given, all packages residing in *device1* will be translated and placed on *device2*.

 If more than one instance of a package resides on *device1*, you must use an instance identifier for *pkg*.

Creating a Datastream Package

Creating a datastream package requires two steps:

1. Create a package using pkgmk.

   Use the default device (the installation spool directory) or name a directory into which the package should be placed. pkgmk creates a package in a fixed directory format. Specify the capacity of the device where the datastream will be placed as an argument to the −l option.

2. After the software is formatted in fixed directory format and is residing in a spool directory, execute pkgtrans.

   This command translates the fixed directory format to the datastream format and places the datastream on the specified medium.

For example, the two steps shown below will create a datastream package.

1. pkgmk −d spooldir −l 1400

(Formats a package into a fixed directory structure and places it in a directory named `spooldir`. Each part of the package will require no more than 1400 blocks.)

2. `pkgtrans spooldir 9track package1`

   (Translates the fixed directory format of `package1` residing in the directory `spooldir` into a datastream format. Places the datastream package on the medium in a device named `9track`.)

OR

3. `pkgtrans -s spooldir diskette package1`

   (Similar to number 2 above, except that it places the datastream package on the medium in a device named `diskette`. `pkgtrans` will prompt for additional volumes if the package requires more than one diskette.)

Translating a Package Instance

When an instance of the package being translated already exists on *device2*, `pkgtrans` will not perform the translation. You can use the −o option to tell `pkgtrans` to overwrite any existing instances on the destination device and the −n option to tell it to create a new instance if one already exists. Note that this check does not apply when *device2* contains a datastream format.

Quick Reference to Packaging Procedures

Before beginning any packaging procedure, you must first have planned your packaging needs based on the information presented in this chapter. "Basic Steps of Packaging" gives a comprehensive list of possible packaging steps and considerations. This section only covers the required steps.

1. **Create a** prototype **file.**

   ■ Create one manually using any editor. There must be one entry for every package component. The format for a prototype file entry is:

   [volno] ftype class pathname [major minor] [mode owner group]

   volno designates the medium volume number on which the object should be placed. If no *volno* is given, pkgmk distributes package components across volumes automatically.

   ftype must be one of these object file types:

   > f (standard executable or data file)
   > e (file to be edited upon installation or removal)
   > v (volatile file, contents will change)
   > d (directory)
   > x (exclusive directory)
   > l (linked file)
   > p (named pipe)
   > c (character special device)
   > b (block special device)
   > i (installation script or package information file)
   > s (symbolic link)

   class defines the class to which the object belongs. Place an object into the class of none if no special handling is required.

   pathname defines the pathname of an object. It can be in one of these formats:

   □ fixed pathname: */src/myfile*

   □ collectively relocatable pathname: *src/myfile* (no beginning slash)

□ individually relocatable pathname: $BIN/*myfile*

This pathname defines where the component should reside on the installation medium and also tells pkgmk where to find it on your machine. If these names differ, use the *path1=path2* format for *pathname*, where *path1* is the name it should have on the installation machine and *path2* is the name it has on your machine.

major minor defines the major and minor numbers for a block or character special device.

mode owner group defines the mode, owner and group for the object. If not defined, the value of the default command is used. If no default value is defined, 644 root other is assigned.

You can use four types of command lines in a prototype file:

search *pathnames* (defines a search path for pkgmk to use when creating your package)

include *filename* (nests prototype files)

default *mode owner group* (defines a default mode owner group for objects defined in this prototype file)

param=value (defines parameter values for pkgmk)

All command lines must begin with an exclamation point (!).

■ Create one using pkgproto.

pkgproto [-i] [-c *class*] [*path1*[=*path2*] ...] > *filename*

where −i tells pkgproto to record symbolic links with an ftype of f (not s), −c defines the class of all objects as *class*, and *path1* defines the object pathname (or names) to be included in the prototype file. If *path1* is a directory, entries for all objects in that directory will be generated.

Use the *path1=path2* format to give an object a different pathname in the prototype file than it has on your machine. *path1* is the pathname where objects can be located on your machine and *path2* is the pathname that should be substituted for those objects.

pkgproto writes its output to the standard output. To create a file, you should redirect the output to a file. That file can be named prototype (although it is not required).

2. **Create a** pkginfo **file.**

   Use any editor. Define one entry per line per parameter in this format:

   PARAM="value"

   where *PARAM* is the name of one of the standard installation parameters defined in the pkginfo manual entry in Appendix B and *value* is the value you assign to it.

   You can also define values for your own installation parameters using the same format. Names for parameters that you create must begin with a capital letter and be followed by only lower-case letters.

   The following five parameters are required in every pkginfo file: PKG, NAME, ARCH, VERSION and CATEGORY. No other restrictions apply concerning which parameters or how many parameters you define.

   The CLASSES parameter dictates which classes are installed and the order of installation. Although the parameter is not required, no classes will be installed without it. Even if you have no class action scripts, the none class must be defined in the CLASSES parameter before objects belonging to that class will be installed.

3. **Execute** pkgmk.

   pkgmk [−d *device*] [−r *rootpath*] [−b *basedir*] [−f *filename*]

   where −d specifies that the package should be copied onto *device*, −r requests that the root directory *rootpath* be used to locate objects on your machine, −b requests that *basedir* be prepended to relocatable paths when searching for them on your machine, and −f names a file, *filename*, to be used as your prototype file. (Other options are described in the pkgmk manual entry in Appendix B.)

Refer to the procedures in this chapter for details on other, optional packaging steps (including how to use pkgtrans to create a package in datastream structure).

9　Modifying the sysadm Interface

Overview of sysadm Modification

UNIX System V Release 4 provides a menu interface to the most common administrative procedures. It is invoked by executing sysadm and so is referred to as the sysadm interface. (A complete description of this interface and instructions on how to use it can be found in the *System Administrator's Guide*.)

You can deliver additions or changes to this interface as part of your application software package. Creating the necessary information for an interface modification is a simple process due to the tools provided by SVR4.

This chapter describes these tools, provides all of the needed background information, and details the procedures necessary to design and write your package administration and to package it so that it will become a part of the administration interface on the installation machine.

 NOTE This chapter assumes you are familiar with the material covered in the "Packaging Application Software" chapter.

Introduction to the Tools

Two commands can be used to create the files necessary to deliver modifications to the sysadm interface as a part of your package.

- edsysadm creates all of the files needed for your interface modifications to be installed along with your package

- delsysadm deletes menus or tasks from the interface

This chapter also provides an overview of a group of tools known as the data validation tools. You can use them when writing your system administration to simplify and standardize the programming of administrative interaction. The tools are described in detail in the "Data Validation Tools" chapter of this book.

The edsysadm Command

edsysadm, which allows you to make changes or additions to the interface, is an interactive command that functions much like the sysadm command itself. It presents a series of prompts for information. (Which prompt appears depends on your response to the previous prompt.)

After you have responded to all the prompts, edsysadm presents a form that you must fill in with information describing the menu or task being changed or added. This form is called the menu (or task) definition form. If you are changing an existing menu or task entry, the definition form will already be filled in with the current values, which you can edit. If you are adding a new menu or task entry, the form will be empty and you will have to fill it in.

When you follow the procedures in this chapter, edsysadm creates all of the files and directories necessary to deliver your interface modifications as a part of your package. The section entitled "Introduction to the Package Modification Files" describes the three files that edsysadm creates.

edsysadm builds the directory structure required by the sysadm interface. You do not need to know this structure and you are not required to have your work directory organized in any predefined way. When you fill in a menu or task definition form, you supply filenames (for example, a file containing help messages) that edsysadm should use when creating the packaging for your interface modifications. edsysadm creates a prototype file and builds the interface directory format by using the *path1=path2* naming convention. *path2* defines where the files reside on your machine and *path1* defines where they should be placed on the installation machine.

The delsysadm Command

delsysadm removes tasks and menus from the interface. When you deliver your modifications as a part of your package, you do not need to use delsysadm to remove them. Any time an interface modification is delivered as a part of a package, those modifications are automatically removed at the same time as the package. This chapter describes the delsysadm command in case you need to use it on your own machine, for example to remove modifications added for testing.

delsysadm checks for dependencies on the entry being removed before deleting the entry. (A dependency exists if the menu being removed contains an entry placed there by an application package.) If delsysadm discovers a dependency, you are asked whether you want to continue with the removal. (If a dependency is found during an automatic removal, the interface entry is not removed.)

When you delete a menu entry with delsysadm, it must already be empty (contain no other menus or tasks) or you can execute delsysadm with the −r option.
This option removes a menu and all its entries at the same time.

 Use delsysadm to remove only those menu or task entries that you have
added to an interface.

The Data Validation Tools

The data validation routines help standardize administration interaction in the
SVR4 environment and also make development easier. The tools are available
as shell commands and as visual modules to be used in a FACE (Framed Access
Command Environment) form. The tools perform the following series of tasks:

- prompt a user for a particular type of input

- validate the response

- format and print help and error messages

- return the input if it passes validation

The type of validation performed is defined by the tool itself. For example, the
shell command ckyorn prompts for and validates an affirmative or negative
response. These tools should be used in your administration programs if they
are to be added to the sysadm interface to maintain consistency within the interface. Refer to the chapter "Data Validation Tools" for full details on these tools
and their uses.

Introduction to the Package Modification Files

When you execute edsysadm to define menus and tasks and save those
definitions to be included in your application software package, it creates three
files:

- the package description file

- the menu information file

- the prototype file

The package description file contains information edsysadm uses to change interface modifications already saved for packaging. When you decide to change your modifications after already creating the packaging (meaning the menu information and prototype files are already created), the package description file provides edsysadm with the information it needs to locate the other package modification files and to make the changes. Without this file, edsysadm cannot make such a change. You are asked to supply a name for this file during the edsysadm interaction and it is created in your current working directory (unless you supply a full pathname to a different directory with the name).

The menu information file contains the menu or task name, where it is located in the interface structure, and, for tasks, what executable to use when the task is invoked. It tells the interface installation software how to modify the interface structures to include the new definitions. The file's name is the hour, minute, second, day-of-year, and year that the file was created, followed by an .mi suffix. It is created in your current working directory.

The prototype file created by edsysadm contains entries for all of the interface modification components that must be packaged with your software (for example, the menu information file and, for tasks, the executables). These entries must be incorporated into your package either by reading the edsysadm-created file into your package prototype file or by using the include command in the main prototype file for your package. The prototype file created by edsysadm is created in your current working directory with the name of prototype.

Overview of the Interface Modification Process

You must take a number of steps to add your package administration to the sysadm interface. This chapter explains each step in detail. The following steps are covered:

- planning your package administration (with details on how to decide if you should modify the interface and where to place it in the interface structure)

■ writing your administration actions (with general information on what your executables can be)

■ writing your help message (with a description of the required help message file)

■ packaging your interface modifications (with procedural details on executing edsysadm and what steps must be taken afterwards)

This chapter also includes instructions on executing delsysadm.

Planning Your Interface Modifications

You will need to plan your interface modifications before executing edsysadm.
Planning begins with deciding if your administration tasks should become a
part of the sysadm interface. If so, you must decide on where your tasks fit into
the interface, what to name your tasks, and the full menu structure involved
with your administrative tasks.

Deciding if You Should Modify the Interface

Any type of task can be added to the sysadm interface with the following two
restrictions:

- Tasks that can be automated should not be added to the interface (for
  example, procedures that can run automatically as part of system booting
  or as part of your package installation).

- Tasks that require the system to be in firmware mode can be added to the
  interface but it is strongly recommended that they not be.

Once you have decided to add your administration tasks to the interface, you
must determine where in the interface you want to locate tasks and menus.

Planning the Location of Your Modifications

To plan your modification you must first become familiar with the interface
organization. Then you must decide how to organize the tasks you want to add
and how to fit your modifications into the overall structure.

An Overview of the Interface Structure

The sysadm interface consists of a hierarchy of menus. At the top of the hierarchy is the main menu (labeled System Administration Menu). It appears on
the screen, immediately after sysadm is invoked, as follows:

```
                    System Administration Menu

applications      -  Administration for Available Applications
backup_service    -  Backup Scheduling, Setup, and Control
diagnostics       -  Diagnosing System Problems
file_systems      -  File System Creation, Checking, and Mounting
machine           -  Machine Configuration Display and Powerdown
networks          -  Network Administration
restore_service   -  Restore From Backup Data
software          -  Software Installation and Removal
storage_devices   -  Storage Device Operations and Definitions
system_setup      -  System Name, Date/Time and Initial Password Setup
users             -  User Login and Group Administration
```

NOTE   The applications menu will not appear on the main sysadm menu until at least one menu or task has been placed under it.

The main menu consists of a list of function-specific menus. The lefthand column notes the menu names (such as machine) and the righthand column gives descriptions of these menus. Each menu offers other menus and/or names of tasks. For example, the machine menu, shown below, contains one menu (configuration) and five tasks.

```
                    Machine Management

configuration  -  System Configuration Display
firmware       -  Stop All Running Programs and Enters Firmware Mode
floppy key     -  Creates a Floppy Key Removable Diskette
powerdown      -  Stops All Running Programs and Turns Off Machine
reboot         -  Stops All Running Programs and Reboots Machine
whos on        -  Displays List of Users Logged onto Machine
```

Choosing the entry configuration from this screen will cause another menu to be presented. Choosing a task entry, such as powerdown, will begin execution of that task.

Planning Your Administration Structure

Planning your administration structure requires three steps:

1. Deciding what tasks to add to the interface.

   You can add any number of tasks. You should have separate entries for each task to be performed. For example, if your administration allowed a log to be changed, added to, and removed, you should create an entry for each task and not combine them into one entry called log administration.

2. Deciding under which menu the tasks should be placed.

   You can create new sysadm menus at any level and you can change or add to any of the original sysadm menus. You should be aware, however, that if you make changes to original menus you might cause problems in the execution of standard sysadm operations. It is therefore recommended (though not mandatory) that you create new menus for your package administration by placing it under the applications menu (located on the main menu) or by creating a new main menu entry.

3. Organizing your tasks.

   You can organize your tasks under one menu or place them in submenu groups. For example, if your package has tasks to be performed daily and weekly, you might create a structure such as the following:

   - Under the applications menu on the main menu, add an entry for your package called pkgAadmin.

   - Under pkgAadmin, add two submenus called daily and weekly.

   - Under the submenu daily, add entries for each of the daily tasks.

   - Under the submenu weekly, add entries for each of the weekly tasks.

It is important that you have your full administrative structure planned before running edsysadm because you must create a menu entry before placing a task or submenu under it.

After you have planned your structure, you should decide on the names for your menus and tasks.

Naming Your Interface Modifications

Naming your interface modifications requires the following three pieces of information described below. This section also details the interface naming requirements and tells you how the system handles naming collisions.

How to Name Your Modifications

When naming your interface modifications, you must decide on these three pieces of information:

Name
: The name of the menu or task as it will appear in the left-hand column of the screen.

Description
: The description of the menu or task as it will appear in the righthand column of the screen.

Location
: The location of a menu or task in the `sysadm` menu hierarchy. This location is a combination, step-by-step, of all the menu names that must be chosen to reach the menu or task. Each step must already exist when the entry is added. For example, when you add a task with a location of `main:applications:mypkg`, you must already have created an entry for the menu `mypkg`.

All locations begin with `main`. When defining a location in the procedures that follow, each step should be separated by a colon. For example, the `powerdown` task is under the menu `machine`, which, in turn, is under the `main` menu. Thus, the location of the `powerdown` task is `main:machine`.

You will supply these pieces of information on the menu (or task) definition form.

Interface Naming Requirements

A menu or task name should be as short as possible in length but, at the same time, be descriptive. It can contain only lower case letters and underscores and has a maximum length of 16 characters.

The description field can contain any character string and has a maximum length of 58 characters. This description field text for a menu is also used as the title for that menu when it is displayed. Use of standard title capitalization rules is recommended.

How the System Handles Naming Collisions

A naming collision might occur under two circumstances:

- When the package being installed is an update to an existing version.

  The administrator will be asked during installation if this is an update, in which case the existing menus and tasks will be overwritten.

- When two packages have created identical interface modifications.

  The colliding menu or task will be renamed by adding the first available numerical suffix (beginning with 2). For example, if an entry for menuA already exists and a package attempts to add an identical entry, the one being added will be renamed to menuA2.

Writing Your Administration Actions

When you execute `edsysadm` to create packaging for a task entry, you will fill in a task definition form. One of the fields on that form asks for the name of the task action file. The task action file is the executable that will run when your task is selected from the interface. Your administrative task can use more than one executable, but, if so, you must create one that is called when the task is selected and call any other executables associated with the task from within it.

The task action can be one of two types:

- Non-interactive

  A non-interactive task action can be any shell executable.

- Interactive

  An interactive task action must be a FACE form. (Refer to the *Programmer's Guide: Character User Interface (FMLI and ETI)* for instructions on writing a FACE form.)

Use the tools described in the chapter "Data Validation Tools" whenever possible when writing administrator interaction.

Writing Your Help Messages

You must write help messages to be packaged with every interface modifications. They are delivered in what is called an item help file. This file has text for two types of messages:

- the help message that will be shown when the user requests help from the parent menu
- the help messages that will be shown for each field when your task action is a FACE form

The format of the item help file allows you to create one item help file for each task, combine all of your help messages for multiple tasks into one file, use the same message for multiple FACE forms, and to define a title hierarchy for the help message screens.

The Item Help File

There are no naming restrictions for the item help file that resides on your machine. However, within the interface structure, the item help file must always be named `Help`. You can use this name if you want to but it is not mandatory since `edsysadm` uses the *path1=path2* naming convention in the prototype file that it creates to define the directory structure required by the interface. Regardless of what the item help file is named on your machine, *path1* in the `prototype` file will have the name `Help`. This means that you can have more than one item help file in your working directory at the same time and `edsysadm` will handle the details of giving it the correct name.

There are three types of entries in an item help file:

- the menu item help
- the default title (can define both a global default and a form default)
- the field item help

A description of each type of entry and its format follows. All of the entries use the colon (`:`) as the keyword delimiter.

The Menu Item Help Message Format

The menu item help message will be shown whenever a user requests help on an entry from the parent menu. Menu item help must be written for each menu and task entry being delivered as an interface modification. For example, if your package administration is adding a menu under main:applications and that menu has three tasks under it, you will need to deliver four menu item help messages.

The format for the menu item help definition is as follows:

```
[task_name:]ABSTRACT:
     <TAB>     Line 1 of message text
     <TAB>     Line 2 of message text
     <TAB>     Line n of message text
```

task_name defines the task (or menu) entry to which this help message belongs. This name must match the name that you have decided should appear in the lefthand column of the menu screen. (Refer back to "Naming Your Interface Modifications" for more details on this name.) *task_name* is not optional when more than one menu item help definition is defined in the same item help file. This helps to distinguish to which task or menu the message belongs.

The message text should be entered beneath the header line. There can be multiple lines of text with a maximum length of 69 characters per line. Each line must begin with a tab character. Blank lines may be included within the message as long as they also begin with a tab character. An example menu item help definition is shown below.

```
task1:ABSTRACT:
          This is line one of the menu item help message.
          This is a second line of message text.

          The preceding line will appear as a blank line
          when the help message is shown because it begins
          with a tab.
```

The title for a menu item help message is always the description text, as it appears in the lefthand column of the menu display, prepended by the string Help on.

The Default Title Format

You can define two types of default titles:

- a global default title to be used on all of the help messages defined in the item help file

- a form default title to be used on all of the help messages defined for a particular form in an item help file with messages defined for numerous forms

Defaults can be overridden, as described in the section "The Title Hierarchy." A default title definition is recommended but not required.

The format for the default title definition is as follows:

[*form_id* :] TITLE : *Title Text*

form_id is the name of the form as it is defined with lininfo in your FACE form definition. When a *form_id* is supplied, this line defines a form default title. When it is not supplied, this line defines a global default title.

The title text defined after the TITLE keyword will have the string HELP on prepended to it when displayed. Keep this in mind when writing the title.

An example form default title definition is shown below.

```
task1:TITLE:Package Administration Task1
```

If task1 had not been added before TITLE, this example would be defining a global default title. The title defined by the example above will be displayed as:

```
HELP on Package Administration Task1
```

The Field Item Help Message Format

The field item help message will be shown whenever a user requests help from within a FACE form. Each field on the form must have a help message defined in the item help file.

The format for the field item help definition is as follows:

```
[form_id:] field_id: [Title Text]
    <TAB>    Line 1 of message text
    <TAB>    Line 2 of message text
    <TAB>    Line n of message text
```

form_id is the name of the form as it is defined with `lininfo` in your FACE form definition. When one item help file contains messages for multiple tasks (and so multiple forms), it is used to distinguish with which form a field belongs. It is optional if the file contains messages for only one task. `field_id` is the name of the field as it is defined with `lininfo` in your FACE form definition. *Title text* defines a title used only with the help message for this field. As with the default title, the text defined here will have the string `HELP on` prepended to it when displayed.

The message text should be entered beneath the header line. There can be multiple lines of text with a maximum length of 69 characters per line. Each line must begin with a tab character. Blank lines may be included within the message as long as they also begin with a tab character. An example field item help definition is shown below.

```
task1:fld1:the Name Field
        This is the text for a field item help for a name
        field.

        The preceding line will appear as a blank line
        when the help message is shown because it begins
        with a tab.
```

The title for this field item help message, as defined above, will be `HELP on the Name Field`

The Title Hierarchy

You can define a global default title, a form default title, and a field title in the item help file. When all three are defined in the same file, the following rules are followed:

- The global default title is used for any message defined in an item help file that does not have a form default title or field title.

- The form default title is used for any message defined in an item help file and that is associated with the form, unless it has a field title.

- The field title is used only for the one field item help message for which it is defined.

In summary, if no field title is defined, the form default title is used. If no form default title is defined, the global default title is used. You always want at least a global default title defined; otherwise, the string HELP on will be displayed with no descriptive text.

To define a global default title, add a line to your item help file in the following format:

> TITLE : *Title Text*

where *Title Text* is the text for the global default title.

To define a form default title, add a line to your item help file in the following format:

> *form_id* : TITLE : *Title Text*

where *form_id* is the name of form as it is defined with lininfo in your FACE form definition and *Title Text* is the text for the form default title.

To define a field title, use the following format for the field item help header line:

> *form_id* : *field_id* : *Title Text*

where *form_id* is the name of the form as it is defined with lininfo in your FACE form definition, *field_id* is the name of the field as it is defined with lininfo in your FACE form definition and *Title Text* is the text for the field title.

In all cases, the text defined as *Title Text* is always prepended with the string
HELP on when displayed to a user.

Setting Up for Item Help in a FACE Object

To help the interface read your item help file and know with which forms and
fields a help message is associated, you must define your help and lininfo
descriptors in your FACE object definition as follows:

- The help descriptor must be defined exactly as shown on the line below:

     help=OPEN TEXT $INTFBASE/Text.itemhelp $LININFO

- The lininfo descriptor for each field must be defined as

     lininfo=[*form_id* :] *field_id*

  where *form_id* and *field_id* are names each no longer than 30 characters.
  The names defined here as *form_id* and *field_id* must match exactly those
  used as *form_id* and *field_id* in the item help file.

 Since you do not create a FACE form definition for a menu entry, you do not
need to take any setup actions. However, you should be certain that the
task_name keyword precedes the ABSTRACT heading line for a menu entry
help message.

Example Item Help Files

This section shows two example item help files. Figure 9-1 shows an item help
file that defines messages for only one form. Figure 9-2 shows an example of
defining messages for multiple forms in one item help file.

Figure 9-1: Item Help File for One Form

```
ABSTRACT:
        The text defined here will be shown to
        users when they request help while
        viewing the parent menu for this
        task.  The task name is "adding users."

TITLE:Adding Users

field1:
        The text defined here will be shown to
        users when they request help from the
        form and the cursor is positioned at
        field1.  The title for this message will
        be ''HELP on Adding Users'' as defined above.

field2:Field 2
        The text defined here will be shown to
        users when they request help from the
        form and the cursor is positioned at
        field2.  The title for this message will
        be ''HELP on Field 2''.
```

Note: The lininfo descriptors in the form definition associated with this file should look like this:

```
        .
        .
        .

lininfo=field1

        .
        .
        .

lininfo=field2
```

System Services and Application Packaging Tools

Figure 9-2: Item Help File for Multiple Forms

```
add:ABSTRACT:
          The text defined here will be shown to
          users when they request help while
          viewing the parent menu for the task
          named add.

add_user:TITLE:Adding Users

add_user:field1:
          The text defined here will be shown to
          users when they request help from the
          form and the cursor is positioned at
          field1.  The title for this message will
          be ''HELP on Adding Users'' as defined above.

add_user:field2:Field 2
          The text defined here will be shown to
          users when they request help from the
          form and the cursor is positioned at
          field2.  The title for this message will
          be ''HELP on Field 2''.

delete:ABSTRACT:
          The text defined here will be shown to
          users when they request help while
          viewing the parent menu for the task
          named delete.

delete_user:TITLE:Deleting Users

delete_user:field1:
          The text defined here will be shown to
          users when they request help from the
          form and the cursor is positioned at
          field1.  The title for this message will
          be ''HELP on Deleting Users'' as defined above.

delete_user:field2:Field 2
          The text defined here will be shown to
          users when they request help from the
          form and the cursor is positioned at
          field2.  The title for this message will
          be ''HELP on Field 2''.
```

(continued on next page)

Figure 9-2: Item Help File for Multiple Forms (continued)

```
    Note: The lininfo descriptors in the form definition associated with this
    file should look like this:


        .
        .
    lininfo-add_user:field1

        .
        .
    lininfo-add_user:field2

        .
        .
    lininfo-delete_user:field1

        .
        .
    lininfo-delete_user:field2
```

Packaging Your Interface Modifications

To prepare your interface modifications for installation, you must create the packaging for your menus and tasks by executing edsysadm. The packaging created by edsysadm consists of two files, a prototype file and a menu information file. This section describes the procedures for creating these files and what to do after they have been created. (It also describes how to change the packaging after it has been created.)

 NOTE edsysadm also creates a package description file. edsysadm uses this file during its execution and is not a part of the packaging.

Basic Steps for Packaging Your Modifications

The procedures described next must be repeated for each menu and task entry being added. Begin with creating the menu entry (or entries) because you cannot add tasks or submenus to a menu that does not exist. Be certain that you use the same package description file name for all of the entries belonging to a package.

After running edsysadm, be certain to follow the steps described in ''Preparing Your Package'' (at the end of this section) to incorporate the modifications into your software package.

For example, if your administration requires the addition of one menu and four tasks, you will need to follow the procedure for creating the packaging for a menu entry, then repeat the procedure for creating the packaging for a task entry four times. Each time, when asked for a package description file name, give the same name to ensure that the packaging created contains all the necessary entries. These procedures will create a menu information file and a prototype file with all of the information necessary to include your interface modifications in your package. The two remaining steps (described in "Preparing Your Package") are to include the edsysadm created prototype file in your package prototype file and to edit the CLASSES parameter in the pkginfo file.

Creating or Changing the Packaging for a Menu Entry

The procedures for creating and changing the packaging for a new menu are similar and both result in the display of a menu definition form. Each procedure is described below, followed by a description of the menu definition form.

Creating the Packaging for a Menu Entry

Before creating the packaging for a new menu entry, you should:

- Select a name and description for the menu.

- Select a location for it in the interface.

- Prepare a help message file for the menu entry (refer to "Writing Your Help Messages" presented earlier in this chapter for instructions).

- Know the name of the package description file to which the information for this menu should be added (if you are adding multiple menus and tasks)

1. Type edsysadm and press <RETURN>.

    NOTE If you do not execute this command from the directory in which the help message file resides, supply the full pathname when prompted for the name of the help message file.

2. You are asked to choose between a menu and a task. Choose menu and press <RETURN>.

3. You are asked to choose between adding a new menu or changing an existing one. Choose add and press <RETURN>.

4. You are given an empty menu definition form. Fill it in and press <SAVE>. (See "The Menu Definition Form" for descriptions of the fields on this form.)

5. You are asked if you want to test the changes before actually making them. Answer either yes or no and press <SAVE>. (If you answer yes, refer to the "Testing Your Menu Changes On-Line" section to learn what the test involves.)

6. You are asked if you want to install the modifications into the interface on your machine or save them for a package. Choose `save` and press <SAVE>.

7. You are asked to supply a file name. Enter a name for the package description file and press <SAVE>.

8. If the file name given for the package description file already exists, you are asked if you want to overwrite it or add to its contents. Answer `overwrite`, `do not overwrite`, or `add` and press <SAVE>.

9. If the file name does not already exist (or after you have completed Step 8) you will see a message stating that the menu information file and `prototype` file have been verified and the top-level `prototype` must be edited to include the new `prototype` file. Press <CANCEL> to return to the menu shown in step 3. Press <CONT> to return to the form shown in step 4.

Changing the Packaging for a Menu Entry

Before changing the packaging for a menu entry, you should:

■ Know the name and description of the menu entry.

■ Know its location in the interface.

■ Change the associated help message file, if necessary, or create a new one (refer to "Writing Your Help Messages" presented earlier in this chapter for instructions).

■ Know the name of the package description file associated with the package being changed (and know that it is available in your current working directory).

1. Type `edsysadm` and press <RETURN>.

NOTE If you have changed a help message file or created a new one and you do not execute this command from the directory in which the help message file resides, supply the full pathname when asked for the name of the file.

2. You are asked to choose between a menu and a task. Choose menu and press <RETURN>.

3. You are asked to choose between adding a new menu and changing an existing one. Choose change and press <RETURN>.

4. You are asked if your change is for an on-line menu or for a menu that has been saved for a package. Choose packaged and press <SAVE>.

5. You are asked to supply the package description file name for the package being changed. Fill in the name of a valid package description file and press <SAVE>.

6. You are given a menu definition form filled in with the current values for the menu named above. Make the desired changes and press <SAVE>. (See the "The Menu Definition Form" for descriptions of the fields on this form.)

7. You are asked if you want to test the changes before actually making them. Answer either yes or no and press <SAVE>. (If you answer yes, refer to the section entitled "Testing Your Menu Changes On-Line" to learn what the test involves.)

8. You are asked if you want to install the modifications into the interface on your machine or save them for a package. Choose save and press <SAVE>.

9. You are asked to supply a file name. Enter a name for the package description file and press <SAVE>. (This must be the same package description file named in Step 5.)

10. If the file name given for the package description file already exists, you are asked if you want to overwrite it or add to its contents. Answer overwrite, do not overwrite, or add and press <SAVE>.

11. If the file name does not already exist (or after you have completed Step 10) you will see a message stating that the menu information file and prototype file have been verified and the top-level prototype must be edited to include the new prototype file. Press <CANCEL> to return to

the menu shown in step 4. Press <CONT> to return to the form shown in step 5.

Testing Your Menu Changes On-Line

Before installing your menu changes, you may want to verify that you've added an entry to a menu. The edsysadm command gives you a chance to do this after you fill in the menu definition form. Follow these steps to perform your test.

1. Type yes when edsysadm presents the following prompt:

   ```
   Do you want to test this modification before continuing?
   ```

2. The parent menu (on which your addition or change is listed) is displayed. Check to make sure your modification has been made correctly.

3. Put the cursor on the new or changed menu entry and press the <HELP> key. The text of the help message for that menu entry is displayed so you can check it. (Press <CANCEL> to return to the menu.)

4. To exit on-line testing, press the <CANCEL> key.

5. You are returned to the prompt:

   ```
   Do you want to test this modification before continuing?
   ```

   If you want to continue executing the change, type no.

   If you want to make additional modifications to the menu definition form, press <CANCEL>. You are returned to the form and can make further changes at that time. (Press <SAVE> when you have finished your editing. You can then retest your changes or continue executing the change.)

The Menu Definition Form

This form contains four fields in which you must provide: a menu name, a menu description, a menu location, and the name of the help message for the menu. Below are descriptions of the information you must provide in each field.

Menu Name   The name of the new menu (as it should appear in the lefthand column of the screen). This field has a maximum length of 16 alphanumeric characters.

Menu Description   A description of the new menu (as it should appear in the righthand column of the screen). This field has a maximum length of 58 characters and can consist of any alphanumeric character except the at sign (@), carat (ˆ), tilde (˜), back grave (´), grave (`), and double quotes (").

Menu Location   The location of the menu in the menu hierarchy, expressed as a menu pathname. The pathname should begin with the main menu followed by all other menus that must be traversed (in the order they are traversed) to access this menu. Each menu name must be separated by colons. For example, the menu location for a menu entry being added to the Applications menu is `main:applications`. *Do not include the menu name in this location definition.* The complete pathname to this menu entry will be the menu location plus the menu name defined at the first prompt.

      This is a scrollable field, showing a maximum of 50 alphanumeric characters at a time.

Menu Help File Name   Pathname to the item help file for this menu entry. If it resides in the directory from which you invoked `edsysadm`, you do not need to give a full pathname. If you name an item help file that does not exist, you are placed in an editor (as defined by $EDITOR) to create one. The new file is created in the current directory and named `Help`.

The following screen shows a filled-in sample menu definition.

```
                Define A Menu

Name:  msvr
Description:  Menu Description
Location:  main:applications
Help Message:  Help
```

Creating or Changing the Packaging for a Task Entry

The procedures for creating and changing the packaging for a new task are similar and both result in the display of a task definition form. Each procedure is described below, followed by a description of the task definition form.

Creating the Packaging for a Task Entry

Before creating the packaging for a task entry, you should:

- Gather all files that will be associated with this task, such as the help file, FACE forms , or other executables. All files should already be prepared.

- Decide on the task name and description.

- Decide on its location in the interface.

- Create a help file (refer to "Writing Your Help Messages" presented earlier in this chapter for instructions).

- Know the name of the package description file to which the information for this task should be added (if you are adding multiple menus and tasks)

1. Type edsysadm and press <RETURN>.

NOTE If you do not execute this command from the same directory in which the files associated with this task reside, enter full pathnames when supplying file names.

2. You are asked to choose between a menu and a task. Choose `task` and press <RETURN>.

3. You are asked to choose between adding a new task or changing an existing one. Choose `add` and press <RETURN>.

4. You are given an empty task definition form. Fill it in and press <SAVE>. (See "The Task Definition Form" for descriptions of the fields on this form. Be aware that, when you name the menu under which you want this new task to reside, that menu must already be packaged.)

5. You are asked if you want to install the modifications into the interface on your machine or save them for a package. Choose `save` and press <SAVE>.

6. You are asked to supply a file name. Enter a name for the package description file and press <SAVE>.

7. If the file name given for the package description file already exists, you are asked if you want to overwrite it or add to its contents. Answer either `overwrite`, `do not overwrite`, or `add` and press <SAVE>.

8. If the file name does not already exist (or after you have completed Step 7) you see a message stating that the menu information file and `proto-type` file have been verified and the top-level `prototype` must be edited to include the new `prototype` file. Press <CANCEL> to return to the menu shown in step 3. Press <CONT> to return to the form shown in step 4.

Changing the Packaging for a Task Entry

Before changing the packaging for a task entry, you should:

■ Gather any of the files associated with this task that have been changed or are new. All files should already be prepared or changed.

- Know the menu name and description.

- Know its location in the interface.

- Change the associated help file, if necessary (refer to "Writing Your Help Messages" presented earlier in this chapter for instructions).

- Know the name of the package description file associated with the package being changed (and know that it is available in your current working directory).

1. Type edsysadm and press <RETURN>.

 If your change requires new files or changes to existing files and you do not execute this command from the directory in which the files reside, enter full pathnames when supplying file names.

2. You are asked to choose between a menu and a task. Choose task and press <RETURN>.

3. You are asked to choose between adding a new task and changing an existing one. Choose change and press <RETURN>.

4. You are asked if your change is for an on-line task or for a task that has been saved for a package. Choose packaged and press <SAVE>.

5. You are asked to supply the package description file name for the package being changed. Fill in the name of a valid package description file and press <SAVE>.

6. You are given a task definition form filled in with the current values for the task named above. Make the desired changes and press <SAVE>. (See "The Task Definition Form" for descriptions of the fields on this form.)

7. You are asked if you want to install the modifications into the interface on your machine or save them for a package. Choose save and press <SAVE>.

8. You are asked to supply a file name. Enter a name for the package description file and press <SAVE>. (This must be the same package description file named in Step 5.)

9. If the file name given for the package description file already exists, you are asked if you want to overwrite it or add to its contents. Answer either overwrite, do not overwrite, or add and press <SAVE>.

10. If the file name does not already exist (or after you have completed Step 9) you see a message stating that the menu information file and prototype file have been verified and the top-level prototype must be edited to include the new prototype file. Press <CANCEL> to return to the menu shown in step 4. Press <CONT> to return to the form shown in step 5.

The Task Definition Form

This form contains six fields in which you must provide: a task name, a task description, a task location, the name of a help message for the task, a task action file, and the files associated with the task. Below are descriptions of the information you must provide in each field.

Task Name   The name of the new task (as it should appear in the left-hand column of the screen). This field has a maximum length of 16 alphanumeric characters.

Task Description   A description of the new task (as it should appear in the righthand column of the screen). This field has a maximum length of 58 characters and can consist of any alphanumeric character except the at sign (@), carat (^), tilde (~), back grave (`), grave ('), and double quotes (").

Task Location   The location of the task in the menu hierarchy, expressed as a pathname. The pathname should begin with the main menu followed by all other menus that must be traversed (in the order they are traversed) to access this task. Each menu name must be separated by colons. For example, the task location for a task entry being added to the applications menu is main:applications. *Do not include the task name in this location definition.* The complete pathname to this task entry will be the task location as well as the task name defined at the first prompt.

                 This is a scrollable field, showing a maximum of 50 alphanumeric characters at a time.

Task Help File Name	Pathname to the item help file for this task entry. If it resides in the directory from which you invoked `edsysadm`, you do not need to give a full pathname. If you name an item help file that does not exist, you are placed in an editor (as defined by $EDITOR) to create one. The new file is created in the current directory and named `Help`.
Task Action	The FACE form name or executable that will be run when this task is selected. This is a scrollable field, showing a maximum of 58 alphanumeric characters at a time. This pathname can be relative to the current directory as well as absolute. (Refer to the "Writing Your Administration Actions" section for details.)
Task Files	Any FACE objects or other executables that support the task action listed above and might be called from within that action. *Do not include the help file name or the task action in this list.* Pathnames can be relative to the current directory as well as absolute. A dot (.) implies "all files in the current directory" and includes files in subdirectories.
	This is a scrollable field, showing a maximum of 50 alphanumeric characters at a time.

The following screen shows a filled-in sample task definition form.

```
          Define A Task

Name: msvrtask
Description:  Task Description
Location:  main:applications:msvr
Help Message:  Help
Action:  Form.msvrtask
Task Files:  Form.task2, Text.task2
```

Preparing Your Package

You must perform two steps, after executing edsysadm, to include your interface modification files in your application package.

1. Include the prototype file

   The prototype file that edsysadm creates must become a part of your package prototype file structure. This means that you must either read it into another prototype file or use the include command in your primary prototype file. For example, adding

   ```
   !include /myproject/admsrc/prototype
   ```

   to a prototype file in the /myproject directory ensures that the prototype file in /myproject/admsrc, and all of the objects it describes, will be included when the packaging tool, pkgmk, creates the package.

2. Change your CLASSES parameter in the pkginfo file

   The components defined in the prototype file that edsysadm creates are placed into the two special classes: OAMmif and OAMadmin. You must edit the pkginfo file for your package and add these to the CLASSES parameter definition. For example, a CLASSES definition before the change might look like this:

   ```
   CLASSES="class1 class2"
   ```

   It should be changed to look like this:

   ```
   CLASSES="class1 class2 OAMmif OAMadmin"
   ```

Your interface modifications are now ready to be included in your package when you create your package using pkgmk. (Details on packaging procedures are discussed in the "Packaging Application Software" chapter.)

Deleting Interface Modifications

Interface modifications can be deleted in two ways. When a package is removed, the modifications installed with the package are removed automatically. Modifications can also be removed online by executing `delsysadm`.

To delete either a menu or task entry online, execute

>   delsysadm   *name*

where *name* is the location of the task or menu in the interface, followed by the menu or task name. For example, to delete a task named `mytask` with the location `main:application:mymenu`, execute

>   delsysadm   main:application:mymenu:mytask

Before an entry for a menu can be removed, that menu must be empty (contain no submenus or tasks). If it is not, you must use the `-r` option with `delsysadm`. This option requests that, in addition to the named menu, all submenus and tasks located under that menu be removed. For example, to remove `main:application:mymenu` and all submenus and tasks that reside under it, execute

>   delsysadm   -r   main:application:mymenu

When you use the `-r` option, `delsysadm` checks for dependencies before removing any subentries. (A dependency exists if the menu being removed contains an entry placed there by an application package.) If a dependency is found, you are shown a list of packages that depend on the menu you want to delete and asked whether you want to continue. If you answer yes, the menu and all of its menus and tasks are removed (even those shown to have dependencies). If you answer no, the menu is not deleted.

 Use `delsysadm` to remove only those menu or task entries that you have added to the interface with `edsysadm`.

10 Data Validation Tools

Introduction to the Tools

The data validation tools are a group of shell level commands that serve two purposes:

- standardize the appearance of administration interaction in the SVR4 environment regardless of who writes it
- simplify development of scripts requiring administrator input

Every tool generates a prompt, validates the answer and returns the response. There are no restrictions on when you should use them. It is recommended that you use them every time your application interacts with an administrator. Using the tools at such a time will make all administrator interaction look alike to the user, regardless of the vendor who created the package. You will see, as well, that using these tools makes writing scripts with administrator interaction much simplier, since the tools do the work based on parameters you provide.

At the very least, it is recommended that you use them in your request script (the packaging script from which you can solicit administrator input) and in the executables you deliver when your package administration will be incorporated into the sysadm interface. See "Modifying the sysadm Interface" for details about writing executables for the sysadm interface and "Packaging Application Software" for details on writing a request script.

This chapter introduces you to the data validation tools and discusses their characteristics. For details on a specific tool, look in Appendix B of this guide. The shell commands and corresponding visual tools are provided as Section 1 manual pages.

Types of Tools

There are two types of data validation tools. Both perform the same series of tasks (described later) but are used in different environments. The two types are:

■ Shell Commands

These tools are invoked from the shell level and used in shell scripts.

■ Visual Tools

These tools are invoked from within the field definition in an FMLI form definition. While the shell commands perform all tasks with one command, the visual tools are broken into separate commands for defining help messages, error messages and performing validation.

Characteristics of the Tools

All of the shell commands perform the same series of tasks (the visual tools each perform a subsection of the full series). Those tasks are:

- Prompt a user for input
- Validate the answer
- Format and print a help message when requested
- Format and present an error message when validation fails
- Return the input if it passes validation
- Allow a user to quit the process

The tool itself defines the type of prompt shown and validation performed is defined. For example, the shell command ckyorn prompts for a yes or no answer and accepts only a positive or negative response. Some tools allow you to supply input during execution to help customize the validation. For example, ckrange prompts for and validates an answer within a given range. The upper and lower limits of the range can be defined when executing ckrange.

 NOTE Leading and trailing white space is stripped from the input before validation is performed.

The Data Validation Tool Prompts

Each tool has a default prompt that you can use as is, add to, or overwrite. The manual page for each tool (see Appendix B) shows the default prompt text. You must use the –p option of a shell command before the default can be overwritten.

For example, executing ckyorn without options produces the following output:

```
Yes or No [y,n,?,q]:
```

The next example shows the use of the −p option and the output that is produced.

```
$ ckyorn -p "Do you want the manual page files installed?"
Do you want the manual page files installed? [y,n,?,q]:
```

The Data Validation Tool Help Messages

Each tool has a default help message that you can use as is, add to, or completely overwrite. The manual page for each tool (see Appendix B) shows the default help message text. You must use the −h option of a shell command before the default can be overwritten.

For example, if you executed ckyorn without options and the user requested a help message by entering ? at the prompt, the following message would be seen:

```
To respond in the affirmative, enter y, yes, Y, or YES.
To respond in the negative, enter n, no, N, or NO.
```

The next example shows the use of the −h option when executing ckyorn. The text defined after the −h will be shown if the user requests a help message.

```
ckyorn -h "Answer yes if you want the manual page files \
installed or no if you do not."
```

If you insert a tilde (˜) at the beginning or end of your definition, the default text will be added at that point. For example,

```
ckyorn -h "The manual page files will be written to your \
system, or not, based on your answer.~"
```

will produce the help message:

```
The manual page files will be written to your system, or not,
based on your answer.  To respond in the affirmative, enter y,
yes, Y, or YES.  To respond in the negative, enter n, no, N, \
or NO.
```

The Data Validation Tool Error Messages

Each tool has a default error message that you can use as is, add to, or completely overwrite. The manual page for each tool (see Appendix B) shows the default error message text. You must use the –e option of a shell command before the default can be overwritten.

For example, if you executed ckyorn without options, and validation failed, the following message would be seen:

        ERROR: Please enter yes or no.

The next example shows the use of the –e option when executing ckyorn. The text defined after the –e will be prepended with ERROR: and shown if validation fails.

        ckyorn –e "You did not respond with yes or no."

If you insert a tilde (˜) at the beginning or end of your definition, the default text will be added at that point.

Message Formatting

All three message types (prompt, error, and help) are limited in length to 78 characters and are automatically formatted. Regardless of how you define them in your code, any white space used (including newline) is stripped during formatting.

You can use the –W option of a shell command (or the ckwidth variable of a function) to define the line length to which your messages should be formatted.

The Shell Commands

Figure 10-1 lists the shell commands and what they are used for. All of the shell commands perform the same series of tasks, as described previously. The table's "Purpose" column describes the type of prompt and validation with which the command deals. Details for each command can be found on the respective manual page in Appendix B.

Figure 10-1: The Shell Commands

Command (and Function)	Purpose
ckdate	Prompts for and validates that the answer is a date (can define format for date).
ckgid	Prompts for and validates that the answer is a group id.
ckint	Prompts for and validates an integer value (can define base for input).
ckitem	Builds a menu, prompts for and validates a menu item (can define characteristics of the menu).
ckkeywd	Adds keywords to a prompt and validates that the return answer matches a keyword.
ckpath	Prompts for and validates a pathname (can define what type of validation to perform, such as "pathname must be readable").

Command (and function)	Purpose
ckrange	Prompts for and validates an integer within a range (can define the upper and lower limits of the range).
ckstr	Prompts for and validates that the answer is a string (can define a regular expression, in which case the string must match the expression).
cktime	Prompts for and validates that the answer is a time (can define format for time).
ckuid	Prompts for and validates that the answer is a user id.
ckyorn	Prompts for and validates a yes/no answer. Input must be y, yes, Y, YES, n, no, N, or NO.
dispgid	Displays a list of all valid group names.
dispuid	Displays a list of all valid user names.

The Visual Tools

The visual tools are invoked from within the field definition of an FMLI form. Because of the nature of FMLI form definitions, it is necessary to divide the tasks performed by only one shell command into sets. The purpose of a visual tool set parallels the purpose of a shell command. For example, ckdate performs a group of tasks for a prompt whose response should be a date. The same group of tasks requires three visual tools:

- errdate (formats and presents an error message)
- helpdate (formats and presents a help message)
- valdate (validates the answer to be a date)

The format and description of each visual tool set is shown on the equivalent shell command manual page in Appendix B. For example, the equivalent shell command for the set described above is ckdate. Refer to the manual page ckdate(1) for details on the three visual tools errdate, helpdate, and valdate.

Figure 10-3 lists the visual tool sets and their associated response type.

Figure 10-2: The Visual Tools

Visual Tool Set	Response Type
erryorn, helpyorn, valyorn	yes or no
errint, helpint, valint	integer
errange, helprange, valrange	integer in a range
errstr, helpstr, valstr	string (potentially matching an expression)
errpath, helppath, valpath	pathname
erritem, helpitem	menu item
errgid, helpgid, valgid	existing group
errtime, helptime, valtime	time of day
errdate, helpdate, valdate	date

There are two other visual tools. dispuid displays a list of login ids and dispgid displays a list of group ids. These two tools can be used with the FMLI rmenu keyword to display a list of ids.

The following example shows a field definition written in FMLI using the visual tools:

```
name="Do you want to install the manual page files?"
value=y
choicemsg='helpyorn'
invalidmsg='erryorn -e "~Enter yes to install the manual page files"'
valid='valyorn $F1'
rows=1
columns=1
```

liber, A Library System

To illustrate the use of UNIX system programming tools in the development of an application, we are going to pretend we are engaged in the development of a computer system for a library. The system is known as liber. The early stages of system development, we assume, have already been completed; feasibility studies have been done, the preliminary design is described in the coming paragraphs. We are going to stop short of producing a complete detailed design and module specifications for our system. You will have to accept that these exist. In using portions of the system for examples of the topics covered in this chapter, we will work from these virtual specifications.

We make no claim as to the efficacy of this design. It is the way it is only in order to provide some passably realistic examples of UNIX system programming tools in use. It is not an application, but rather is code fragments only.

liber is a system for keeping track of the books in a library. The hardware consists of a single computer with terminals throughout the library. One terminal is used for adding new books to the data base. Others are used for checking out books and as electronic card catalogs.

The design of the system calls for it to be brought up at the beginning of the day and remain running while the library is in operation. Associated with each terminal is a program specific to the function of that terminal, each running as a separate UNIX process. The system has one master index that contains the unique identifier of each title in the library. When the system is running the index is mapped into the address space of each process. Semaphores are used to synchronize access to the index. In the pages that follow fragments of some of the system's programs are shown to illustrate the way they work together. The startup program performs the system initialization; opening the semaphores and the index file; mapping the index file into memory; and kicking off the other programs. The id numbers for the semaphores (wrtsem, and rdsem) are written to a file during initialization, this file is then read by all the subsidiary programs so that all use the same semaphores.

All the programs share access to the index file. They gain access to it with the following code:

```
/*
 * Gain access to the index file, map it in.
 * After mapping, free the file descriptor so
 * that it will be available for other uses --
 * the mapping will remain until the program
 * exits, or until the mapping is removed either
 * by munmap() or by mapping over top of this one
 * with another call to mmap().  Note the use of
 * the read/write open mode -- all programs but
 * "add-books" should open just for read-only.
 */
if ((index_fd = open("index.file", O_RDWR)) == -1)
{
        (void) fprintf(stderr, "index open failed: %d\n", errno);
        exit(1);
}
/*
 * Establish the mapping.  As with the call to
 * open(), all programs but "add-books" should
 * map with PROT_READ for read-only access.
 */
if ((int)(index = (INDEX *)mmap(0, sizeof (INDEX), PROT_READ|PROT_WRITE,
    MAP_SHARED, index_fd, 0) == -1)
{
        (void) fprintf(stderr, "shmat failed: %d\n", errno);
        exit(1);
}
(void) close(index_fd);
```

The preceding code fragment establishes a mapping to the index file in the address space of the program. Access to the addresses at which the file is mapped affect the file directly, no further file operations are required. For instance, if the access deposits data at the accessed address, then the file will be modified by operation. If the access examines data, then the file will be accessed. In either case, the portion of the file containing the information will be obtained or restored to secondary storage automatically by the system and transparently to the application.

Of the programs shown, add-books is the only one that alters the index. The semaphores are used to ensure that no other programs will try to read the index while add-books is altering it. The checkout program locks the file record for the book, so that each copy being checked out is recorded separately and the book cannot be checked out at two different checkout stations at the same time.

The program fragments do not provide any details on the structure of the index or the book records in the data base.

```
                        /* liber.h - header file for the
                         *           library system.
                         */
typedef ... INDEX;      /* data structure for book file index */
typedef struct {        /* type of records in book file */
        char title[30];
        char author[30];
        .
        .
        .
} BOOK;
int index_fd;
int wrtsem;
int rdsem;
INDEX *index;

int book_file;
BOOK book_buf;

/*      startup program  */

/*
 * 1. Open index file and map it in.
 * 2. Open two semaphores for providing exclusive write access to index.
 * 3. Stash id's for shared memory segment and semaphores in a file
 *    where they can be accessed by the programs.
 * 4. Start programs:  add-books, card-catalog, and checkout running
 *    on the various terminals throughout the library.
 */

#include    <stdio.h>
#include    <sys/types.h>
#include    <sys/ipc.h>
#include    <sys/shm.h>
#include    <sys/sem.h>
#include    "liber.h"

void exit();
extern int errno;

key_t key;
int shmid;
int wrtsem;
```

(continued on next page)

```
int rdsem;
FILE *ipc_file;

main()
{
        .
        .
        .
    /*
     * Open index file and map it.
     */

    /* See previous example */

    /*
     * Get the read/write semaphores.
     */
    if ((wrtsem = semget(key, 1, IPC_CREAT | 0666)) == -1)
    {
        (void) fprintf(stderr, "startup: semget failed: errno=%d\n", errno);
        exit(1);
    }

    if ((rdsem = semget(key, 1, IPC_CREAT | 0666)) == -1)
    {
        (void) fprintf(stderr, "startup: semget failed: errno=%d\n", errno);
        exit(1);
    }
    (void) fprintf(ipc_file, "%d\n%d\n", wrtsem, rdsem);

    /*
     * Start the add-books program running on the terminal in the
     * basement.  Start the checkout and card-catalog programs
     * running on the various other terminals throughout the library.
     */
        .
        .
        .
}

/*    card-catalog program*/

/*
 * 1. Read screen for author and title.
 * 2. Use semaphores to prevent reading index while it is being written.
 * 3. Use index to get position of book record in book file.
```

(continued on next page)

```
 * 4. Print book record on screen or indicate book was not found.
 * 5. Go to 1.
 */

#include        <stdio.h>
#include        <sys/types.h>
#include        <sys/ipc.h>
#include        <sys/sem.h>
#include    <fcntl.h>
#include    "liber.h"

void exit();
extern int errno;
struct sembuf sop[1];

main() {
    .
    .
    .

    while (1)
    {
        /*
         * Read author/title/subject information from screen.
         */

        /*
         * Wait for write semaphore to reach 0 (index not being written).
         */
        sop[0].sem_op = 1;
        if (semop(wrtsem, sop, 1) == -1)
        {
                (void) fprintf(stderr, "semop failed: %d\n", errno);
                exit(1);
        }
        /*
         * Increment read semaphore so potential writer will wait
         * for us to finish reading the index.
         */
        sop[0].sem_op = 0;
        if (semop(rdsem, sop, 1) == -1)
        {
                (void) fprintf(stderr, "semop failed: %d\n", errno);
                exit(1);
        }
```

(continued on next page)

```
                    /* Use index to find file pointer(s) for book(s) */

                    /* Decrement read semaphore */
                    sop[0].sem_op = -1;
                    if (semop(rdsem, sop, 1) == -1)
                    {
                                (void) fprintf(stderr, "semop failed: %d\n", errno);
                                exit(1);
                    }

                    /*
                     * Now we use the file pointers found in the index to
                     * read the book file.  Then we print the information
                     * on the book(s) to the screen.
                     */

                    /*
                     * Note design alternatives for this portion of the
                     * the code: the book file could be accessed by
                     * lseek()s to the portion of the file containing
                     * the record, and then read() could be used to
                     * obtain the file information.  Alternatively, the
                     * entire book file could be mapped into memory, and the
                     * the record accessed directly without further
                     * file operations, or the area of the file containing
                     * the book record could just be mapped and then unmapped
                     * when the access is complete.
                     */
                    .
                    .
                    .

            } /* while */
    }
    /*    checkout program */

    /*
     * 1. Read screen for Dewey Decimal number of book to be checked out.
     * 2. Use semaphores to prevent reading index while it is being written.
     * 3. Use index to get position of book record in book file.
     * 4. If book not found print message on screen, otherwise lock
     *    book record and read.
     * 5. If book already checked out print message on screen, otherwise
     *    mark record "checked out" and write back to book file.
     * 6. Unlock book record.
     * 7. Go to 1.
```

(continued on next page)

```
    */

#include        <stdio.h>
#include        <sys/types.h>
#include        <sys/ipc.h>
#include        <sys/sem.h>
#include     <fcntl.h>
#include     "liber.h"

void exit();
long lseek();
extern int errno;
struct flock flk;
struct sembuf sop[1];
long bookpos;

main()
{
        .
        .
        .
      while (1)
      {
          /*
           * Read Dewey Decimal number from screen.
           */

          /*
           * Wait for write semaphore to reach 0 (index not being written).
           */
          sop[0].sem_flg = 0;
          sop[0].sem_op = 0;
          if (semop(wrtsem, sop, 1) == -1)
          {
                  (void) fprintf(stderr, "semop failed: %d\n", errno);
                  exit(1);
          }
          /*
           * Increment read semaphore so potential writer will wait
           * for us to finish reading the index.
           */
          sop[0].sem_op = 1;
          if (semop(rdsem, sop, 1) == -1)
          {
                  (void) fprintf(stderr, "semop failed: %d\n", errno);
                  exit(1);
```

(continued on next page)

```
        }

        /*
         * Now we can use the index to find the book's record position.
         * Assign this value to "bookpos".
         */

        /* Decrement read semaphore */
        sop[0].sem_op = -1;
        if (semop(rdsem, sop, 1) == -1)
        {
                (void) fprintf(stderr, "semop failed: %d\n", errno);
                exit(1);
        }

        /*
         * Lock the book's record in book file, read the record.
         * Here again we have the design option of deciding to
         * access and update the database through the use of
         * seeks, read()s and write()s; or file mapping can
         * be used to access the file.  File mapping has the
         * disadvantage that it does not interact well with
         * enforcement-mode locking, although semaphores
         * could be used as an alternative synchronization
         * mechanism to file locking.  File mapping would have
         * potential efficiency advantages, eliminating the need
         * for repetitive file access operations and attendant
         * data copying.  For this example, however, we choose
         * not to use mapping to demonstrate the use of other
         * system facilities.
         */
        flk.l_type = F_WRLCK;
        flk.l_whence = 0;
        flk.l_start = bookpos;
        flk.l_len = sizeof(BOOK);
        if (fcntl(book_file, F_SETLKW, &flk) == -1)


        {
                (void) fprintf(stderr, "trouble locking: %d\n", errno);
                exit(1);
        }
        if (lseek(book_file, bookpos, 0) == -1)
        {
                (Error processing for lseek);
        }
        if (read(book_file, &book_buf, sizeof(BOOK)) == -1)
```

(continued on next page)

```
                {
                        (Error processing for read);
                }

                /*
                 * If the book is checked out inform the client, otherwise
                 * mark the book's record as checked out and write it
                 * back into the book file.
                 */

                /* Unlock the book's record in book file. */
                flk.l_type = F_UNLCK;
                if (fcntl(book_file, F_SETLK, &flk) == -1)
                {
                        (void) fprintf(stderr, "trouble unlocking: %d\n", errno);
                        exit(1);
                }
        } /* while */
}

/*      add-books program*/

/*
 * 1. Read a new book entry from screen.
 * 2. Insert book in book file.
 * 3. Use semaphore "wrtsem" to block new readers.
 * 4. Wait for semaphore "rdsem" to reach 0.
 * 5. Insert book into index.
 * 6. Decrement wrtsem.
 * 7. Go to 1.
 */

#include <stdio.h>
#include    <sys/types.h>
#include    <sys/ipc.h>
#include    <sys/sem.h>
#include    "liber.h"

void exit();
extern int errno;
struct sembuf sop[1];
BOOK bookbuf;

main()
{
        .
```

(continued on next page)

```
        .
        .
    for (;;)
    {

        /*
         * Read information on new book from screen.
         */

        addscr(&bookbuf);

        /* write new record at the end of the bookfile.
         * Code not shown, but
         * addscr() returns a 1 if title information has
         * been entered, 0 if not.
         */

        /*
         * Increment write semaphore, blocking new readers from
         * accessing the index.
         */
        sop[0].sem_flg = 0;
        sop[0].sem_op = 1;
        if (semop(wrtsem, sop, 1) == -1)
        {
                (void) fprintf(stderr, "semop failed: %d\n", errno);
                exit(1);
        }

        /*
         * Wait for read semaphore to reach 0 (all readers to finish
         * using the index).
         */
        sop[0].sem_op = 0;
        if (semop(rdsem, sop, 1) == -1)
        {
                (void) fprintf(stderr, "semop failed: %d\n", errno);
                exit(1);
        }
        /*
         * Now that we have exclusive access to the index we
         * insert our new book with its file pointer.
         */

        /* Decrement write semaphore, permitting readers to read index. */
        sop[0].sem_op = -1;
```

(continued on next page)

```
            if (semop(wrtsem, sop, 1) == -1)
            {
                        (void) fprintf(stderr, "semop failed: %d\n", errno);
                        exit(1);
            }
    } /* for */
    .
    .
    .
}
```

The example following, addscr(), illustrates two significant points about curses screens:

1. Information read in from a curses window can be stored in fields that are part of a structure defined in the header file for the application.

2. The address of the structure can be passed from another function where the record is processed.

```
                         /*  addscr is called from add-books.
                          *  The user is prompted for title
                          *  information.
                          */
#include <curses.h>

WINDOW *cmdwin;

addscr(bb)
struct BOOK *bb;
{
      int c;

      initscr();
      nonl();
      noecho();
      cbreak();

      cmdwin = newwin(6, 40, 3, 20);
      mvprintw(0, 0, "This screen is for adding titles to the data base");
      mvprintw(1, 0, "Enter  a  to add;  q  to quit: ");
      refresh();
      for (;;)
      {
            refresh();
            c = getch();
            switch (c) {
              case 'a':
                       werase(cmdwin);
                       box(cmdwin, '|', '-');
                       mvwprintw(cmdwin, 1, 1, "Enter title: ");
                       wmove(cmdwin, 2, 1);
                       echo();
                       wrefresh(cmdwin);
                       wgetstr(cmdwin, bb->title);
                       noecho();
                       werase(cmdwin);
                       box(cmdwin, '|', '-');
                       mvwprintw(cmdwin, 1, 1, "Enter author: ");
                       wmove(cmdwin, 2, 1);
                       echo();
                       wrefresh(cmdwin);
                       wgetstr(cmdwin, bb->author);
                       noecho();
                       werase(cmdwin);
                       wrefresh(cmdwin);
```

(continued on next page)

```
                    endwin();
                    return(1);
            case 'q':
                    erase();
                    endwin();
                    return(0);
            }
     }
}

#
# Makefile for liber library system
#

CC = cc
CFLAGS = -O
all: startup add-books checkout card-catalog

startup: liber.h startup.c
     $(CC) $(CFLAGS) -o startup startup.c

add-books: add-books.o addscr.o
     $(CC) $(CFLAGS) -o add-books add-books.o addscr.o

add-books.o: liber.h

checkout: liber.h checkout.c
     $(CC) $(CFLAGS) -o checkout checkout.c

card-catalog: liber.h card-catalog.c
     $(CC) $(CFLAGS) -o card-catalog card-catalog.c
```

MANUAL PAGES

Manual Pages

The manual pages included in this appendix are unique to the *Programmer's Guide: System Services and Appplication Packaging Tools*. Other manual pages may be applicable as well, but won't be duplicated here; they may be referred to in the appropriate *Reference Manual*.

NAME

ckdate, errdate, helpdate, valdate – prompts for and validates a date

SYNOPSIS

ckdate [–Q] [–W *width*] [–f *format*] [–d *default*] [–h *help*] [–e *error*] [–p *prompt*]
[–k *pid* [–s *signal*]]

errdate [–W] [–e *error*] [–f *format*]
helpdate [–W] [–h *help*] [–f *format*]
valdate [–f *format*] *input*

DESCRIPTION

ckdate prompts a user and validates the response. It defines, among other
things, a prompt message whose response should be a date, text for help and
error messages, and a default value (which will be returned if the user responds
with a carriage return). The user response must match the defined format for a
date.

All messages are limited in length to 70 characters and are formatted automatically. Any white space used in the definition (including newline) is stripped.
The –W option cancels the automatic formatting. When a tilde is placed at the
beginning or end of a message definition, the default text will be inserted at that
point, allowing both custom text and the default text to be displayed.

If the prompt, help or error message is not defined, the default message (as
defined under NOTES) will be displayed.

Three visual tool modules are linked to the ckdate command. They are errdate
(which formats and displays an error message), helpdate (which formats and
displays a help message), and valdate (which validates a response). These
modules should be used in conjunction with FML objects. In this instance, the
FML object defines the prompt. When *format* is defined in the errdate and
helpdate modules, the messages will describe the expected format.

The options and arguments for this command are:

–Q	Specifies that quit will not be allowed as a valid response.
–W *width*	Specifies that prompt, help and error messages will be formatted to a line length of *width*.
–f *format*	Specifies the format against which the input will be verified. Possible formats and their definitions are:

%b = abbreviated month name
%B = full month name
%d = day of month (01 - 31)
%D = date as %m/%d/%y (the default format)
%e = day of month (1 - 31; single digits are preceded by a blank)
%h = abbreviated month name (jan, feb, mar)
%m = month number (01 - 12)
%y = year within century (e.g. 89)
%Y = year as CCYY (e.g. 1989)

−d *default*	Defines the default value as *default*. The default does not have to meet the format criteria.
−h *help*	Defines the help messages as *help*.
−e *error*	Defines the error message as *error*.
−p *prompt*	Defines the prompt message as *prompt*.
−k *pid*	Specifies that process ID *pid* is to be sent a signal if the user chooses to abort.
−s *signal*	Specifies that the process ID *pid* defined with the −k option is to be sent signal `signal` when quit is chosen. If no signal is specified, `SIGTERM` is used.
input	Input to be verified against format criteria.

EXIT CODES

0 = Successful execution
1 = EOF on input
2 = Usage error
3 = User termination (quit)
4 = Garbled format argument

NOTES

The default prompt for ckdate is:

    Enter the date [?,q]:

The default error message is:

    ERROR - Please enter a date, using the following format: *<for-
    mat>*.

The default help message is:

    Please enter a date, using the following format: *<format>*.

When the quit option is chosen (and allowed), q is returned along with the return
code 3. The `valdate` module will not produce any output. It returns zero for
success and non-zero for failure.

NAME

ckgid, errgid, helpgid, valgid – prompts for and validates a group id

SYNOPSIS

ckgid [-Q] [-W *width*] [-m] [-d *default*] [-h *help*] [-e *error*] [-p *prompt*]
[-k *pid* [-s *signal*]]

errgid [-W] [-e *error*]
helpgid [-W] [-m] [-h *help*]
valgid *input*

DESCRIPTION

ckgid prompts a user and validates the response. It defines, among other things,
a prompt message whose response should be an existing group ID, text for help
and error messages, and a default value (which will be returned if the user
responds with a carriage return).

All messages are limited in length to 70 characters and are formatted automatically. Any white space used in the definition (including newline) is stripped.
The -W option cancels the automatic formatting. When a tilde is placed at the
beginning or end of a message definition, the default text will be inserted at that
point, allowing both custom text and the default text to be displayed.

If the prompt, help or error message is not defined, the default message (as
defined under NOTES) will be displayed.

Three visual tool modules are linked to the ckgid command. They are errgid
(which formats and displays an error message), helpgid (which formats and
displays a help message), and valgid (which validates a response). These
modules should be used in conjunction with FML objects. In this instance, the
FML object defines the prompt.

The options and arguments for this command are:

-Q	Specifies that quit will not be allowed as a valid response.
-W *width*	Specifies that prompt, help and error messages will be formatted to a line length of *width*.
-m	Displays a list of all groups when help is requested or when the user makes an error.
-d *default*	Defines the default value as *default*. The default is not validated and so does not have to meet any criteria.
-h *help*	Defines the help messages as *help*.
-e *error*	Defines the error message as *error*.
-p *prompt*	Defines the prompt message as *prompt*.
-k *pid*	Specifies that process ID *pid* is to be sent a signal if the user chooses to abort.
-s *signal*	Specifies that the process ID *pid* defined with the -k option is to be sent signal **signal** when quit is chosen. If no signal is specified, SIGTERM is used.
input	Input to be verified against /etc/group

EXIT CODES

    0 = Successful execution
    1 = EOF on input
    2 = Usage error
    3 = User termination (quit)

NOTES

The default prompt for ckgid is:

```
Enter the name of an existing group [?,q]:
```

The default error message is:

```
ERROR - Please enter the name of an existing group.
```
(if the −m option of ckgid *is used, a list of valid groups is displayed here)*

The default help message is:

```
Please enter an existing group name.
```
(if the −m option of ckgid *is used, a list of valid groups is displayed here)*

When the quit option is chosen (and allowed), q is returned along with the return code 3. The valgid module will not produce any output. It returns zero for success and non-zero for failure.

NAME

ckint – display a prompt; verify and return an integer value

SYNOPSIS

ckint [–Q] [–W width] [–b base] [–d default] [–h help] [–e error] [–p prompt]
[–k pid [–s signal]]

errint [–W] [–b base] [–e error]
helpint [–W] [–b base] [–h help]
valint [–b base] input

DESCRIPTION

ckint prompts a user, then validates the response. It defines, among other things, a prompt message whose response should be an integer, text for help and error messages, and a default value (which will be returned if the user responds with a carriage return).

All messages are limited in length to 70 characters and are formatted automatically. Any white space used in the definition (including newline) is stripped. The –W option cancels the automatic formatting. When a tilde is placed at the beginning or end of a message definition, the default text will be inserted at that point, allowing both custom text and the default text to be displayed.

If the prompt, help or error message is not defined, the default message (as defined under NOTES) will be displayed.

Three visual tool modules are linked to the ckint command. They are errint (which formats and displays an error message), helpint (which formats and displays a help message), and valint (which validates a response). These modules should be used in conjunction with FML objects. In this instance, the FML object defines the prompt. When base is defined in the errint and helpint modules, the messages will include the expected base of the input.

The options and arguments for this command are:

–Q   Specifies that quit will not be allowed as a valid response.

–W   Specifies that prompt, help and error messages will be formatted to a line length of width.

–b   Defines the base for input. Must be 2 to 36, default is 10.

–d   Defines the default value as default. The default is not validated and so does not have to meet any criteria.

–h   Defines the help messages as help.

–e   Defines the error message as error.

–p   Defines the prompt message as prompt.

–k   Specifies that process ID pid is to be sent a signal if the user chooses to abort.

–s   Specifies that the process ID pid defined with the –k option is to be sent signal signal when quit is chosen. If no signal is specified, SIGTERM is used.

input   Input to be verified against *base* criterion.

EXIT CODES
0 = Successful execution
1 = EOF on input
2 = Usage error
3 = User termination (quit)

NOTES
The default base 10 prompt for `ckint` is:

    Enter an integer [?,q]:

The default base 10 error message is:

    ERROR - Please enter an integer.

The default base 10 help message is:

    Please enter an integer.

The messages are changed from "integer" to "base *base* integer" if the base is set to a number other than 10.

When the quit option is chosen (and allowed), q is returned along with the return code **3**. The `valint` module will not produce any output. It returns zero for success and non-zero for failure.

NAME

ckitem – build a menu; prompt for and return a menu item

SYNOPSIS

ckitem [–Q] [–W *width*] [–uno] [–f *file*] [–1 *label*] [[–i *invis*] [, ...]] [–m *max*]
[–d *default*] [–h *help*] [–e *error*] [–p *prompt*] [–k *pid* [–s *signal*]] [*choice* [...]]

erritem [–W] [–e *error*] [*choice* [...]]
helpint [–W] [–h *help*] [*choice* [...]]

DESCRIPTION

ckitem builds a menu and prompts the user to choose one item from a menu of
items. It then verifies the response. Options for this command define, among
other things, a prompt message whose response will be a menu item, text for
help and error messages, and a default value (which will be returned if the user
responds with a carriage return).

By default, the menu is formatted so that each item is prepended by a number
and is printed in columns across the terminal. Column length is determined by
the longest choice. Items are alphabetized.

All messages are limited in length to 70 characters and are formatted automatically. Any white space used in the definition (including newline) is stripped.
The –W option cancels the automatic formatting. When a tilde is placed at the
beginning or end of a message definition, the default text will be inserted at that
point, allowing both custom text and the default text to be displayed.

If the prompt, help or error message is not defined, the default message (as
defined under NOTES) will be displayed.

Two visual tool modules are linked to the ckitem command. They are erritem
(which formats and displays an error message) and helpitem (which formats and
displays a help message). These modules should be used in conjunction with
FML objects. In this instance, the FML object defines the prompt. When *choice* is
defined in these modules, the messages will describe the available menu choice
(or choices).

The options and arguments for this command are:

–Q   Specifies that quit will not be allowed as a valid response.

–W   Specifies that prompt, help and error messages will be formatted to a line
          length of *width*.

–u   Specifies that menu items should be displayed as an unnumbered list.

–n   Specifies that menu items should not be displayed in alphabetical order.

–o   Specifies that only one menu token will be returned.

–f   Defines a file, *file*. which contains a list of menu items to be displayed.
          [The format of this file is: token<tab>description. Lines beginning
          with a pound sign (#) are designated as comments and ignored.]

–1   Defines a label, *label*, to print above the menu.

-i   Defines invisible menu choices (those which will not be printed in the menu). (For example, "all" used as an invisible choice would mean it is a legal option but does not appear in the menu. Any number of invisible choices may be defined.) Invisible choices should be made known to a user either in the prompt or in a help message.

-m   Defines the maximum number of menu choices allowed.

-d   Defines the default value as *default*. The default is not validated and so does not have to meet any criteria.

-h   Defines the help messages as *help*.

-e   Defines the error message as *error*.

-p   Defines the prompt message as *prompt*.

-k   Specifies that the process ID *pid* is to be sent a signal if the user chooses to abort.

-s   Specifies that process ID *pid* defined with the **-k** option is to be sent signal **signal** when quit is chosen. If no signal is specified, SIGTERM is used.

choice   Defines menu items. Items should be separated by white space or newline.

SEE ALSO

allocmenu(3X)
printmenu(3X)
setinvis(3X)
setitems(3X)

EXIT CODES

0 = Successful execution
1 = EOF on input
2 = Usage error
3 = User termination (quit)
4 = No choices from which to choose

NOTES

The user may input the number of the menu item if choices are numbered or as much of the string required for a unique identification of the item. Long menus are paged with 10 items per page.

When menu entries are defined both in a file (by using the -f option) and also on the command line, they are usually combined alphabetically. However, if the -n option is used to suppress alphabetical ordering, then the entries defined in the file are shown first, followed by the options defined on the command line.

The default prompt for ckitem is:

Enter selection [?,??,q]:

One question mark will give a help message and then redisplay the prompt. Two question marks will give a help message and then redisplay the menu label, the menu and the prompt.

The default error message is:

```
ERROR - Does not match an available menu selection.
Enter one of the following:
- the number of the menu item you wish to select
- the token associated withe the menu item,
- partial string which uniquely identifies the token for the
menu item
- ?? to reprint the menu
```

The default help message is:

```
Enter one of the following:
- the number of the menu item you wish to select
- the token associated with the menu item,
- partial string which uniquely identifies the token for the
menu item
- ?? to reprint the menu
```

When the quit option is chosen (and allowed), q is returned along with the return code 3.

NAME

ckkeywd – prompts for and validates a keyword

SYNOPSIS

ckkeywd [-Q] [-W *width*] [-d *default*] [-h *help*] [-e *error*] [-p *prompt*]
[-k *pid* [-s *signal*]] [*keyword* [...]]

DESCRIPTION

ckkeywd prompts a user and validates the response. It defines, among other
things, a prompt message whose response should be one of a list of keywords,
text for help and error messages, and a default value (which will be returned if
the user responds with a carriage return). The answer returned from this command must match one of the defined list of keywords.

All messages are limited in length to 70 characters and are formatted automatically. Any white space used in the definition (including newline) is stripped.
The -W option cancels the automatic formatting. When a tilde is placed at the
beginning or end of a message definition, the default text will be inserted at that
point, allowing both custom text and the default text to be displayed.

If the prompt, help or error message is not defined, the default message (as
defined under NOTES) will be displayed.

-Q   Specifies that quit will not be allowed as a valid response.

-W   Specifies that prompt, help and error messages will be formatted to a line
     length of *width*.

-d   Defines the default value as *default*. The default is not validated and so
     does not have to meet any criteria.

-h   Defines the help messages as *help*.

-e   Defines the error message as *error*.

-p   Defines the prompt message as *prompt*.

-k   Specifies that process ID *pid* is to be sent a signal if the user chooses to
     abort.

-s   Specifies that the process ID *pid* defined with the -k option is to be sent
     signal `signal` when quit is chosen. If no signal is specified, SIGTERM is
     used.

keyword
     Defines the keyword, or list of keywords, against which the answer will
     be verified.

EXIT CODES

0 = Successful execution
1 = EOF on input
2 = Usage error
3 = User termination (quit)
4 = No keywords from which to choose

NOTES

The default prompt for **ckkeywd** is:

```
Enter selection [keyword,[...],?,q]:
```

The default error message is:

```
ERROR - Does not match any of the valid selections.
Please enter one of the following keywords:
keyword[,...]
```

The default help message is:

```
Please enter one of the following keywords:
keyword[,...]
```

When the quit option is chosen (and allowed), q is returned along with the return code 3.

NAME

ckpath – display a prompt; verify and return a pathname

SYNOPSIS

ckpath [–Q] [–W *width*] [–a | l] [–b | c | g | y] [–n | [o | z]] [–rtwx] [–d *default*]
[–h *help*] [–e *error*] [–p *prompt*] [–k *pid* [–s *signal*]]

errpath [–W] [–a | l] [–b | c | g | y] [–n | [o | z]] [–rtwx] [–e *error*]
helppath [–W] [–a | l] [–b | c | g | y] [–n | [o | z]] [–rtwx] [–h *help*]
valpath [–a | l] [–b | c | g | y] [–n | [o | z]] [–rtwx] *input*

DESCRIPTION

ckpath prompts a user and validates the response. It defines, among other
things, a prompt message whose response should be a pathname, text for help
and error messages, and a default value (which will be returned if the user
responds with a carriage return).

The pathname must obey the criteria specified by the first group of options. If no
criteria is defined, the pathname must be for a normal file that does not yet exist.
If neither –a (absolute) or –l (relative) is given, then either is assumed to be
valid.

All messages are limited in length to 70 characters and are formatted automatically. Any white space used in the definition (including newline) is stripped.
The –W option cancels the automatic formatting. When a tilde is placed at the
beginning or end of a message definition, the default text will be inserted at that
point, allowing both custom text and the default text to be displayed.

If the prompt, help or error message is not defined, the default message (as
defined under NOTES) will be displayed.

Three visual tool modules are linked to the ckpath command. They are errpath
(which formats and displays an error message), helppath (which formats and
displays a help message), and valpath (which validates a response). These
modules should be used in conjunction with FACE objects. In this instance, the
FACE object defines the prompt.

The options and arguments for this command are:

–Q   Specifies that quit will not be allowed as a valid response.

–W   Specifies that prompt, help and error messages will be formatted to a line
        length of *width*.

–a   Pathname must be an absolute path.

–l   Pathname must be a relative path.

–b   Pathname must be a block special file.

–c   Pathname must be a character special file.

–g   Pathname must be a regular file.

–y   Pathname must be a directory.

-n   Pathname must not exist (must be new).

-o   Pathname must exist (must be old).

-z   Pathname must have a length greater than 0 bytes.

-r   Pathname must be readable.

-t   Pathname must be creatable (touchable). Pathname will be created if it does not already exist.

-w   Pathname must be writable.

-x   Pathname must be executable.

-d   Defines the default value as *default*. The default is not validated and so does not have to meet any criteria.

-h   Defines the help messages as *help*.

-e   Defines the error message as *error*.

-p   Defines the prompt message as *prompt*.

-k   Specifies that process ID *pid* is to be sent a signal if the user chooses to abort.

-s   Specifies that the process ID *pid* defined with the -k option is to be sent signal `signal` when quit is chosen. If no signal is specified, SIGTERM is used.

input   Input to be verified against validation options.

EXIT CODES

    0 = Successful execution
    1 = EOF on input
    2 = Usage error
    3 = User termination (quit)
    4 = Mutually exclusive options

NOTES

The text of the default messages for ckpath depends upon the criteria options that have been used. An example default prompt for ckpath (using the -a option) is:

```
Enter a pathname [?,q]:
```

An example default error message (using the -a option) is:

```
ERROR - Invalid pathname entered. A pathname is a filename,
optionally preceded by parent directories.
```

An example default help message is:

```
A pathname is a filename, optionally preceded by parent direc-
tories. The pathname you enter:
- must contain 1 to {NAME_MAX} characters
- must not contain a spaces or special characters
```

NAME_MAX is a system variable that is defined in `limits.h`.

When the quit option is chosen (and allowed), `q` is returned along with the return code 3. The **valpath** module will not produce any output. It returns zero for success and non-zero for failure.

NAME

ckrange – prompts for and validates an integer

SYNOPSIS

ckrange [-Q] [-W *width*] [-l *lower*] [-u *upper*] [-b *base*] [-d *default*] [-h *help*]
[-e *error*] [-p *prompt*] [-k *pid* [-s *signal*]]

errange [-W] [-l *lower*] [-u *upper*] [-e *error*]
helprange [-W] [-l *lower*] [-u *upper*] [-h *help*]
valrange [-l *lower*] [-u *upper*] [-b *base*] *input*

DESCRIPTION

ckrange prompts a user and validates the response. It defines, among other
things, a prompt message whose response should be an integer in the range
specified, text for help and error messages, and a default value (which will be
returned if the user responds with a carriage return).

This command also defines a range for valid input. If either the lower or upper
limit is left undefined, then the range is bounded on only one end.

All messages are limited in length to 70 characters and are formatted automatically. Any white space used in the definition (including newline) is stripped.
The -W option cancels the automatic formatting. When a tilde is placed at the
beginning or end of a message definition, the default text will be inserted at that
point, allowing both custom text and the default text to be displayed.

If the prompt, help or error message is not defined, the default message (as
defined under NOTES) will be displayed.

Three visual tool modules are linked to the ckrange command. They are
errange (which formats and displays an error message), helprange (which formats and displays a help message), and valrange (which validates a response).
These modules should be used in conjunction with FACE objects. In this
instance, the FACE object defines the prompt.

The options and arguments for this command are:

-Q   Specifies that quit will not be allowed as a valid response.

-W   Specifies that prompt, help and error messages will be formatted to a line
          length of *width*.

-l   Defines the lower limit of the range as *lower*. Default is the machine's
          largest negative integer or long.

-u   Defines the upper limit of the range as *upper*. Default is the machine's
          largest positive integer or long.

-b   Defines the base for input. Must be 2 to 36, default is 10.

-d   Defines the default value as *default*. The default is not validated and so
          does not have to meet any criteria.

-h   Defines the help messages as *help*.

-e   Defines the error message as *error*.

-p   Defines the prompt message as *prompt*.

-k   Specifies that process ID *pid* is to be sent a signal if the user chooses to abort.

-s   Specifies that the process ID *pid* defined with the -k option is to be sent signal `signal` when quit is chosen. If no signal is specified, `SIGTERM` is used.

input Input to be verified against upper and lower limits and base.

EXIT CODES

    0 = Successful execution
    1 = EOF on input
    2 = Usage error
    3 = User termination (quit)

NOTES

The default base 10 prompt for `ckrange` is:

`Enter an integer between` *lower_bound* `and` *upper_bound* [q,?]:

The default base 10 error message is:

`ERROR` – `Please enter an integer between` *lower_bound* `and` *upper_bound*.

The default base 10 help message is:

`Please enter an integer between` *lower_bound* `and` *upper_bound*.

The messages are changed from "integer" to "base *base* integer" if the base is set to a number other than 10.

When the quit option is chosen (and allowed), q is returned along with the return code 3. The `valrange` module will not produce any output. It returns zero for success and non-zero for failure.

NAME
ckstr – display a prompt; verify and return a string answer

SYNOPSIS
ckstr [–Q] [–W *width*] [[–r *regexp*] [...]] [–l *length*] [–d *default*] [–h *help*] [–e *error*]
[–p *prompt*] [–k *pid* [–s *signal*]]

errstr [–W] [–e *error*]
helpstr [–W] [–h *help*]
valstr *input*

DESCRIPTION
ckstr prompts a user and validates the response. It defines, among other things, a prompt message whose response should be a string, text for help and error messages, and a default value (which will be returned if the user responds with a carriage return).

The answer returned from this command must match the defined regular expression and be no longer than the length specified. If no regular expression is given, valid input must be a string with a length less than or equal to the length defined with no internal, leading or trailing white space. If no length is defined, the length is not checked. Either a regular expression or a length must be given with the command.

All messages are limited in length to 70 characters and are formatted automatically. Any white space used in the definition (including newline) is stripped. The –W option cancels the automatic formatting. When a tilde is placed at the beginning or end of a message definition, the default text will be inserted at that point, allowing both custom text and the default text to be displayed.

If the prompt, help or error message is not defined, the default message (as defined under NOTES) will be displayed.

Three visual tool modules are linked to the ckstr command. They are errstr (which formats and displays an error message), helpstr (which formats and displays a help message), and valstr (which validates a response). These modules should be used in conjunction with FACE objects. In this instance, the FACE object defines the prompt.

The options and arguments for this command are:

–Q   Specifies that quit will not be allowed as a valid response.

–W   Specifies that prompt, help and error messages will be formatted to a line length of *width*.

–r   Specifies a regular expression, regexp, against which the input should be validated. May include white space. If multiple expressions are defined, the answer must match only one of them.

–l   Specifies the maximum length of the input.

–d   Defines the default value as *default*. The default is not validated and so does not have to meet any criteria.

       −h   Defines the help messages as *help*.

       −e   Defines the error message as *error*.

       −p   Defines the prompt message as *prompt*.

       −k   Specifies that process ID *pid* is to be sent a signal if the user chooses to abort.

       −s   Specifies that the process ID *pid* defined with the **−k** option is to be sent signal **signal** when quit is chosen. If no signal is specified, **SIGTERM** is used.

      input   Input to be verified against format length and/or regular expression criteria.

EXIT CODES

    0 = Successful execution
    1 = EOF on input
    2 = Usage error
    3 = User termination (quit)

NOTES

    The default prompt for **ckstr** is:

        `Enter an appropriate value [?,q]:`

    The default error message is dependent upon the type of validation involved. The user will be told either that the length or the pattern matching failed.

    The default help message is also dependent upon the type of validation involved. If a regular expression has been defined, the message is:

        `Please enter a string which matches the following pattern:`
        `regexp`

    Other messages define the length requirement and the definition of a string.

    When the quit option is chosen (and allowed), **q** is returned along with the return code **3**. The **valstr** module will not produce any output. It returns zero for success and non-zero for failure.

NAME

　　　cktime – display a prompt; verify and return a time of day

SYNOPSIS

　　　cktime [–Q] [–W *width*] [–f *format*] [–d *default*] [–h *help*] [–e *error*] [–p *prompt*]
　　　[–k *pid* [–s *signal*]]

　　　errtime [–W] [–e *error*] [–f *format*]
　　　helptime [–W] [–h *help*] [–f *format*]
　　　valtime [–f *format*] *input*

DESCRIPTION

　　　cktime prompts a user and validates the response. It defines, among other
　　　things, a prompt message whose response should be a time, text for help and
　　　error messages, and a default value (which will be returned if the user responds
　　　with a carriage return). The user response must match the defined format for the
　　　time of day.

　　　All messages are limited in length to 70 characters and are formatted automati-
　　　cally. Any white space used in the definition (including newline) is stripped.
　　　The –W option cancels the automatic formatting. When a tilde is placed at the
　　　beginning or end of a message definition, the default text will be inserted at that
　　　point, allowing both custom text and the default text to be displayed.

　　　If the prompt, help or error message is not defined, the default message (as
　　　defined under NOTES) will be displayed.

　　　Three visual tool modules are linked to the cktime command. They are errtime
　　　(which formats and displays an error message), helptime (which formats and
　　　displays a help message), and valtime (which validates a response). These
　　　modules should be used in conjunction with FML objects. In this instance, the
　　　FML object defines the prompt. When *format* is defined in the errtime and
　　　helptime modules, the messages will describe the expected format.

　　　The options and arguments for this command are:

　　　–Q　　　Specifies that quit will not be allowed as a valid response.

　　　–W　　　Specifies that prompt, help and error messages will be formatted to a line
　　　　　　　length of *width*.

　　　–f　　　Specifies the format against which the input will be verified. Possible for-
　　　　　　　mats and their definitions are:

　　　　　　　%H　=　hour (00 - 23)
　　　　　　　%I　=　hour (00 - 12)
　　　　　　　%M　=　minute (00 - 59)
　　　　　　　%p　=　ante meridian or post meridian
　　　　　　　%r　=　time as %I:%M:%S %p
　　　　　　　%R　=　time as %H:%M (the default format)
　　　　　　　%S　=　seconds (00 - 59)
　　　　　　　%T　=　time as %H:%M:%S

-d   Defines the default value as *default*. The default is not validated and so does not have to meet any criteria.

-h   Defines the help messages as *help*.

-e   Defines the error message as *error*.

-p   Defines the prompt message as *prompt*.

-k   Specifies that process ID *pid* is to be sent a signal if the user chooses to abort.

-s   Specifies that the process ID *pid* defined with the -k option is to be sent signal `signal` when quit is chosen. If no signal is specified, `SIGTERM` is used.

input   Input to be verified against format criteria.

EXIT CODES

    0 = Successful execution
    1 = EOF on input
    2 = Usage error
    3 = User termination (quit)
    4 = Garbled format argument

NOTES

The default prompt for `cktime` is:

```
Enter the time of day [?,q]:
```

The default error message is:

```
ERROR - Please enter the time of day, using the following for-
mat:
<format>
```

The default help message is:

```
Please enter the time of day, using the following format:
<format>
```

When the quit option is chosen (and allowed), q is returned along with the return code 3. The `valtime` module will not produce any output. It returns zero for success and non-zero for failure.

NAME

ckuid – prompts for and validates a user ID

SYNOPSIS

ckuid [–Q] [–W *width*] [–m] [–d *default*] [–h *help*] [–e *error*] [–p *prompt*]
[–k *pid* [–s *signal*]]

erruid [–W] [–e *error*]
helpuid [–W] [–m] [–h *help*]
valuid *input*

DESCRIPTION

ckuid prompts a user and validates the response. It defines, among other things,
a prompt message whose response should be an existing user ID, text for help
and error messages, and a default value (which will be returned if the user
responds with a carriage return).

All messages are limited in length to 70 characters and are formatted automatically. Any white space used in the definition (including newline) is stripped.
The –W option cancels the automatic formatting. When a tilde is placed at the
beginning or end of a message definition, the default text will be inserted at that
point, allowing both custom text and the default text to be displayed.

If the prompt, help or error message is not defined, the default message (as
defined under NOTES) will be displayed.

Three visual tool modules are linked to the ckuid command. They are erruid
(which formats and displays an error message), helpuid (which formats and
displays a help message), and valuid (which validates a response). These
modules should be used in conjunction with FML objects. In this instance, the
FML object defines the prompt.

The options and arguments for this command are:

–Q   Specifies that quit will not be allowed as a valid response.

–W   Specifies that prompt, help and error messages will be formatted to a line
            length of *width*.

–m   Displays a list of all logins when help is requested or when the user
            makes an error.

–d   Defines the default value as *default*. The default is not validated and so
            does not have to meet any criteria.

–h   Defines the help messages as *help*.

–e   Defines the error message as *error*.

–p   Defines the prompt message as *prompt*.

–k   Specifies that process ID *pid* is to be sent a signal if the user chooses to
            abort.

–s   Specifies that the process ID *pid* defined with the –k option is to be sent
            signal signal when quit is chosen. If no signal is specified, SIGTERM is
            used.

    input   Input to be verified against **/etc/passwd.**

EXIT CODES

    0 = Successful execution
    1 = EOF on input
    2 = Usage error
    3 = User termination (quit)

NOTES

The default prompt for ckuid is:

```
Enter the login name of an existing user [?,q]:
```

The default error message is:

```
ERROR - Please enter the login name of an existing user.
Select the help option (?) for a list of valid login names.
```
(Last line appears only if the —m option of ckuid *is used)*

The default help message is:

```
Please enter the login name of an existing user.
```
(If the —m option of ckuid *is used, a list of valid groups is also displayed.)*

When the quit option is chosen (and allowed), q is returned along with the return code 3. The valuid module will not produce any output. It returns zero for success and non-zero for failure.

NAME

ckyorn – prompts for and validates yes/no

SYNOPSIS

ckyorn [–Q] [–W *width*] [–d *default*] [–h *help*] [–e *error*] [–p *prompt*]
[–k *pid* [–s *signal*]]

erryorn [–W] [–e *error*]
helpyorn [–W] [–h *help*]
valyorn *input*

DESCRIPTION

ckyorn prompts a user and validates the response. It defines, among other things, a prompt message for a yes or no answer, text for help and error messages, and a default value (which will be returned if the user responds with a carriage return).

All messages are limited in length to 70 characters and are formatted automatically. Any white space used in the definition (including newline) is stripped. The –W option cancels the automatic formatting. When a tilde is placed at the beginning or end of a message definition, the default text will be inserted at that point, allowing both custom text and the default text to be displayed.

If the prompt, help or error message is not defined, the default message (as defined under NOTES) will be displayed.

Three visual tool modules are linked to the ckyorn command. They are erryorn (which formats and displays an error message), helpyorn (which formats and displays a help message), and valyorn (which validates a response). These modules should be used in conjunction with FACE objects. In this instance, the FACE object defines the prompt.

The options and arguments for this command are:

–Q Specifies that quit will not be allowed as a valid response.

–W Specifies that prompt, help and error messages will be formatted to a line length of *width*.

–d Defines the default value as *default*. The default is not validated and so does not have to meet any criteria.

–h Defines the help messages as *help*.

–e Defines the error message as *error*.

–p Defines the prompt message as *prompt*.

–k Specifies that process ID *pid* is to be sent a signal if the user chooses to abort.

–s Specifies that the process ID *pid* defined with the –k option is to be sent signal signal when quit is chosen. If no signal is specified, SIGTERM is used.

input Input to be verified as y, **yes**, Y, Yes, YES or n, no, N, No, NO.

EXIT CODES
>   0 = Successful execution
>   1 = EOF on input
>   2 = Usage error
>   3 = User termination (quit)

NOTES
>   The default prompt for ckyorn is:
>
>   `Yes or No [y,n,?,q]:`
>
>   The default error message is:
>
>   `ERROR - Please enter yes or no.`
>
>   The default help message is:
>
>   `To respond in the affirmative, enter y, yes, Y, or YES.`
>   `To respond in the negative, enter n, no, N, or NO.`
>
>   When the quit option is chosen (and allowed), q is returned along with the return code 3. The `valyorn` module will not produce any output. It returns zero for success and non-zero for failure.

NAME

dispgid – displays a list of all valid group names

SYNOPSIS

dispgid

DESCRIPTION

dispgid displays a list of all group names on the system (one group per line).

EXIT CODES

0 = Successful execution
1 = Cannot read the group file

NAME

       `dispuid` – displays a list of all valid user names

SYNOPSIS

       `dispuid`

DESCRIPTION

       `dispuid` displays a list of all user names on the system (one line per name).

EXIT CODES

       0 = Successful execution

       1 = Cannot read the password file

NAME

pkginfo – display software package information

SYNOPSIS

pkginfo [–q|x|l] [–p|i] [–a *arch*] [–v *version*]
[–c *category1*, [*category2*[, ...]]] [*pkginst*[,*pkginst*[, ...]]]

pkginfo [–d *device* [–q|x|l] [–a *arch*] [–v *version*]
[–c *category1*, [*category2*[, ...]]] [*pkginst*[,*pkginst*[, ...]]]

DESCRIPTION

pkginfo displays information about software packages which are installed on the
system (with the first synopsis) or which reside on a particular device or directory (with the second synopsis). Only the package name and abbreviation for
pre-SVR4 packages will be included in the display.

The options for this command are:

–q   Does not list any information, but can be used from a program to
check (*i.e.*, query) whether or not a package has been installed.

–x   Designates an extracted listing of package information. It contains the
package abbreviation, package name, package architecture (if available)
and package version (if available).

–l   Designates long format, which includes all available information about
the designated package(s).

–p   Designates that information should be presented only for partially
installed packages.

–i   Designates that information should be presented only for fully
installed packages.

–a   Specifies the architecture of the package as *arch*.

–v   Specifies the version of the package as *version*. "All compatible versions" can be requested by preceding the version name with a tilde (˜).
Multiple white space is replaced with a single space during version
comparison.

–c   Selects packages to be display based on the category *category*.
(Categories are defined in the category field of the pkginfo file.) If
more than one category is supplied, the package must only match one
of the list of categories. The match is not case specific.

pkginst   Designates a package by its instance. An instance can be the package
abbreviation or a specific instance (for example, inst.1 or
inst.beta). All instances of package can be requested by inst.*.

–d   Defines a device, *device*, on which the software resides. *device* can be a
directory pathname or the identifiers for tape, floppy disk, removable
disk, *etc.* The special token "spool" may be used to indicate the
default installation spool directory.

NOTES

Without options, `pkginfo` lists the primary category, package instance, and name of all completely installed and partially installed packages. One line per package selected is produced.

The −p and −i options are meaningless if used in conjunction with the −d option.

The options −q, −x, and −l are mutually exclusive.

`pkginfo` cannot tell if a pre-SVR4 package is only partially installed. It is assumed that all pre-SVR4 packages are fully installed.

SEE ALSO

pkgadd(1M), pkgask(1M), pkgchk(1M), pkgrm(1M), pkgtrans(1).

NAME

pkgmk – produce an installable package

SYNOPSIS

pkgmk [–o] [–d *device*] [–r *rootpath*] [–b *basdir*] [–l *limit*] [–a *arch*]
        [–v *version*] [–p *pstamp*] [–f *prototype*] [*variable=value* . . .] [*pkginst*]

DESCRIPTION

pkgmk produces an installable package to be used as input to the pkgadd command. The package contents will be in directory structure format.

The command uses the package prototype file as input and creates a pkgmap file. The contents for each entry in the prototype file is copied to the appropriate output location. Information concerning the contents (checksum, file size, modification date) is computed and stored in the pkgmap file, along with attribute information specified in the prototype file.

–o	Overwrites the same instance, package instance will be overwritten if it already exists.
–d	Creates the package on *device*. *device* can be a directory pathname or the identifiers for a floppy disk or removable disk (for example, /dev/diskette). The default device is the installation spool directory.
–r	Ignores destination paths in the prototype file. Instead, uses the indicated *rootpath* with the source pathname appended to locate objects on the source machine.
–b	Prepends the indicated *basedir* to locate relocatable objects on the source machine.
–l	Specifies the maximum size in 512 byte blocks of the output device as *limit*. By default, if the output file is a directory or a mountable device, pkgmk will employ the df command to dynamically calculate the amount of available space on the output device. Useful in conjunction with pkgtrans to create package with datastream format.
–a	Overrides the architecture information provided in the pkginfo file with *arch*.
–v	Overrides version information provided in the pkginfo file with *version*.
–p	Overrides the production stamp definition in the pkginfo file with *pstamp*.
–f	Uses the file prototype as input to the command. The default prototype filename is [Pp]rototype.
variable=value	Places the indicated variable in the packaging environment. [See prototype(4) for definitions of packaging variables.]
pkginst	Specifies the package by its instance. An instance can be the package abbreviation or a specific instance (for example, inst.1).

NOTES

Architecture information is provided on the command line with the −a option or in the prototype file. If no architecture information is supplied at all, the output of uname −m will be used.

Version information is provided on the command line with the −v option or in the prototype file. If no version information is supplied, a default based on the current date will be provided.

Command line definitions for both architecture and version override the prototype definitions.

SEE ALSO

pkgparam(1), pkgproto(1), pkgtrans(1).

NAME

pkgparam – displays package parameter values

SYNOPSIS

pkgparam [–v][–d *device*] *pkginst* [*param*[...]]

pkgparam –f *file* [–v] [*param*[...]]

DESCRIPTION

pkgparam displays the value associated with the parameter or parameters requested on the command line. The values are located in either the pkginfo file for *pkginst* or from the specific file named with the –f option.

One parameter value is shown per line. Only the value of a parameter is given unless the –v option is used. With this option, the output of the command is in this format:

>   *parameter1='value1'*
>   *parameter2='value2'*
>   *parameter3='value3'*

If no parameters are specified on the command line, values for all parameters associated with the package are shown.

Options and arguments for this command are:

–v   Specifies verbose mode. Displays name of parameter and its value.

–d   Specifies the *device* on which a *pkginst* is stored. It can be a directory pathname or the identifiers for tape, floppy disk or removable disk (for example, /var/tmp, /dev/diskette, and /dev/dsk/c1d0s0). The default device is the installation spool directory. If no instance name is given, parameter information for all packages residing in *device* is shown.

–f   Requests that the command read *file* for parameter values.

pkginst Defines a specific package instance for which parameter values should be displayed. The format *pkginst*.* can be used to indicate all instances of a package.

param   Defines a specific parameter whose value should be displayed.

ERRORS

If parameter information is not available for the indicated package, the command exits with a non-zero status.

NOTES

The –f synopsis allows you to specify the file from which parameter values should be extracted. This file should be in the same format as a pkginfo file. As an example, such a file might be created during package development and used while testing software during this stage.

SEE ALSO

pkgmk(1), pkgparam(3x), pkgproto(1), pgktrans(1).

NAME
      pkgproto – generate a prototype file
SYNOPSIS
      pkgproto [-i] [-c class] [path1[=path2] ...]
DESCRIPTION
      pkgproto scans the indicated paths and generates a prototype file that may be
      used as input to the pkgmk command.

      -i   Ignores symbolic links and records the paths as ftype=f (a file) versus
                  ftype=s(symbolic link)

      -c   Maps the class of all paths to class.

      path1   Pathname where objects are located.

      path2   Pathname which should be substituted on output for path1.

      If no paths are specified on the command line, standard input is assumed to be a
      list of paths. If the pathname listed on the command line is a directory, the con-
      tents of the directory is searched. However, if input is read from stdin, a direc-
      tory specified as a pathname will not be searched.

NOTES
      By default, pkgproto creates symbolic link entries for any symbolic link encoun-
      tered (ftype=s). When you use the -i option, pkgproto creates a file entry for
      symbolic links (ftype=f). The prototype file would have to be edited to assign
      such file types as "v" (volatile), "e" (editable), or "x" (exclusive directory).
      pkgproto detects linked files. If multiple files are linked together, the first path
      encountered is considered the source of the link.

EXAMPLE
      The following two examples show uses of pkgproto and a parial listing of the
      output produced.

      Example 1:
            $ pkgproto /usr/bin=bin /usr/usr/bin=usrbin /etc=etc
            f none bin/sed=/bin/sed 0775 bin bin
            f none bin/sh=/bin/sh 0755 bin daemon
            f none bin/sort=/bin/sort 0755 bin bin
            f none usrbin/sdb=/usr/bin/sdb 0775 bin bin
            f none usrbin/shl=/usr/bin/shl 4755 bin bin
            d none etc/master.d 0755 root daemon
            f none etc/master.d/kernel=/etc/master.d/kernel 0644 root daemon
            f none etc/rc=/etc/rc 0744 root daemon
      Example 2:
            $ find / -type d -print | pkgproto
            d none / 755 root root
            d none /usr/bin 755 bin bin
            d none /usr 755 root root
            d none /usr/bin 775 bin bin
            d none /etc 755 root root
            d none /tmp 777 root root

SEE ALSO
      pkgmk(1), pkgparam(1), pkgtrans(1).

NAME

pkgtrans – translate package format

SYNOPSIS

pkgtrans [-ions] *device1* *device2* [*pkginst1* [*pkginst2* [...]]]

DESCRIPTION

pkgtrans translates an installable package from one format to another. It translates:

a file system format to a datastream

a datastream to a file system format

a file system format to another file system format

The options and arguments for this command are:

-i   Copies only the pkginfo and pkgmap files.

-o   Overwrites the same instance on the destination device, package instance will be overwritten if it already exists.

-n   Creates a new instance if any instance of this package already exists.

-s   Indicates that the package should be written to *device2* as a datastream rather than as a file system. The default behavior is to write a file system format on devices that support both formats.

device1   Indicates the source device. The package or packages on this device will be translated and placed on *device2*.

device2   Indicates the destination device. Translated packages will be placed on this device.

pkginst   Specifies which package instance or instances on *device1* should be translated. The token all may be used to indicate all packages. *pkginst*.* can be used to indicate all instances of a package. If no packages are defined, a prompt shows all packages on the device and asks which to translate.

NOTES

Device specifications can be either the special node name (/dev/diskette) or the device alias (diskette1). The device spool indicates the default spool directory. Source and destination devices may not be the same.

By default, pkgtrans will not transfer any instance of a package if any instance of that package already exists on the destination device. Use of the –n option will create a new instance if an instance of this package already exists. Use of the –o option will overwrite the same instance if it already exists. Neither of these options are useful if the destination device is a datastream.

EXAMPLE

The following example translates all packages on the floppy drive /dev/diskette and places the translations on /tmp.

```
pkgtrans /dev/diskette /tmp all
```

The next example translates packages pkg1 and pkg2 on /tmp and places their translations (i.e., a datastream) on the 9track1 output device.

```
pkgtrans /tmp 9track1 pkg1 pkg2
```

The next example translates pkg1 and pkg2 on tmp and places them on the diskette in a datastream format.

```
pkgtrans -s /tmp /dev/diskette pkg1 pkg2
```

SEE ALSO

installf(1M), pkgadd(1M), pkgask(1M), pkginfo(1), pkgmk(1), pkgparam(1), pkgproto(1), pkgrm(1M), removef(1M).

NAME
delsysadm – sysadm interface menu or task removal tool

SYNOPSIS
delsysadm *task* | [–r] *menu*

DESCRIPTION
The delsysadm command deletes a *task* or *menu* from the sysadm interface and modifies the interface directory structure on the target machine.

task | menu   The logical name and location of the menu or task within the interface menu hierarchy. Begin with the top menu main and proceed to where the menu or the task resides, separating each name with colons. See EXAMPLES.

If the –r option is used, this command will recursively remove all sub-menus and tasks for this menu. If the –r option is not used, the menu must be empty.

delsysadm should only be used to remove items added as "on-line" changes with the edsysadm command. Such an addition will have a package instance tag of ONLINE. If the task or menu (and its sub-menus and tasks) have any package instance tags other than ONLINE, you are asked whether to continue with the removal or to exit. Under these circumstances, you probably do not want to continue and you should rely on the package involved to take the necessary actions to delete this type of entry.

The command exits successfully or provides the error code within an error message.

EXAMPLES
To remove the nformat task, execute:

delsysadm main:applications:ndevices:nformat.

DIAGNOSTICS
0 Successful execution
2 Invalid syntax
3 Menu or task does not exist
4 Menu not empty
5 Unable to update interface menu structure

NOTES
Any menu that was originally a placeholder menu (one that only appears if sub-menus exist under it) will be returned to placeholder status when a deletion leaves it empty.

When the –r option is used, delsysadm checks for dependencies before removing any subentries. (A dependency exists if the menu being removed contains an entry placed there by an application package). If a dependency is found, the user is shown a list of packages that depend on the menu being deleted and asked whether or not to continue. If the answer is yes, the menu and all of its menus and tasks are removed (even those shown to have dependencies). If the answer is no, the menu is not deleted.

delsysadm should only be used to remove menu or task entries that have been added to the interface with edsysadm.

SEE ALSO

edsysadm(1M), sysadm(1M).

NAME

　　edsysadm – sysadm interface editing tool

SYNOPSIS

　　edsysadm

DESCRIPTION

　　edsysadm is an interactive tool that adds or changes either menu and task definitions in the sysadm interface. It can be used to make changes directly on-line on a specific machine or to create changes that will become part of a software package. The command creates the administration files necessary to achieve the requested changes in the interface and either places them in the appropriate place for on-line changes or saves them to be included in a software package.

　　edsysadm presents several screens, first prompting for which type of menu item you want to change, menu or task, and then for what type of action to take, add or change. When you select add, a blank menu or task definition (as described below) is provided for you to fill in. When you select change, a series of screens is presented to help identify the definition you wish to change. The final screen presented is the menu or task definition filled in with its current values, which you can then edit.

　　The menu definition prompts and their descriptions are:

Menu Name	The name of the new menu (as it should appear in the lefthand column of the screen). This field has a maximum length of 16 alphanumeric characters.
Menu Description	A description of the new menu (as it should appear in the righthand column of the screen). This field has a maximum length of 58 characters and can consist of any alphanumeric character except at sign (@), carat (^), tilde (~), back grave (`), grave ('), and double quotes (").
Menu Location	The location of the menu in the menu hierarchy, expressed as a menu pathname. The pathname should begin with the main menu followed by all other menus that must be traversed (in the order they are traversed) to access this menu. Each menu name must be separated by colons. For example, the menu location for a menu entry being added to the Applications menu is main:applications. *Do not include the menu name in this location definition.* The complete pathname to this menu entry will be the menu location plus the menu name defined at the first prompt.
	This is a scrollable field, showing a maximum of 50 alphanumeric characters at a time.

Menu Help File Name   Pathname to the item help file for this menu entry. If it resides in the directory from which you invoked **edsysadm**, you do not need to give a full pathname. If you name an item help file that does not exist, you are placed in an editor (as defined by $EDITOR) to create one. The new file is created in the current directory and named **Help**.

The task definition prompts and their descriptions are:

Task Name   The name of the new task (as it should appear in the lefthand column of the screen). This field has a maximum length of 16 alphanumeric characters.

Task Description   A description of the new task (as it should appear in the righthand column of the screen). This field has a maximum length of 58 characters and can consist of any alphanumeric character except at sign (@), carat (^), tilde (~), back grave (`), grave ('), and double quotes (").

Task Location   The location of the task in the menu hierarchy, expressed as a pathname. The pathname should begin with the main menu followed by all other menus that must be traversed (in the order they are traversed) to access this task. Each menu name must be separated by colons. For example, the task location for a task entry being added to the applications menu is **main:applications**. *Do not include the task name in this location definition.* The complete pathname to this task entry will be the task location as well as the task name defined at the first prompt.

This is a scrollable field, showing a maximum of 50 alphanumeric characters at a time.

Task Help File Name   Pathname to the item help file for this task entry. If it resides in the directory from which you invoked **edsysadm**, you do not need to give a full pathname. If you name an item help file that does not exist, you are placed in an editor (as defined by $EDITOR) to create one. The new file is created in the current directory and named **Help**.

Task Action   The FACE form name or executable that will be run when this task is selected. This is a scrollable field, showing a maximum of 58 alphanumeric characters at a time. This pathname can be relative to the current directory as well as absolute.

Task Files   Any FACE objects or other executables that support the task action listed above and might be called from within that action. *Do not include the help file name or the task action in this list.* Pathnames can be relative to the current directory as well as absolute. A dot (.) implies "all files in the current directory" and includes files in subdirectories.

This is a scrollable field, showing a maximum of 50 alphanumeric characters at a time.

Once the menu or task has been defined, screens for installing the menu or task or saving them for packaging are presented. The package creation or on-line installation is verified and you are informed upon completion.

NOTES

For package creation or modification, this command automatically creates a menu information file and a prototype file in the current directory (the directory from which the command is executed). The menu information file is used during package installation to modify menus in the menu structure. A prototype file is an installation file which gives a listing of package contents. The prototype file created by edsysadm lists the files defined under task action and gives them the special installation class of "admin". The contents of this prototype file must be incorporated in the package prototype file.

For on-line installation, edsysadm automatically creates a menu information file and adds or modifies the interface menu structure directly.

The item help file must follow the format shown in the *Application Programmer's Guide* in the "Customizing the Administration Interace" chapter or in the *System Administrator's Guide* in the "Customizing the sysadm Interface" appendix.

SEE ALSO

delsysadm(1M), pkgmk(1), prototype(4), sysadm(1M)

NAME

installf – add a file to the software installation database

SYNOPSIS

installf [–c *class*] *pkginst pathname* [*ftype* [[*major minor*]
[*mode owner group*]]]

installf [–c *class*] *pkginst* –

installf –f [–c *class*] *pkginst*

DESCRIPTION

installf informs the system that a pathname not listed in the pkgmap file is being created or modified. It should be invoked before any file modifications have occurred.

When the second synopsis is used, the pathname descriptions will be read from standard input. These descriptions are the same as would be given in the first synopsis but the information is given in the form of a list. (The descriptions should be in the form: *pathname* [*ftype* [[*major minor*] [*mode owner group*]]].)

After all files have been appropriately created and/or modified, installf should be invoked with the –f synopsis to indicate that installation is final. Links will be created at this time and, if attribute information for a pathname was not specified during the original invocation of installf or was not already stored on the system, the current attribute values for the pathname will be stored. Otherwise, installf verifies that attribute values match those given on the command line, making corrections as necessary. In all cases, the current content information is calculated and stored appropriately.

–c *class*   Class to which installed objects should be associated. Default class is none.

pkginst   Name of package instance with which the pathname should be associated.

pathname   Pathname that is being created or modified.

ftype   A one-character field that indicates the file type. Possible file types include:

f	a standard executable or data file
e	a file to be edited upon installation or removal
v	volatile file (one whose contents are expected to change)
d	directory
x	an exclusive directory
l	linked file
p	named pipe
c	character special device
b	block special device
s	symbolic link

major   The major device number. The field is only specified for block or character special devices.

minor   The minor device number. The field is only specified for block or character special devices.

mode   The octal mode of the file (for example, 0664). A question mark (?) indicates that the mode will be left unchanged, implying that the file already exists on the target machine. This field is not used for linked or symbolically linked files.

owner   The owner of the file (for example, `bin` or `root`). The field is limited to 14 characters in length. A question mark (?) indicates that the owner will be left unchanged, implying that the file already exists on the target machine. This field is not used for linked or symbolically linked files.

group   The group to which the file belongs (for example, `bin` or `sys`). The field is limited to 14 characters in length. A question mark (?) indicates that the group will be left unchanged, implying that the file already exists on the target machine. This field is not used for linked or symbolically linked files.

−f   Indicates that installation is complete. This option is used with the final invocation of `installf` (for all files of a given class).

NOTES

When *ftype* is specified, all applicable fields, as shown below, must be defined:

ftype	*Required Fields*
p x d f v or e	mode owner group
c or b	major minor mode owner group

The `installf` command will create directories, named pipes and special devices on the original invocation. Links are created when `installf` is invoked with the −f option to indicate installation is complete.

Links should be specified as *path1=path2*. *path1* indicates the destination and *path2* indicates the source file.

Files installed with `installf` will be placed in the class *none*, unless a class is defined with the command. Subsequently, they will be removed when the associated package is deleted. If this file should not be deleted at the same time as the package, be certain to assign it to a class which is ignored at removal time. If special action is required for the file before removal, a class must be defined with the command and an appropriate class action script delivered with the package.

When classes are used, `installf` must be used as follows:

```
installf −c class1 ...
installf −f −c class1 ...
installf −c class2 ...
installf −f −c class2 ...
```

EXAMPLE

The following example shows the use of installf invoked from an optional preinstall or postinstall script:

```
#create /dev/xt directory
#(needs to be done before drvinstall)
installf $PKGINST /dev/xt d 755 root sys ||
          exit 2
majno=`/usr/sbin/drvinstall -m /etc/master.d/xt
     -d $BASEDIR/data/xt.o -v1.0` ||
          exit 2
i=00
while [ $i -lt $limit ]
do
    for j in 0 1 2 3 4 5 6 7
    do
        echo /dev/xt$i$j c $majno `expr $i * 8 + $j`
            644 root sys |
        echo /dev/xt$i$j=/dev/xt/$i$j
    done
    i=`expr $i + 1`
    [ $i -le 9 ] && i="0$i" #add leading zero
done | installf $PKGINST - || exit 2
# finalized installation, create links
installf -f $PKGINST || exit 2
.ft 1
```

SEE ALSO

pkgadd(1M), pkgask(1M), pkgchk(1), pkginfo(1), pkgmk(1), pkgparam(1), pkgproto(1), pkgtrans(1), pkgrm(1M), removef(1M).

NAME

pkgadd – transfer software package to the system

SYNOPSIS

pkgadd [–d *device*] [–r *response*] [–n] [–a *admin*] [*pkginst1* [*pkginst2*[...]]]

pkgadd –s *spool* [–d *device*] [*pkginst1* [*pkginst2*[...]]]

DESCRIPTION

pkgadd transfers the contents of a software package from the distribution medium or directory to install it onto the system. Used without the –d option, pkgadd looks in the default spool directory for the package (var/spool/pkg). Used with the –s option, it reads the package to a spool directory instead of installing it.

–d   Installs or copies a package from *device*. *device* can be a full path name to a directory or the identifiers for tape, floppy disk or removable disk (for example, /var/tmp, /dev/diskette, or diskette1). It can also be the device alias.

–r   Identifies a file or directory, *response*, which contains output from a previous pkgask session. This file supplies the interaction responses that would be requested by the package in interactive mode. *response* must be a full pathname.

–n   Installation occurs in non-interactive mode. The default mode is interactive.

–a   Defines an installation administration file, *admin*, to be used in place of the default administration file. The token none overrides the use of any *admin* file, and thus forces interaction with the user. Unless a full path name is given, pkgadd looks in the var/sadm/install/admin directory for the file.

pkginst   Specifies the package instance or list of instances to be installed. The token all may be used to refer to all packages available on the source medium. The format *pkginst*.* can be used to indicate all instances of a package.

–s   Reads the package into the directory *spool* instead of installing it.

When executed without options, pkgadd users /var/spool/pkg (the default spool directory).

NOTES

When transferring a package to a spool directory, the –r, –n, and –a options cannot be used.

The –r option can be used to indicate a directory name as well as a filename. The directory can contain numerous *response* files, each sharing the name of the package with which it should be associated. This would be used, for example, when adding multiple interactive packages with one invocation of pkgadd. Each package would need a *response* file. If you create response files with the same name as the package (*i.e. package1* and *package2*), then name the directory in which these files reside after the –r.

The −n option will cause the installation to halt if any interaction is needed to complete it.

NAME
     pkgask – stores answers to a request script

SYNOPSIS
     pkgask [–d *device*] –r *response pkginst* [*pkginst* [...]]

DESCRIPTION
     pkgask allows the administrator to store answers to an interactive package (one
     with a request script). Invoking this command generates a *response* file that is
     then used as input at installation time. The use of this *response* file prevents any
     interaction from occurring during installation since the file already contains all of
     the information the package needs.

     –d   Runs the request script for a package on *device*. *device* can be a direc-
                 tory pathname or the identifiers for tape, floppy disk or removable
                 disk (for example, /var/tmp, /dev/diskette, and /dev/dsk/c1d0s0).
                 The default device is the installation spool directory.

     –r   Identifies a file or directory, which should be created to contain the
                 responses to interaction with the package. The name must be a full
                 pathname. The file, or directory of files, can later be used as input to
                 the pkgadd command.

     pkginst   Specifies the package instance or list of instances for which request
                 scripts will be created. The token all may be used to refer to all
                 packages available on the source medium.

NOTES
     The –r option can be used to indicate a directory name as well as a filename.
     The directory name is used to create numerous *response* files, each sharing the
     name of the package with which it should be associated. This would be used, for
     example, when you will be adding multiple interactive packages with one invoca-
     tion of pkgadd. Each package would need a *response* file. To create multiple
     response files with the same name as the package instance, name the directory in
     which the files should be created and supply multiple instance names with the
     pkgask command. When installing the packages, you will be able to identify this
     directory to the pkgadd command.

SEE ALSO
     installf(1M), pkgadd(1M), pkgchk(1), pkgmk(1), pkginfo(1), pkgparam(1),
     pkgproto(1), pkgtrans(1), pkgrm(1M), removef(1M).

NAME

pkgchk – check accuracy of installation

SYNOPSIS

pkgchk [−l | −acfqv] [−nx] [−p path1[, path2 ...] [−i file] [pkginst...]

pkgchk −d device [−l | v] [−p path1[, path2 ...] [−i file] [pkginst...]

pkgchk −m pkgmap [−e envfile] [−l | −acfqv] [−nx] [−i file]
      [−p path1[, path2 ...]]

DESCRIPTION

pkgchk checks the accuracy of installed files or, by use of the −l option, displays information about package files. The command checks the integrity of directory structures and the files. Discrepancies are reported on stderr along with a detailed explanation of the problem.

The first synopsis defined above is used to list or check the contents and/or attributes of objects that are currently installed on the system. Package names may be listed on the command line, or by default the entire contents of a machine will be checked.

The second synopsis is used to list or check the contents of a package which has been spooled on the specified device, but not installed. Note that attributes cannot be checked for spooled packages.

The third synopsis is used to list or check the contents and/or attributes of objects which are described in the indicated pkgmap.

The option definitions are:

−l   Lists information on the selected files that make up a package. It is not compatible with the a, c, f, g, and v options.

−a   Audits the file attributes only, does not check file contents. Default is to check both.

−c   Audits the file contents only, does not check file attributes. Default is to check both.

−f   Corrects file attributes if possible. If used with the −x option, it removes hidden files. When pkgchk is invoked with this option it creates directories, named pipes, links and special devices if they do not already exist.

−q   Quiet mode. Does not give messages about missing files.

−v   Verbose mode. Files are listed as processed.

−n   Does not check volatile or editable files. This should be used for most post-installation checking.

−x   Searches exclusive directories, looking for files which exist that are not in the installation software database or the indicated pkgmap file.

−p   Only checks the accuracy of the pathname or pathnames listed. pathname can be one or more pathnames separated by commas (or by white space, if the list is quoted).

-i   Reads a list of pathnames from *file* and compares this list against the installation software database or the indicated *pkgmap* file. Pathnames which are not contained in *inputfile* are not checked.

-d   Specifies the device on which a spooled package resides. *device* can be a directory pathname or the identifiers for tape, floppy disk or removable disk (for example, `/var/tmp` or `/dev/diskette`).

-m   Requests that the package be checked against the pkgmap file *pkgmap*.

-e   Requests that the pkginfo file named as *envfile* be used to resolve parameters noted in the specified pkgmap file.

pkginst
        Specifies the package instance or instances to be checked. The format *pkginst.** can be used to check all instances of a package. The default is to display all information about all installed packages.

SEE ALSO
        pkgadd(1M), pkgask(1M), pkginfo(1), pkgrm(1M), pkgtrans(1).

NAME
     pkgrm – removes a package from the system

SYNOPSIS
     pkgrm [–n] [–a *admin*] [*pkginst1* [*pkginst2*[...]]]

     pkgrm –s *spool* [*pkginst*]

DESCRIPTION
     pkgrm will remove a previously installed or partially installed package from the
     system. A check is made to determine if any other packages depend on the one
     being removed. The action taken if a dependency exists is defined in the admin
     file.

     The default state for the command is in interactive mode, meaning that prompt
     messages are given during processing to allow the administrator to confirm the
     actions being taken. Non-interactive mode can be requested with the –n option.

     The –s option can be used to specify the directory from which spooled packages
     should be removed.

     The options and arguments for this command are:

     –n   Non-interactive mode. If there is a need for interaction, the com-
                 mand will exit. Use of this option requires that at least one pack-
                 age instance be named upon invocation of the command.

     –a   Defines an installation administration file, *admin*, to be used in
                 place of the default *admin* file.

     –s   Removes the specified package(s) from the directory "spool."

     pkginst   Specifies the package to be removed. The format *pkg_abbrev.** can
                 be used to remove all instances of a package.

SEE ALSO
     installf(1M), pkgadd(1M), pkgask(1M), pkgchk(1), pkginfo(1), pkgmk(1),
     pkgparam(1), pkgproto(1), pkgtrans(1), removef(1M).

NAME

removef – remove a file from software database

SYNOPSIS

removef pkginst path1 [path2 ...]

removef -f pkginst

DESCRIPTION

removef informs the system that the user, or software, intends to remove a path-name. Output from removef is the list of input pathnames that may be safely removed (no other packages have a dependency on them).

After all files have been processed, removef should be invoked with the −f option to indicate that the removal phase is complete.

EXAMPLE

The following shows the use of removef in an optional pre-install script:

```
echo "The following files are no longer part of this package
        and are being removed."
removef $PKGINST /dev/xt[0-9][0-9][0-9] |
while read pathname
do
        echo "$pathname"
        rm -f $pathname
done
removef -f $PKGINST || exit 2
```

SEE ALSO

installf(1M), pkgadd(1M), pkgask(1M), pkgchk(1), pkginfo(1), pkgmk(1), pkgproto(1), pkgtrans(1), pkgparam(3X).

NAME

compver – compatible versions file

DESCRIPTION

compver is an ASCII file used to specify previous versions of the associated package which are upward compatible. It is created by a package developer.

Each line of the file specifies a previous version of the associated package with which the current version is backward compatible.

Since some packages may require installation of a specific version of another software package, compatibility information is extremely crucial. Consider, for example, a package called "A" which requires version "1.0" of application "B" as a prerequisite for installation. If the customer installing "A" has a newer version of "B" (version 1.3), the compver file for "B" must indicate that "1.3" is compatible with version "1.0" in order for the customer to install package "A".

NOTES

The comparison of the version string disregards white space and tabs. It is performed on a word-by-word basis. Thus "Version   1.3" and "Version 1.3" would be considered the same.

EXAMPLE

A sample compver file is shown below.

```
Version 1.3
Version 1.0
```

NAME

copyright – copyright information file

DESCRIPTION

copyright is an ASCII file used to provide a copyright notice for a package. The text may be in any format. The full file contents (including comment lines) is displayed on the terminal at the time of package installation.

NAME

depend – software dependencies files

DESCRIPTION

depend is an ASCII file used to specify information concerning software dependencies for a particular package. The file is created by a software developer.

Each entry in the depend file describes a single software package. The instance of the package is described after the entry line by giving the package architecture and/or version. The format of each entry and subsequent instance definition is:

> *type pkg name*
>   *(arch)version*
>   *(arch)version*
>   ...

The fields are:

type   Defines the dependency type. Must be one of the following characters:

        P   Indicates a prerequisite for installation, for example, the referenced package or versions must be installed.

        I   Implies that the existence of the indicated package or version is incompatible.

        R   Indicates a reverse dependency. Instead of defining the package's own dependencies, this designates that another package depends on this one. This type should be used only when an old package does not have a depend file but it relies on the newer package nonetheless. Therefore, the present package should not be removed if the designated old package is still on the system since, if it is removed, the old package will no longer work.

pkg   Indicates the package abbreviation.

name   Specifies the full package name.

(arch)version   Specifies a particular instance of the software. A version name cannot begin with a left parenthesis. The instance specifications, both *arch* and *version*, are completely optional but must each begin on a new line that begins with white space. A null version set equates to any version of the indicated package.

EXAMPLE

Here is a sample depend file:

```
I msvr 3B2 Messaging Server
P ctc Cartridge Tape Utilities
P dfm Directory and File Management Utilities
P ed Editing Utilities
P ipc Inter-Process Communication Utilities
P lp Line Printer Spooling Utilities
P shell Shell Programming Utilities
P sys System Header Files
          Release 3.0
P sysadm System Administration Utilities
P term Terminal Filters Utilities
P terminfo Terminal Information Utilities
P usrenv User Environment Utilities
P uucp Basic Networking Utilities
P x25 X.25 Network Interface
          Issue 1 Version 1
          Issue 1 Version 2
P windowing AT&T Windowing Utilities
          (3B2)Version 1
R cms 3B2 Call Management System
```

NAME

pkginfo – package characteristics file

DESCRIPTION

pkginfo is an ASCII file that describes the characteristics of the package along with information that helps control the flow of installation. It is created by the software package developer.

Each entry in the pkginfo file is a line that establishes the value of a parameter in the following form:

PARAM="value"

There is no required order in which the parameters must be specified within the file. Each parameter is described below. Only fields marked with an asterisk are mandatory.

PKG*	Abbreviation for the package being installed, generally three characters in length (for example, dir or pkg). All characters in the abbreviation must be alphanumeric and the first may not be numeric. The abbreviation is limited to a maximum length of nine characters. install, new, and all are reserved abbreviations.
NAME*	Text that specifies the package name (maximum length of 256 ASCII characters).
ARCH*	A comma-separated list of alphanumeric tokens that indicate the architecture (for example, 3B2) associated with the package. The pkgmk tool may be used to create or modify this value when actually building the package. The maximum length of a token is 16 characters and it cannot include a comma.
VERSION*	Text that specifies the current version associated with the software package. The maximum length is 256 ASCII characters and the first character cannot be a left parenthesis. The pkgmk tool may be used to create or modify this value when actually building the package.
CATEGORY*	A comma-separated list of categories under which a package may be displayed. A package must at least belong to the system or application category. Categories are case-insensitive and may contain only alphanumerics. Each category is limited in length to 16 characters.
DESC	Text that describes the package (maximum length of 256 ASCII characters).
VENDOR	Used to identify the vendor that holds the software copyright (maximum length of 256 ASCII characters).
HOTLINE	Phone number and/or mailing address where further information may be received or bugs may be reported (maximum length of 256 ASCII characters).

EMAIL   An electronic address where further information is available or bugs may be reported (maximum length of 256 ASCII characters).

VSTOCK   The vendor stock number, if any, that identifies this product (maximum length of 256 ASCII characters).

CLASSES   A space-separated list of classes defined for a package. The order of the list determines the order in which the classes are installed. Classes listed first will be installed first (on a media by media basis). This parameter may be modified by the request script.

ISTATES   A list of allowable run states for package installation (for example, "S s 1").

RSTATES   A list of allowable run states for package removal (for example, "S s 1").

BASEDIR   The pathname to a default directory where "relocatable" files may be installed. If blank, the package is not relocatable and any files that have relative pathnames will not be installed. An administrator can override the default directory.

ULIMIT   If set, this parameter is passed as an argument to the ulimit command, which establishes the maximum size of a file during installation.

ORDER   A list of classes defining the order in which they should be put on the medium. Used by pkgmk in creating the package. Classes not defined in this field are placed on the medium using the standard ordering procedures.

MAXINST   The maximum number of package instances that should be allowed on a machine at the same time. By default, only one instance of a package is allowed. This parameter must be set in order to have multiple instances of a package.

PSTAMP   Production stamp used to mark the pkgmap file on the output volumes. Provides a means for distinguishing between production copies of a version if more than one is in use at a time. If PSTAMP is not defined, the default is used. The default consists of the UNIX system machine name followed by the string "YYMMDDHHMM" (year, month, date, hour, minutes).

INTONLY   Indicates that the package should only be installed interactively when set to any non-NULL value.

PREDEPEND   Used to maintain compatibility with pre-SVR4 package dependency checking. Pre-SVR4 dependency checks were based on whether or not the name file for the required package existed in the /var/options directory. This directory is not maintained for SVR4 packages since the depend file is used for checking dependencies. However, entries can be created in this directory to maintain compatibility. Setting the PREDEPEND parameter to y or yes creates a /usr/option entry for the package.

(Packages that are new for SVR4 do not need to use this parameter.)

EXAMPLES

Here is a sample pkginfo:

```
PKG="oam"
NAME="OAM Installation Utilities"
VERSION="3"
VENDOR="AT&T"
HOTLINE="1-800-ATT-BUGS"
EMAIL="attunix!olsen"
VSTOCK="0122c3f5566"
CATEGORY="system.essential"
ISTATES="S 2"
RSTATES="S 2"
```

NOTES

Developers may define their own installation parameters by adding a definition to this file. A developer-defined parameter must begin with a capital letter.

NAME

pkgmap – package contents description file

DESCRIPTION

pkgmap is an ASCII file that provides a complete listing of the package contents. It is automatically generated by pkgmk(1) using the information in the prototype file.

Each entry in pkgmap describes a single "deliverable object file." A deliverable object file includes shell scripts, executable objects, data files, directories, etc. The entry consists of several fields of information, each field separated by a space. The fields are described below and must appear in the order shown.

part   An optional field designating the part number in which the object resides. A part is a collection of files, and is the atomic unit by which a package is processed. A developer can choose the criteria for grouping files into a part (e.g., based on class). If no value is defined in this field, part 1 is assumed.

ftype   A one-character field that indicates the file type. Valid values are:

        f   a standard executable or data file
        e   a file to be edited upon installation or removal
        v   volatile file (one whose contents are expected to change)
        d   directory
        x   an exclusive directory
        l   linked file
        p   named pipe
        c   character special device
        b   block special device
        i   installation script or information file
        s   symbolic link

class   The installation class to which the file belongs. This name must contain only alphanumeric characters and be no longer than 12 characters. It is not specified if the ftype is i (information file).

pathname The pathname where the object will reside on the target machine, such as /usr/bin/mail. Relative pathnames (those that do not begin with a slash) indicate that the file is relocatable.

For linked files (ftype is either l or s), pathname must be in the form of *path1=path2*, with *path1* specifying the destination of the link and *path2* specifying the source of the link.

pathname may contain variables which support relocation of the file. A $*parameter* may be embedded in the pathname structure. $BASEDIR can be used to identify the parent directories of the path hierarchy, making the entire package easily relocatable. Default values for *parameter* and BASEDIR must be supplied in the pkginfo file and may be overridden at installation.

major   The major device number. The field is only specified for block or character special devices.

minor   The minor device number. The field is only specified for block or character special devices.

mode   The octal mode of the file (for example, 0664). A question mark (?) indicates that the mode will be left unchanged, implying that the file already exists on the target machine. This field is not used for linked files, packaging information files or non-installable files.

owner   The owner of the file (for example, bin or root). The field is limited to 14 characters in length. A question mark (?) indicates that the owner will be left unchanged, implying that the file already exists on the target machine. This field is not used for linked files or non-installable files. It is used optionally with a package information file. If used, it indicates with what owner an installation script will be executed.

Can be a variable specification in the form of $[A-Z]. Will be resolved at installation time.

group   The group to which the file belongs (for example, "bin" or "sys"). The field is limited to 14 characters in length. A question mark (?) indicates that the group will be left unchanged, implying that the file already exists on the target machine. This field is not used for linked files or non-installable files. It is used optionally with a package information file. If used, it indicates with what group an installation script will be executed.

Can be a variable assignment in the form of $[A-Z]. Will be resolved at installation time.

size   The actual size of the file in bytes. This field is not specified for named pipes, special devices, directories or linked files.

cksum   The checksum of the file contents. This field is not specified for named pipes, special devices, directories or linked files.

modtime   The time of last modification, as reported by the stat(2) function call. This field is not specified for named pipes, special devices, directories or linked files.

Each pkgmap must have one line that provides information about the number and maximum size (in 512-byte blocks) of parts that make up the package. This line is in the following format:

> :*number_of_parts maximum_part_size*

Lines that begin with "#" are comment lines and are ignored.

When files are saved during installation before they are overwritten, they are normally just copied to a temporary pathname. However, for files whose mode includes execute permission (but which are not editable), the existing version is linked to a temporary pathname and the original file is removed. This allows processes which are executing during installation to be overwritten.

EXAMPLES

The following is an example of a **pkgmap** file.

```
:2 500
1 i pkginfo 237 1179 541296672
1 b class1 /dev/diskette 17 134 0644 root other
1 c class1 /dev/rdiskette 17 134 0644 root other
1 d none bin 0755 root bin
1 f none bin/INSTALL 0755 root bin 11103 17954 541295535
1 f none bin/REMOVE 0755 root bin 3214 50237 541295541
1 l none bin/UNINSTALL=bin/REMOVE
1 f none bin/cmda 0755 root bin 3580 60325 541295567
1 f none bin/cmdb 0755 root bin 49107 51255 541438368
1 f class1 bin/cmdc 0755 root bin 45599 26048 541295599
1 f class1 bin/cmdd 0755 root bin 4648 8473 541461238
1 f none bin/cmde 0755 root bin 40501 1264 541295622
1 f class2 bin/cmdf 0755 root bin 2345 35889 541295574
1 f none bin/cmdg 0755 root bin 41185 47653 541461242
2 d class2 data 0755 root bin
2 p class1 data/apipe 0755 root other
2 d none log 0755 root bin
2 v none log/logfile 0755 root bin 41815 47563 541461333
2 d none save 0755 root bin
2 d none spool 0755 root bin
2 d none tmp 0755 root bin
```

NOTES

The **pkgmap** file may contain only one entry per unique pathname.

NAME

prototype – package information file

DESCRIPTION

prototype is an ASCII file used to specify package information. Each entry in the
file describes a single deliverable object. An object may be a data file, directory,
source file, executable object, etc. This file is generated by the package developer.

Entries in a prototype file consist of several fields of information separated by
white space. Comment lines begin with a "#" and are ignored. The fields are
described below and must appear in the order shown.

part   An optional field designating the part number in which the object
resides. A part is a collection of files, and is the atomic unit by which a
package is processed. A developer can choose criteria for groupig files
into a part (e.g., based on class). If this field is not used, part 1 is
assumed.

ftype   A one-character field which indicates the file type. Valid values are:

        f   a standard executable or data file
        e   a file to be edited upon installation or removal
        v   volatile file (one whose contents are expected to change)
        d   directory
        x   an exclusive directory
        l   linked file
        p   named pipe
        c   character special device
        b   block special device
        i   installation script or information file
        s   symbolic link

class   The installation class to which the file belongs. This name must contain only alphanumeric characters and be no longer than 12 characters.
The field is not specified for installation scripts. (admin and all classes
beginning with capital letters are reserved class names.)

pathname The pathname where the file will reside on the target machine, e.g.,
/usr/bin/mail or bin/ras_proc. Relative pathnames (those that do
not begin with a slash) indicate that the file is relocatable. The form

        path1=path2

may be used for two purposes: to define a link and to define local
pathnames.

For linked files, *path1* indicates the destination of the link and *path2*
indicates the source file. (This format is mandatory for linked files.)

For local pathnames, *path1* indicates the pathname an object should
have on the machine where the entry is to be installed and *path2* indicates either a relative or fixed pathname to a file on the host machine
which contains the actual contents.

A pathname may contain a variable specification, which will be resolved at the time of installation. This specification should have the form $[A-Z].

major The major device number. The field is only specified for block or character special devices.

minor The minor device number. The field is only specified for block or character special devices.

mode The octal mode of the file (for example, 0664). A question mark (?) indicates that the mode will be left unchanged, implying that the file already exists on the target machine. This field is not used for linked files or packaging information files.

owner The owner of the file (for example, bin or root). The field is limited to 14 characters in length. A question mark (?) indicates that the owner will be left unchanged, implying that the file already exists on the target machine. This field is not used for linked files or packaging information files.

Can be a variable specification in the form of $[A-Z]. Will be resolved at installation time.

group The group to which the file belongs (for example, bin or sys). The field is limited to 14 characters in length. A question mark (?) indicates that the group will be left unchanged, implying that the file already exists on the target machine. This field is not used for linked files or packaging information files.

Can be a variable specification in the form of $[A-Z]. Will be resolved at installation time.

An exclamation point (!) at the beginning of a line indicates that the line contains a command. These commands are used to incorporate files in other directories, to locate objects on a host machine, and to set permanent defaults. The following commands are available:

search Specifies a list of directories (separated by white space) to search for when looking for file contents on the host machine. The basename of the *path* field is appended to each directory in the ordered list until the file is located.

include Specifies a pathname which points to another prototype file to include. Note that search requests do not span include files.

default Specifies a list of attributes (mode, owner, and group) to be used by default if attribute information is not provided for prototype entries which require the information. The defaults do not apply to entries in include prototype files.

param=value Places the indicated parameter in the current environment.

The above commands may have variable substitutions embedded within them, as demonstrated in the two example prototype files below.

Before files are overwritten during installation, they are copied to a temporary pathname. The exception to this rule is files whose mode includes execute permission, unless the file is editable (i.e, *ftype* is **e**). For files which meet this exception, the existing version is linked to a temporary pathname, and the original file is removed. This allows processes which are executing during installation to be overwritten.

EXAMPLES

Example 1:

```
!PROJDIR=/usr/proj
!BIN=$PROJDIR/bin
!CFG=$PROJDIR/cfg
!LIB=$PROJDIR/lib
!HDRS=$PROJDIR/hdrs
!search /usr/myname/usr/bin /usr/myname/src /usr/myname/hdrs
i pkginfo=/usr/myname/wrap/pkginfo
i depend=/usr/myname/wrap/depend
i version=/usr/myname/wrap/version
d none /usr/wrap 0755 root bin
d none /usr/wrap/usr/bin 0755 root bin
! search $BIN
f none /usr/wrap/bin/INSTALL 0755 root bin
f none /usr/wrap/bin/REMOVE 0755 root bin
f none /usr/wrap/bin/addpkg 0755 root bin
!default 755 root bin
f none /usr/wrap/bin/audit
f none /usr/wrap/bin/listpkg
f none /usr/wrap/bin/pkgmk
# the following file starts out zero length but grows
v none /usr/wrap/logfile=/dev/null 0644 root bin
# the following specifies a link (dest=src)
l none /usr/wrap/src/addpkg=/usr/wrap/bin/rmpkg
! search $SRC
!default 644 root other
f src /usr/wrap/src/INSTALL.sh
f src /usr/wrap/src/REMOVE.sh
f src /usr/wrap/src/addpkg.c
f src /usr/wrap/src/audit.c
f src /usr/wrap/src/listpkg.c
f src /usr/wrap/src/pkgmk.c
d none /usr/wrap/data 0755 root bin
d none /usr/wrap/save 0755 root bin
d none /usr/wrap/spool 0755 root bin
d none /usr/wrap/tmp 0755 root bin
d src /usr/wrap/src 0755 root bin
```

Example 2:

```
# this prototype is generated by 'pkgproto' to refer
# to all prototypes in my src directory
!PROJDIR=/usr/dew/projx
!include $PROJDIR/src/cmd/prototype
!include $PROJDIR/src/cmd/audmerg/protofile
!include $PROJDIR/src/lib/proto
```

SEE ALSO

pkginfo(4), pkgmk(1).

NOTES

Normally, if a file is defined in the prototype file but does not exist, that file is created at the time of package installation. However, if the file pathname includes a directory that does not exist, the file will not be created. For example, if the prototype file has the following entry:

```
f none /usr/dev/bin/command
```

and that file does not exist, it will be created if the directory /usr/dev/bin already exists or if the prototype also has an entry defining the directory:

```
d none /usr/dev/bin
```

NAME

space – disk space requirement file

DESCRIPTION

space is an ASCII file that gives information about disk space requirements for the target environment. It defines space needed beyond that which is used by objects defined in the prototype file—for example, files which will be installed with the installf command. It should define the maximum amount of additional space which a package will require.

The generic format of a line in this file is:

pathname blocks inodes

Definitions for the fields are as follows:

pathname   Specifies a directory name which may or may not be the mount point for a filesystem. Names that do not begin with a slash (/) indicate relocatable directories.

blocks   Defines the number of disk blocks required for installation of the files and directory entries contained in the pathname (using a 512-byte block size).

inodes   Defines the number of inodes required for installation of the files and directory entries contained in the pathname.

EXAMPLE

```
# extra space required by config data which is
# dynamically loaded onto the system
data 500   1
```

SEE ALSO

installf(1M), prototype(4)

C Package Installation Case Studies

Introduction

This appendix presents packaging case study in order to show packaging techniques such as installing objects conditionally, determining at run time how many files to create, and how to modify an existing data file during package installation and removal.

Each case begins with a description of the study, followed by a list of the packaging techniques it uses and a narrative description of the approach taken when using those techniques. After this material, sample files and scripts associated with the case study are shown.

Case #1

This package has three types of objects. The installer may choose which of the three types to install and where to locate the objects on the installation machine.

Techniques

This case study shows examples of the following techniques:

- using variables in object pathnames
- using the request script to solicit input from the installer
- setting conditional values for an installation parameter

Approach

To set up selective installation, you must:

- Define a class for each type of object which can be installed.

  In this case study, the three object types are the package executables, the manual pages, and the emacs executables. Each type has its own class: bin, man, and emacs, respectively. Notice in the prototype file, shown in Figure C-2, that all of the object files belong to one of these three classes.

- Initialize the CLASSES parameter in the pkginfo file as null.

  Normally when you define a class, you want the CLASSES parameter to list all classes that will be installed. Otherwise, no objects in that class will be installed. For this example, the parameter is initially set to null. CLASSES will be given values by the request script, based on the package pieces chosen by the installer. This way, CLASSES is set to only those object types that the installer wants installed. Figure C-1 shows the pkginfo file associated with this package. Notice that the CLASSES parameter is set to null.

- Define object pathnames in the prototype file with variables.

  These variables will be set by the request script to the value which the installer provides. pkgadd resolves these variables at installation time and so knows where to install the package.

The three variables used in this example are:

- $NCMPBIN (defines location for object executables)

- $NCMPMAN (defines location for manual pages)

- $EMACS (defines location for emacs executables)

Look at the example prototype file (Figure C-2) to see how to define the object pathnames with variables.

■ Create a request script to ask the installer which parts of the package should be installed and where they should be placed.

The request script for this package, shown in Figure C-3, asks two questions:

- Should this part of the package be installed?

    When the answer is yes, then the appropriate class name is added to the CLASSES parameter. For example, when the question "Should the manual pages associated with this package be installed" is answered yes, the class man is added to the CLASSES parameter.

- If so, where should that part of the package be placed?

    The appropriate variable is given the value of the response to this question. In the manual page example, the variable $NCMPMAN is set to this value.

These two questions are repeated for each of the three object types.

At the end of the request script, the parameters are made available to the installation environment for pkgadd and any other packaging scripts. In the case of this example, no other scripts are provided.

When looking at the request script for this example, notice that the questions are generated by the data validation tools ckyorn and ckpath.

Sample Files

Figure C-1: Case #1 `pkginfo` **File**

```
PKG='ncmp'
NAME='NCMP Utilities'
CATEGORY='applications,tools'
ARCH='3b2'
VERSION='Release 1.0, Issue 1.0'
CLASSES=''
```

Figure C-2: Case #1 `prototype` **File**

```
i pkginfo
i request
x bin $NCMPBIN 0755 root other
f bin $NCMPBIN/dired=/usr/ncmp/bin/dired 0755 root other
f bin $NCMPBIN/less=/usr/ncmp/bin/less 0755 root other
f bin $NCMPBIN/ttype=/usr/ncmp/bin/ttype 0755 root other
f emacs $NCMPBIN/emacs=/usr/ncmp/bin/emacs 0755 root other
x emacs $EMACS 0755 root other
f emacs $EMACS/ansii=/usr/ncmp/lib/emacs/macros/ansii 0644 root other
f emacs $EMACS/box=/usr/ncmp/lib/emacs/macros/box 0644 root other
f emacs $EMACS/crypt=/usr/ncmp/lib/emacs/macros/crypt 0644 root other
f emacs $EMACS/draw=/usr/ncmp/lib/emacs/macros/draw 0644 root other
f emacs $EMACS/mail=/usr/ncmp/lib/emacs/macros/mail 0644 root other
f emacs $NCMPMAN/man1/emacs.1=/usr/ncmp/man/man1/emacs.1 0644 root other
d man $NCMPMAN 0755 root other
d man $NCMPMAN/man1 0755 root other
f man $NCMPMAN/man1/dired.1=/usr/ncmp/man/man1/dired.1 0644 root other
f man $NCMPMAN/man1/ttype.1=/usr/ncmp/man/man1/ttype.1 0644 root other
f man $NCMPMAN/man1/less.1=/usr/ncmp/man/man1/less.1 0644 inixmr other
```

Figure C-3: Case Study #1 Request Script

```
trap 'exit 3' 15

# determine if and where general executables should be placed
ans=`ckyorn -d y \
        -p "Should executables included in this package be installed"
` || exit $?
if [ "$ans" = y ]
then
        CLASSES="$CLASSES bin"
        NCMPBIN=`ckpath -d /usr/ncmp/bin -aoy \
                -p "Where should executables be installed"
        ` || exit $?
fi

# determine if emacs editor should be installed, and if it should
# where should the associated macros be placed
ans=`ckyorn -d y \
        -p "Should emacs editor included in this package be installed"
` || exit $?
if [ "$ans" = y ]
then
        CLASSES="$CLASSES emacs"
        EMACS=`ckpath -d /usr/ncmp/lib/emacs -aoy \
                -p "Where should emacs macros be installed"
        ` || exit $?
fi

# determine if and where manual pages should be installed
ans=`ckyorn \
        -d y \
        -p "Should manual pages associated with this package be installed"
` || exit $?
if [ "$ans" = y ]
then
        CLASSES="$CLASSES man"
        NCMPMAN=`ckpath -d /usr/ncmp/man -aoy \
                -p "Where should manual pages be installed"
        ` || exit $?
fi

# make parameters available to installation service,
# and so to any other packaging scripts
cat >$1 <<!
CLASSES='$CLASSES'
```

(continued on next page)

Figure C-3: Case Study #1 Request Script (continued)

```
NCMPBIN='$NCMPBIN'
EMACS='$EMACS'
NCMPMAN='$NCMPMAN'
!

exit 0
```

Case #2

This package installs a driver. A set of device nodes associated with that driver needs to be created, but the installer will decide how many nodes to create. After installation, the system needs to be rebooted so that the driver is properly configured.

Techniques

This case study shows examples of the following techniques:

- installing a driver with a postinstall script
- using an exit code to reboot the system
- allowing the installer to define how many device nodes to create at installation time

Approach

To install a driver at the time of installation, you must:

- Include the object and master files for the driver in the prototype file.

  In this example, the object file for the driver is a data file named qz.o. This is the file on which the standard UNIX driver install command, drvinstall, operates. The master.d file is named qz and is used by drvinstall to help configure the driver.

  Looking at Figure C-4 (the prototype file for this example), notice the following:

  - Since no special treatment is required for these files, you can put them into the standard none class. The CLASSES parameter is set to none in the pkginfo file (Figure C-5).

  - The pathname for qz.o begins with the variable $BOOTDIR. This variable will be set in the request script and allows the administrator to decide where the object file should be installed. The default directory will be /boot.

  □ There is an entry for the postinstall script (the script that will per-
    form the driver installation).

■ Create a request script.

  The request script, shown in Figure C-6, has two major functions:

  □ to determine how many device nodes to create for this driver

    This is accomplished by questioning the installer and then assigning
    the answer to the parameter $NDEVICES. Notice that the data vali-
    dation tool ckrange is used and that it limits the response to a
    number between 0 and 32. It sets the default number to 8.

    If the installer chooses not to install any devices, the CLASSES
    parameter is set to null. This means that no classes are defined and
    therefore no objects will be installed.

  □ to determine where the installer wants the driver objects to be
    installed

    This is accomplished by questioning the installer and assigning the
    answer to the $BOOTDIR parameter.

  The script ends with a routine to make the three parameters CLASSES,
  NDEVICES, and BOOTDIR available to the installation environment and so
  to the postinstall script.

■ Create a postinstall script.

  The postinstall script, shown in Figure C-7, actually performs the driver
  installation. It is executed after the two files qz and qz.o have been
  installed. The postinstall shown for this example performs the following
  actions:

  □ checks to see if any devices should be installed (if not, it exits)

  □ creates the /dev/qz directory using the installf command (this
    directory could also be created by putting an entry for it in the pro-
    totype file)

  □ executes the drvinstall command using the two files installed
    with this package (the major number is returned to the script at this
    time)

    □ calculates the minor numbers for installed devices

    □ installs the device using `installf`

    □ creates a link for the device also using `installf`

    □ finalizes the installation using `installf -f`

- Reboot the system upon installation.

   This is accomplished by exiting from the postinstall script with an exit code of 10, meaning that the system should be rebooted upon completing an error-free installation.

Sample Files

Figure C-4: Case #2 prototype **File**

```
i pkginfo
i request
i postinstall
f none $BOOTDIR/qz.o 444 root root
f none /etc/master.d/qz 444 root root
```

Figure C-5: Case #2 pkginfo **File**

```
PKG='qzdev'
NAME='qz Devices'
CATEGORY='system'
ARCH='3b2'
VERSION='Software Issue #19'
CLASSES='none'
```

Figure C-6: Case #2 Request Script

```
trap 'exit 3' 15

# determine if and where general executables should be placed
NDEVICES=`ckrange -10 -u32 -d 8 \
        -p "How many qz devices do you want configured"
` || exit $?

# if user chose to install no devices, don't install anything
if [ $NDEVICES -eq 0 ]
then
        CLASSES=
else
        # determine where driver object should be placed; location
        # must be an absolute pathname which is an existing directory
        BOOTDIR=`ckpath -aoy -d /boot \
                -p "Where do you want driver object installed"
        ` || exit $?
fi

# make parameters available to installation service,
# and so to any other packaging scripts
cat >$1 <<!
CLASSES='$CLASSES'
NDEVICES='$NDEVICES'
BOOTDIR='$BOOTDIR'
!
exit 0
```

Figure C-7: Case #2 Postinstall Script

```
# PKGINST parameter provided by installation service
# NDEVICES parameter provided by 'request' script
# BOOTDIR parameter provided by 'request' script

[ $NDEVICES -eq 0 ] && exit 0

err_code=1   # an error is considered fatal

# need to create the /dev/qz directory
installf $PKGINST /dev/qz d 755 root sys ||
        exit $err_code

# install the driver object and determine major device number
majno=`/usr/sbin/drvinstall -m /etc/master.d/qz -d $BOOTDIR/qz.o -v1.0` ||
        exit $err_code

i=00
while [ $i -lt $NDEVICES ]
do
        for j in 0 1 2 3 4 5 6 7
        do
                # calculate minor number based on loop variables
                minno=`expr $i \* 8 + $j` || exit $err_code

                # install character device with appropriate major/minor
                # device numbers and correct permissions (installf will
                # do all of work here - you need only provide the info!)
                installf $PKGINST /dev/qz/$i$j c $majno $minno 644 root sys ||
                        exit $err_code

                # create a link from /dev/qz/xx to /dev/qzxx
                installf $PKGINST /dev/qz$i$j=/dev/qz/$i$j ||
                        exit $err_code
        done
        i=`expr $i + 1`

        # add leading zero if necessary
        [ $i -le 9 ] && i="0$i"
done

# finalize installation; the installf command will now
# attempt to create the links that was requested above
installf -f $PKGINST || exit $err_code

exit 10   # requests a reboot from user
```

Case #3

This study creates a database file at the time of installation and saves a copy of the database when the package is removed.

Techniques

This case study shows examples of the following techniques:

- using classes and class action scripts to perform special actions on different sets of objects

- using the `space` file to inform `pkgadd` that extra space will be required to install this package properly

- using the `installf` command

Approach

To create a database file at the time of installation and save a copy on removal, you must:

- Create three classes.

  This package requires three classes:

    □ the standard class of none (contains a set of processes belonging in the subdirectory `bin`)

    □ the `admin` class (contains an executable file `config` and a directory containing data files)

    □ the `cfgdata` class (contains a directory)

- Make the package collectively relocatable.

  Notice in the `prototype` file (Figure C-9) that none of the pathnames begin with a slash or a variable. This indicates that they are collectively relocatable.

- Calculate the amount of space the database file will require and create a `space` file to deliver with the package. This file notifies `pkgadd` that this package requires extra space and how much extra space. Figure C-10 shows the `space` file for this package.

- Create an installation class action script for the admin class.

  The script, shown in Figure C-11, initializes a database using the data files belonging to the admin class. To perform this task, it:

  □ copies the source data file to its proper destination

  □ creates an empty file named config.data and assigns it to a class of cfgdata

  □ executes the bin/config command (delivered with the package and already installed) to populate the database file config.data using the data files belonging to the admin class

  □ executes installf -f to finalize installation

  No special action is required for the admin class at removal time so no removal class action script is created. This means that all files and directories in the admin class will simply be removed from the system.

- Create a removal class action script for the cfgdata class.

  The script, shown in Figure C-12, makes a copy of the database file before it is deleted during package removal. No special action is required for this class at installation time, so no installation class action script is needed.

  Remember that the input to a removal script is a list of pathnames to remove. Pathnames always appear in lexical order with the directories appearing first. This script captures directory names so that they can be acted upon later and copies any files to a directory named /tmp. When all of the pathnames have been processed, the script then goes back and removes all directories and files associated with the cfgdata class.

  The outcome of this removal script is to copy config.data to /tmp and then remove the config.data file and the data directory.

Sample Files

Figure C-8: Case #3 `pkginfo` **File**

```
PKG='krazy'
NAME='KrAzY Applications'
CATEGORY='applications'
ARCH='3b2'
VERSION='Version 1'
CLASSES='none cfgdata admin'
```

Figure C-9: Case #3 `prototype` **File**

```
i pkginfo
i request
i i.admin
i r.cfgdata
d none bin 555 root sys
f none bin/process1 555 root other
f none bin/process2 555 root other
f none bin/process3 555 root other
f admin bin/config 500 root sys
d admin cfg 555 root sys
f admin cfg/datafile1 444 root sys
f admin cfg/datafile2 444 root sys
f admin cfg/datafile3 444 root sys
f admin cfg/datafile4 444 root sys
d cfgdata data 555 root sys
```

Case #3

Figure C-10: Case #3 space **File**

```
# extra space required by config data which is
# dynamically loaded onto the system
data 500 1
```

System Services and Application Packaging Tools

Figure C-11: Case #3 Installation Class Action Script (i.admin)

```
# PKGINST parameter provided by installation service
# BASEDIR parameter provided by installation service

while read src dest
do
        # the installation service provides '/dev/null' as the
        # pathname for directories, pipes, special devices, etc
        # which it knows how to create
        [ "$src" = /dev/null ] && continue

        cp $src $dest || exit 2
done

# if this is the last time this script will
# be executed during the installation, do additional
# processing here
if [ "$1" = ENDOFCLASS ]
then
        # our config process will create a data file based on any changes
        # made by installing files in this class; make sure
        # the data file is in class 'cfgdata' so special rules can apply
        # to it during package removal
        installf -c cfgdata $PKGINST $BASEDIR/data/config.data f 444 root sys ||
                exit 2
        $BASEDIR/bin/config > $BASEDIR/data/config.data ||
                exit 2
        installf -f -c cfgdata $PKGINST ||
                exit 2
fi
exit 0
```

Figure C-12: Case #3 Removal Class Action Script (r.cfgdata)

```
# the product manager for this package has suggested that
# the configuration data is so valuable that it should be
# backed up to /tmp before it is removed!

while read path
do
        # pathnames appear in lexical order, thus directories
        # will appear first; you can't operate on directories
        # until done, so just keep track of names until
        # later
        if [ -d $path ]
        then
                dirlist="$dirlist $path"
                continue
        fi
        mv $path /tmp || exit 2
done
if [ -n "$dirlist" ]
then
        rm -rf $dirlist || exit 2
fi
exit 0
```

System Services and Application Packaging Tools

Case #4

This package uses the optional packaging files to define package compatibilities and dependencies and to present a copyright message during installation.

Techniques

This case study shows examples of the following techniques:

- using the `copyright` file
- using the `compver` file
- using the `depend` file

Approach

To meet the requirements in the description, you must:

- Create a `copyright` file.

  A `copyright` file contains the ASCII text of a copyright message. The message shown in Figure C-14 will be displayed on the screen during package installation (and also during package removal).

- Create a `compver` file.

  The `pkginfo` file shown in Figure C-13 defines this package version as version 3.0. The `compver` file, shown in Figure C-15, defines version 3.0 as being compatible with versions 2.3, 2.2, 2.1, 2.1.1, 2.1.3 and 1.7.

- Create a `depend` file.

  Files listed in a `depend` file must already be installed on the system when a package is installed. The example shown in Figure C-16 has 11 packages which must already be on the system at installation time.

Sample Files

Figure C-13: Case #4 `pkginfo` **File**

```
PKG='case4'
NAME='Case Study #4'
CATEGORY='application'
ARCH='3b2'
VERSION='Version 3.0'
CLASSES='none'
```

Figure C-14: Case #4 `copyright` **File**

```
Copyright (c) 1989 AT&T
All Rights Reserved.

THIS PACKAGE CONTAINS UNPUBLISHED PROPRIETARY SOURCE CODE OF AT&T.

The copyright notice above does not evidence any
actual or intended publication of such source code.
```

System Services and Application Packaging Tools

Figure C-15: Case #4 compver File

```
Version 2.3
Version 2.2
Version 2.1
Version 2.1.1
Version 2.1.3
Version 1.7
```

Figure C-16: Case #4 depend File

```
P  acu    Advanced C Utilities
          Issue 4 Version 1
P  cc     C Programming Language
          Issue 4 Version 1
P  dfm    Directory and File Management Utilities
P  ed     Editing Utilities
P  esg    Extended Software Generation Utilities
          Issue 4 Version 1
P  graph  Graphics Utilities
P  rfs    Remote File Sharing Utilities
          Issue 1 Version 1
P  rx     Remote Execution Utilities
P  sgs    Software Generation Utilities
          Issue 4 Version 1
P  shell  Shell Programming Utilities
P  sys    System Header Files
          Release 3.1
```

Case #5a

This study modifies a file which exists on the installation machine during package installation. It uses one of three modification methods. The other two methods are shown in Cases 5b and 5c. The file modified is /sbin/inittab.

Techniques

This case study shows examples of the following techniques:

- using the sed class
- using a postinstall script

Approach

To modify /sbin/inittab at the time of installation, you must:

- Add the sed class script to the prototype file.

  The name of a script must be the name of the file that will be edited. In this case, the file to be edited is /sbin/inittab and so our sed script is named /sbin/inittab. There are no requirements for the mode owner group of a sed script (represented in the sample prototype by question marks). The file type of the sed script must be e (indicating that it is editable). The prototype file for this case study is shown in Figure C-17.

- Set the CLASSES parameter to include 4sed.

  In the case of the example shown in Figure C-18, sed is the only class being installed. However, it could be one of any number of classes.

- Create a sed class action script.

  You cannot deliver a copy of /sbin/inittab that looks the way you need for it to, since /sbin/inittab is a dynamic file and you have no way of knowing how it will look at the time of package installation. Using a sed script allows us to modify the /sbin/inittab file during package installation.

  As already mentioned, the name of a sed script should be the same as the name of the file it will edit. A sed script contains sed commands to remove and add information to the file. See Figure C-19 for an example sed script.

■ Create a postinstall script.

You need to inform the system that /sbin/inittab has been modified by executing init q. The only place you can perform that action in this example is in a postinstall script. Looking at the example postinstall script, shown in Figure C-20, you will see that its only purpose is to execute init q.

This approach to editing /sbin/inittab during installation has two drawbacks. First of all, you have to deliver a full script (the postinstall script) simply to perform init q. In addition to that, the package name at the end of each comment line is hardcoded. It would be nice if this value could be based on the package instance so that you could distinguish between the entries you add for each package.

Sample Files

Figure C-17: Case #5a `pkginfo` **File**

```
PKG='case5a'
NAME='Case Study #5a'
CATEGORY='applications'
ARCH='3b2'
VERSION='Version 1d05'
CLASSES='sed'
```

Figure C-18: Case #5a prototype File

```
i pkginfo
i postinstall
e sed /sbin/inittab ? ? ?
```

Figure C-19: Case #5a sed Script (/sbin/inittab)

```
!remove
# remove all entries from the table that are associated
# with this package, though not necessarily just
# with this package instance
/^[^:]*:[^:]*:[^:]*:[^#]*#ROBOT$/d

!install
# remove any previous entry added to the table
# for this particular change
/^[^:]*:[^:]*:[^:]*:[^#]*#ROBOT$/d

# add the needed entry at the end of the table;
# sed(1) does not properly interpret the '$a'
# construct if you previously deleted the last
# line, so the command
#        $a\
#            rb:023456:wait:/usr/robot/bin/setup #ROBOT
# will not work here if the file already contained
# the modification.  Instead, you will settle for
# inserting the entry before the last line!
$i\
rb:023456:wait:/usr/robot/bin/setup #ROBOT
```

System Services and Application Packaging Tools

Figure C-20: Case #5a Postinstall Script

```
# make init re-read inittab
/sbin/init q ||
        exit 2
exit 0
```

Case #5b

This study modifies a file which exists on the installation during package installation. It uses one of three modification methods. The other two methods are shown in Cases 5a and 5c. The file modified is /sbin/inittab.

Techniques

This case study shows examples of the following techniques:

- creating classes
- using installation and removal class action scripts

Approach

To modify /sbin/inittab during installation, you must:

- Create a class.

  Create a class called inittab. You must provide an installation and a removal class action script for this class. Define the inittabl class in the CLASSES parameter in the pkginfo file (as shown in Figure C-21).

- Create an inittab file.

  This file contains the information for the entry that you will add to /sbin/inittab. Notice in the prototype file (Figure C-22) that inittab is a member of the inittab class and has a file type of e for editable. Figure C-25 shows what inittab looks like.

- Create an installation class action script.

  Since class action scripts must be multiply executable (meaning you get the same results each time they are executed), you can't just add our text to the end of the file. The script, shown in Figure C-23, performs the following procedures:

  □ checks to see if this entry has been added before

  □ if it has, removes any previous versions of the entry

- edits the `inittab` file file and adds the comment lines so you know where the entry is from

- moves the temporary file back into `/sbin/inittab`

- executes `init q` when it receives the end-of-class indicator

Note that `init q` can be performed by this installation script. A one-line postinstall script is not needed by this approach.

- Create a removal class action script.

The removal script, shown in Figure C-24, is very similar to the installation script. The information added by the installation script is removed and `init q` is executed.

This case study resolves the drawbacks to Case 5a. You can support multiple package instances since the comment at the end of the `inittab` entry is now based on package instance. Also, you no longer need a one-line postinstall script. However, this case has a drawback of its own. You must deliver two class action scripts and the `inittab` file to add one line to a file. Case 5c shows a more streamlined approach to editing `/sbin/inittab` during installation.

Sample Files

Figure C-21: Case #5b `pkginfo` **File**

```
PKG='case5b'
NAME='Case Study #5b'
CATEGORY='applications'
ARCH='3b2'
VERSION='Version 1d05'
CLASSES='inittab'
```

Figure C-22: Case #5b prototype **File**

```
i pkginfo
i i.inittab
i r.inittab
e inittab /sbin/inittab ? ? ?
```

Figure C-23: Case #5b Installation Class Action Script (i.inittab)

```
# PKGINST parameter provided by installation service

while read src dest
do
        # remove all entries from the table that
        # associated with this PKGINST
        sed -e "/^[^:]*:[^:]*:[^:]*:[^#]*#$PKGINST$/d" $dest > /tmp/$$itab ||
                exit 2

        sed -e "s/$/#$PKGINST" $src >> /tmp/$$itab ||
                exit 2

        mv /tmp/$$itab $dest ||
                exit 2
done
if [ "$1" = ENDOFCLASS ]
then
        /sbin/init q ||
                exit 2
fi
exit 0
```

System Services and Application Packaging Tools

Figure C-24: Case #5b Removal Class Action Script (r.inittab)

```
# PKGINST parameter provided by installation service

while read src dest
do
        # remove all entries from the table that
        # are associated with this PKGINST
        sed -e "/^[^:]*:[^:]*:[^:]*:[^#]*#$PKGINST$/d" $dest > /tmp/$$itab ||
                exit 2

        mv /tmp/$$itab $dest ||
                exit 2
done
/sbin/init q ||
        exit 2
exit 0
```

Figure C-25: Case #5b `inittab` **File**

```
rb:023456:wait:/usr/robot/bin/setup
```

Case #5c

This study modifies a file which exists on the installation machine during package installation. It uses one of three modification methods. The other two methods are shown in Cases 5a and 5b. The file modified is /sbin/inittab.

Techniques

This case study shows examples of the following technique:

- using the build class

Approach

This approach to modifying /sbin/inittab uses the build class. A build class file is executed as a shell script and its output becomes the new version of the file being executed. In other words, the data file inittab that is delivered with this package will be executed and the output of that execution will become /sbin/inittab.

The build class file is executed during package installation and package removal. The argument install is passed to the file if it is being executed at installation time. Notice in the sample build file in Figure C-28 that installation actions are defined by testing for this argument.

To edit /sbin/inittab using the build class, you must:

- Define the build file in the prototype file.

  The entry for the build file in the prototype file should place it in the build class and define its file type as e. Be certain that the CLASSES parameter in the pkginfo file is defined as build. Figure C-26 shows the pkginfo file for this example and Figure C-27 shows the prototype file.

- Create the build file.

  The build file shown in Figure C-28 performs the following procedures:

  □ Edits /sbin/inittab to remove any changes already existing for this package. Notice that the filename /sbin/inittab is hard-coded into the sed command.

□ If the package is being installed, adds the new line to the end of
   /sbin/inittab. A comment tag is included in this new entry to
   remind us from where that entry came.

□ Executes init q.

This solution addresses the drawbacks in case studies 5a and 5b. Only one file
is needed (beyond the pkginfo and prototype files), that file is short and
simple, it works with multiple instances of a package since the $PKGINST
parameter is used, and no postinstall script is required since init q can be executed from the build file.

Figure C-26: Case #5c pkginfo **File**

```
PKG='case5c'
NAME='Case Study #5c'
CATEGORY='applications'
ARCH='3b2'
VERSION='Version 1d05'
CLASSES='build'
```

Figure C-27: Case #5c prototype **File**

```
i pkginfo
e build /sbin/inittab ? ? ?
```

Figure C-28: Case #5c build **Script** (/sbin/init)

```
# PKGINST parameter provided by installation service

# remove all entries from the existing table that
# are associated with this PKGINST
sed -e "/^[^:]*:[^:]*:[^:]*:[^#]*#$PKGINST$/d" /sbin/inittab ||
        exit 2

if [ "$1" = install ]
then
        # add the following entry to the table
        echo "rb:023456:wait:/usr/robot/bin/setup #$PKGINST" ||
                exit 2
fi
/sbin/init q ||
        exit 2
exit 0
```

System Services and Application Packaging Tools

Case #6

This case study modifies a number `crontab` files during package installation.

Techniques

This case study shows examples of the following techniques:

- using classes and class action scripts
- using the `crontab` command within a class action script

Approach

You could use the `build` class and follow the approach shown for editing `/sbin/inittab` in case study 5c except that you want to edit more than one file. If you used the `build` class approach, you would need to deliver one for each `cron` file edited. Defining a `cron` class provides a more general approach. To edit a `crontab` file with this approach, you must:

- Define the `cron` files that will be edited in the `prototype` file.

  Create an entry in the `prototype` file for each `crontab` file which will be edited. Define their class as `cron` and their file type as `e`. Use the actual name of the file to be edited, as shown in Figure C-30.

- Create the `crontab` files that will be delivered with the package.

  These files contain the information you want added to the existing `crontab` files of the same name. See Figures C-33 and C-34 for examples of what these files look like.

- Create an installation class action script for the `cron` class.

  The `i.cron` script (Figure C-31) performs the following procedures:

  - Calculates the user id.

    This is done by setting the variable *user* to the base name of the cron class file being processed. That name equates to the user id. For example, the basename of `/var/spool/cron/crontabs/root` is root (which is also the user id).

      □ Executes crontab using the user id and the −l option.

        Using the −l options tells crontab to send the standard output the contents of the crontab for the defined user.

      □ Pipes the output of the crontab command to a sed script that removes any previous entries that have been added using this installation technique.

      □ Puts the edited output into a temporary file.

      □ Adds the data file for the root user id (that was delivered with the package) to the temporary file and adds a tag so that you will know from where these entries came.

      □ Executes crontab with the same user id and give it the temporary file as input.

■ Create a removal class action script for the cron class.

The removal script, shown in Figure C-32, is the same as the installation script except that there is no procedure to add information to the crontab file.

These procedures are performed for every file in the cron class.

Sample Files

Figure C-29: Case #3 pkginfo File

```
PKG='case6'
NAME='Case Study #6'
CATEGORY='application'
ARCH='3b2'
VERSION='Version 1.0'
CLASSES='cron'
```

Figure C-30: Case #6 prototype **File**

```
i pkginfo
i i.cron
i r.cron
e cron /var/spool/cron/crontabs/root ? ? ?
e cron /var/spool/cron/crontabs/sys ? ? ?
```

Figure C-31: Case #6 Installation Class Action Script (i.cron)

```
# PKGINST parameter provided by installation service

while read src dest
do
        user=`basename $dest` ||
                exit 2

        (crontab -l $user |
        sed -e "/#$PKGINST$/d" > /tmp/$$crontab) ||
                exit 2

        sed -e "s/$/ #$PKGINST/" $src >> /tmp/$$crontab ||
                exit 2

        crontab $user < /tmp/$$crontab ||
                exit 2
        rm -f /tmp/$$crontab
done
exit 0
```

Figure C-32: Case #6 Removal Class Action Script (r.cron)

```
# PKGINST parameter provided by installation service

while read path
do
        user=`basename $path` ||
                exit 2

        (crontab -l $user |
        sed -e "/#$PKGINST$/d" > /tmp/$$crontab) ||
                exit 2

        crontab $user < /tmp/$$crontab ||
                exit 2
        rm -f /tmp/$$crontab
done
exit 0
```

Figure C-33: Case #6 Root `crontab` **File (delivered with package)**

```
41,1,21 * * * /usr/lib/uucp/uudemon.hour > /dev/null
45 23 * * * ulimit 5000; /usr/bin/su uucp -c "/usr/lib/uucp/uudemon.cleanup" >
/dev/null 2>&1
11,31,51 * * * /usr/lib/uucp/uudemon.poll > /dev/null
```

System Services and Application Packaging Tools

Figure C-34: Case #6 Sys crontab **File (delivered with package)**

```
0 * * * 0-6 /usr/lib/sa/sa1
20,40 8-17 * * 1-5 /usr/lib/sa/sa1
5 18 * * 1-5 /usr/lib/sa/sa2 -s 8:00 -e 18:01 -i 1200 -A
```

INDEX

Index

System Services and Application Packaging Tools

System Services and Application Packaging Tools